Service-Learning and Educating in Challenging Contexts

Also available from Continuum

Subject Knowledge and Teacher Education, Viv Ellis
Teacher Development, Qing Gu
Teacher Education and the Development of Practical Judgement, Ruth Heilbronn

Service-Learning and Educating in Challenging Contexts

International Perspectives

Edited by

Timothy Murphy and Jon E. C. Tan

continuum

Continuum International Publishing Group
A Bloomsbury company

50 Bedford Square   80 Maiden Lane
London   New York
WC1B 3DP   NY 10038

www.continuumbooks.com

British Library Cataloguing-in-Publication Data
A catalogue record for this book is available from the British Library.

ISBN: 978-1-4411-2074-8 (hardcover)
978-1-4411-1800-4 (PDF)

Library of Congress Cataloging-in-Publication Data
Service-learning and educating in challenging contexts : international perspectives / edited by Timothy Murphy and Jon Tan.
p. cm.
Summary: "Explores best practice for engagement with challenging educational contexts through service-learning drawing on the contributors' international experience"– Provided by publisher.
Includes bibliographical references and index.
ISBN 978-1-4411-2074-8 (hardback)– ISBN 978-1-4411-1800-4 ()
1. Service learning–Cross-cultural studies. I. Murphy, Timothy, Dr. II. Tan, Jon.
LC220.5.S4547 2012
361.3'7–dc23
2012011313

Typeset by Fakenham Prepress Solutions, Fakenham, Norfolk NR21 8NN
Printed and bound in Great Britain

Contents

Contributors

Phil Bamber is a Senior Lecturer in the Faculty of Education at Liverpool Hope University, UK. He has extensive experience embedding local and international community engagement projects in the higher education curriculum, with an emphasis on teacher education. His research explores the transformative potential of this pedagogical approach with relation to local and global citizenship. Phil is a research fellow of the Institute of Research in Education and Society at St Xavier's College, Mumbai, India, and founding Director of the Centre for International and Development Education based at Liverpool Hope University, UK.

Roser Batlle specializes in Service-Learning, Non-formal Education, Human Values Education and Citizenship Education. She was previously an educator and trainer in non-formal education at the NGO and local government levels. She also worked as a teacher in special education and was co-founder of a number of educational youth movements and social foundations. Roser has written several books in the field of Service-Learning and related educational programs, including citizenship textbooks for both primary and high school levels. She is on the board of *Centre Promotor Aprenentatge Servei* and *Fundación Zerbikas*, both of which are involved in Service-Learning promotion. She is also a founding member of the *Spanish Service-Learning Network*. At an international level, Roser collaborates with *Fundación SES* in Argentina and with *Cátedra Medellín-Barcelona*, a programme of cooperation between Colombia and Spain, and is a member of the *Service-Learning Iberoamericana Network*.

Josephine Boland is Senior Lecturer in the School of Education at the National University of Ireland, Galway. Josephine's professional experience spans both further and higher education and education policy development at national level. She currently facilitates Service-Learning within teacher education (Learning to Teach for Social Justice) and is a lead partner in Community Engaged Research in Action (CORA). She is a member of Supporting Service-Learning and Civic Engagement in Jordan and Lebanon (Tawasol) and a board member of Campus Engage – a network promoting civic engagement in higher education. Her research and publications centre on civic engagement, higher education policy and academic practice. Josephine provides staff development in curriculum design for civic engagement within higher education, nationally and internationally.

Noah Borrero is Assistant Professor of Teacher Education at the University of San Francisco, USA, where he developed a new Masters programme in Urban Education and Social Justice at the University of San Francisco. Noah teaches courses in bilingual education, critical pedagogy, action research, and teaching for diversity and social justice. His book, *Closing the Achievement Gap: How to Pinpoint Student Strengths to Differentiate Instruction and Help Your Striving Readers Succeed* (Scholastic, 2009), reflects his scholarly interests in urban education, English learner (EL) literacy and adolescent development. Noah taught middle and high school English in the San Francisco Bay Area and developed a 'young interpreters' programme where bilingual youth served as interpreters and translators for their school and community.

Helen Dunbar-Krige is a registered educational psychologist and Head of the Department of Educational Psychology at the University of Johannesburg, South Africa. She has varied teaching responsibilities at graduate level in the department's programmes. The BEd Hons and postgraduate MEd Educational Psychology programmes have been recognized as strong programmes in the university and received a very positive review from the Health Professions Council of South Africa. She has supervised about 40 masters' students and is involved in the SANPAD research programme focusing on child-headed households. Her main research focus is on community engagement in the form of Service-Learning, and professional practice supervision within this area. She has published nationally and internationally in a number of books and journals. Helen is the secretary of the educational psychology division of the Psychological Association of South Africa as well as the secretary of the Educational Psychology Forum.

Rhoda Frumkin is Associate Professor in the School of Education at Wagner College, New York, USA. She has particular expertise in literacy/reading and special education. Her areas of research include literacy acquisition for diverse learners, Service-Learning, and professional development for teachers.

Andrew Furco is Associate Vice President for Public Engagement at the University of Minnesota, USA, where he also serves as Associate Professor of Higher Education and Director of the International Center for Research on Community Engagement. He conducts research focused on studying the impacts and institutionalization of Service-Learning and community engagement in primary, secondary and tertiary education. Previously, Andrew served for 14 years as the Founding Director of the Service-Learning Research and Development Center at the University of California-Berkeley, USA.

Katia Gonzalez is Assistant Professor in the School of Education and Faculty Scholar for Teaching and Learning at Wagner College, New York, USA. She has developed expertise in early childhood education, curriculum and special education. Her research interests include curriculum design and implementation for diverse learners, Service-Learning, and the use of collaborative groupings and techniques for the professional development of educators.

Elaine Keane is a Lecturer in the School of Education at the National University of Ireland, Galway. Her teaching focuses on the sociology of education and research methods. Her research and publications centre on social class and education, widening participation in higher education, and qualitative research methodologies. Elaine is a former post-primary teacher and has experience of managing institutional, national and transnational projects in this area. She also works closely with local and national community and non-governmental organizations in a civic engagement capacity and offers a teacher education Service-Learning module within the School of Education. Currently the Director of the Master of Education programme, Elaine is deeply committed to the advancement of social justice through education.

Britta Klopsch is a Lecturer in the Department of Education at Heidelberg University of Education, Germany. A former primary and secondary school-teacher in Germany, she is involved in research and various projects to develop and promote the holistic learning of students and to equip them with the necessary skills for the twenty-first century.

Jennifer Lauria is Associate Professor in the School of Education at Wagner College, New York, USA. She has a particular interest in childhood education and her areas of research include theory and practice, individualized instruction and technology in education.

Jenna Londy is a graduate of Hamline University, USA, where she completed her academic career in K-12 ESL Education and Religion. She was a student leader for the *Each One Teach One* programme, organizing service trips to New Orleans with fellow classmates. Jenna is a very active member in the community, volunteering in urban classrooms and mentoring students through high school.

Terence Lovat is Professor Emeritus at the University of Newcastle, Australia, Visiting Professor at the University of Bristol, UK, and Academic Dean at the Broken Bay Institute of Theology, Australia. He is a former Pro Vice-Chancellor and Dean of Education at University of Newcastle, Australia. Terence is a highly experienced researcher with over Austral\$2m. of funded grant work, multiple research texts and more than 100 refereed publications. He was the chief investigator on the major research projects emanating from the Australian Values Education Program (2005–2010), work that culminated in three books published by Springer Press of Dordrecht, including *International Research Handbook on Values Education and Student Wellbeing* (2010) and *Values Pedagogy and Student Achievement* (2011). Among his many publications is a special issue on values education in *International Journal of Educational Research* (2011), for which he was the guest editor.

Esther Luna is a Professor and Researcher in the Department of Diagnostic and Research Methods in Education at the University of Barcelona, Spain. She has done research on the civic participation of young people by linking the school and the community. Her main areas of research are active, critical, responsible and intercultural citizenship together with mediation and social inclusion. She has made several visits to research centres in the USA, Sweden, the UK, Argentina and Portugal. These visits invited research and development of a new pedagogical approach that engages youth with their surrounding communities which has resulted in publications such as 'From school to the community: developing materials for active citizenship' (2007), in M. Bartolomé and F. Cabrera (ed.), *Building an Intercultural and Responsible Citizenship. Guide to High School Teacher* (Madrid: Narcea), pp. 77–140.

Timothy Murphy is a Senior Lecturer in the School of Education and Childhood at Leeds Metropolitan University, UK. Previously, he worked as a post-doctoral researcher for the Centre for Excellence in Learning & Teaching (CELT) at the National University of Ireland, Galway, where he was also a lecturer in Education. While at the National University of Ireland, he developed his initial interest in Service-Learning through active involvement with the Community Knowledge Initiative (CKI) and for the past decade he has been extensively involved as both a researcher and as a practitioner. Timothy's work has been disseminated widely in peer-reviewed journals, as well as in various book chapter contributions. He is a member of the Board of Directors of the International Center for Service-Learning in Teacher Education (ICSLTE). He is currently involved in integrating a Service-Learning oriented approach at Leeds Metropolitan University, UK, referred to as Directed Experiential Learning (DEL).

Ana Panone is a preschool teacher at the Minnesota Literacy Council Learning Center-Northeast, where she teaches English as a Second Language. She is Student Leader for the *Each One Teach One*, travelling to New Orleans to help clean parks and mentor students.

Nadine Petersen is a Senior Lecturer in the Department of Education Studies at the University of Johannesburg, South Africa. She is interested in researching teacher education students' engagement with social justice and care in Service-Learning and was one of the lead researchers in a national Community Higher Education Service Partnerships-funded research project at the University of Johannesburg, in 2006–8. Nadine has been extending her research in Service-Learning to include the integration of advanced academic reading and writing in the (re-)design of an existing Service-Learning curriculum using the methodology of design-based research. In 2011, she was awarded a National Research Foundation (NRF) grant in teacher education in which she focuses on the influence of an educational excursion on the development of campus learning communities.

Anne Power is a Senior Lecturer at the University of Western Sydney, Australia, where she is Course Adviser for Master of Teaching and Master of Teaching Honours. She has made significant contributions to research and community engagement projects in Western Sydney, having an impact on the social, academic and creative education of youth. Her research is informed by Wenger's theoretical concepts of community of practice, valuing both informal and formal learning that occurs in learning communities, emerging in writing about musical experience as serious play. Her research is integrally connected with quality teaching and learning, along with evaluation of new policy directions. In projects such as Boys' Motivation and Engagement, Anne contributed significant case study expertise and has published from this research, focusing on engagement within a music education perspective. She convenes the unit Professional Experience 3 which provides opportunities for Service-Learning experience to pre-service teachers. This unit has won the Australian Learning and Teaching Council Award for programmes that enhance learning. Anne's research interests have focused on professional learning for music teachers, globalization through music in work with AusAid, the relationship of leadership and mentoring, and community-based learning. She both edits journals and serves on several editorial boards.

Gonzalo Silió Sáiz is an Assistant Teacher in the Department of Education at the University of Cantabria, Spain. He has participated in different activities from ZERBIKAS, CLAYSS and University of Barcelona, Spain, and is a member of the Red Española de Aprendizaje y Servicio. Gonzalo works as a tutor in several community-based organizations in Cantabria, and collaborates with educators in Germany, USA and Brazil.

Anne Sliwka is Professor of Education at Heidelberg University of Education, Germany. Her research focuses on citizenship education and school development in an international perspective. She has been instrumental in introducing Service-Learning to higher education in Germany and has published extensively on Service-Learning in schools and universities.

Jean Strait is Professor and Director of the Center for Excellence in Urban Teaching at Hamline University, USA. She is a critical component of the Center for Excellence in Urban Teaching and the School of Education's Service-Learning development director. The university's 20-year partnership with Hancock-Hamline elementary school, where over 60 per cent of faculty, staff and students participate in Service-Learning, has led to two top-five finalist positions in the Minnesota Jimmy Carter Partnership awards.

Jon E. C. Tan is a Senior Lecturer and Research Coordinator in the field of education and childhood at Carnegie Faculty, Leeds Metropolitan University, UK. His work draws from a range of disciplines including social welfare, education and critical social theory. Jon's current research foregrounds issues of professional identities and dispositions and the ways in which critical reflective pedagogies and an inquiry-stance can inform socially-sensitive readings of cultural and social difference. Working with both in-service educators and those entering the educationally-oriented professions, Jon's work is committed to collaborative approaches that develop critical awareness and action in addressing inequalities.

Foreword

Andrew Furco, Associate Vice President for Public Engagement at the University of Minnesota, USA

The recent substantial rise in Service-Learning programming within primary, secondary and tertiary educational systems across the globe has brought with it a growing interest in understanding how Service-Learning is best operationalized across diverse settings, communities and cultures. With more than 20 countries having instituted Service-Learning practice into their educational systems, we are finally beginning to realize more fully the complex nature of this multifaceted instructional practice.

Within national contexts, Service-Learning is implemented and practised in unique ways. Indeed, the purposes, intentions, focus and operationalization of the practice vary substantially from country to country. Yet, no matter where it occurs, the essence of Service-Learning is visible and recognizable. Its distinctive character, defined by the interplay of its three fundamental components – *intentional learning objectives, meaningful service and organized reflection activities that connect the learning and service components* – distinguish this pedagogy from other community-based learning practices.

The extant 30-year literature on Service-Learning has focused primarily on intra-national analyses of the pedagogy. Despite Service-Learning's universal appeal, not much is known about how this instructional practice is able to retain the essence of its character when it is used to serve a vast array of purposes and to achieve a broad cross-section of educational goals. And while a set of best practices for high quality Service-Learning has been identified, there is still no real understanding of which combination of these so-called 'best practice' components should be incorporated in particular Service-Learning contexts or community settings.

As more countries promote the practice of Service-Learning in their educational systems, we need to build a more robust understanding of the elements and components that best contribute to the development of high-quality

Service-Learning practice in specific contexts. This is important for several reasons. First, there is no uniform mechanism for administering a national Service-Learning initiative; the focus and organizational structure of a country's educational system influence where and how Service-Learning is incorporated within the educational enterprise. While in some countries the responsibility for implementing Service-Learning rests squarely with the educational system, in other countries Service-Learning programming is primarily the responsibility of community-based organizations that are responsible for providing students with educational, community service experiences. Consequently, the Service-Learning components that might be considered best practices in one type of Service-Learning system might not be best practices in another system.

Second, the particular educational purposes and goals that are ascribed to Service-Learning vary substantially from country to country. For example, in Australia, Service-Learning is tied to a national values education curriculum. In the United Kingdom, it is aligned more closely to a national citizenship education agenda. In Argentina, Service-Learning is designed to advance youth empowerment and promote community-building, while in South Africa, there is a strong emphasis on building stronger campus–community partnerships. These diverse, intended purposes and intentions lead to varied sets of desired educational outcomes, ultimately influencing how successful, high quality Service-Learning is defined.

Third, the term 'service' carries with it many meanings and connotations that are rooted in cultural, religious, political and societal norms and practices. Depending on what actions or activities qualify as 'service' within a particular national context ultimately affects the structure and focus of the community-based activities in which Service-Learning students engage. For a number of countries, the literal translation of the English term 'Service-Learning' has been problematic, either because the word 'service' connotes other meanings (e.g., in certain societies, 'service' is equated with domestic help) or the term 'learning' has a political or religious subtext (e.g., in certain societies, 'learning' that is delivered through formal schooling is viewed as government-sponsored indoctrination or propaganda). For the languages and the cultural contexts in which the literal translation of 'Service-Learning' detracts from the true meaning of the practice, new terms have been adopted to capture more fully the true essence of the pedagogy (e.g., educación *solidaria* in Argentina, *educazione sociale* in Italy). The persistent 'What is Service-Learning?' question, which almost every volume in the field addresses to some degree, becomes even more difficult to answer as we begin to examine Service-Learning in a global context. Such examination raises questions about how students and faculty from different cultures, who might assign different intentions and meanings to *service* and/or *learning*, will approach their community-based work. It also raises questions about how they, in turn, ultimately interpret meaning from their Service-Learning experiences.

Regardless of where the activities take place, most if not all high-quality Service-Learning experiences are situated in multifaceted and complex community contexts. Service-Learning participants are asked to act 'in the moment' and respond accordingly to the various situations and issues that arise. It is this authentic, real-time work that is considered to promote the powerful, transformational learning experiences that are widely touted in the Service-Learning literature. So how do Service-Learning participants in different countries engage and respond to the community contexts in which their service occurs? Is there a common, universal framework that Service-Learning participants from different backgrounds can apply to help them better navigate and negotiate the complexities of their Service-Learning settings? How do the prevailing definitions and purposes of Service-Learning affect the manner in which Service-Learning participants approach their community-based work? These are the kinds of questions that the next phase of Service-Learning inquiry needs to address.

The next phase of research also needs to expand the focus of the inquiry beyond student participants. Currently, 85 per cent of the more than 600 published research studies in the Service-Learning field focus on assessing the experiences of the students who participate in the practice. These studies and the resulting literature have examined and unpacked important issues regarding students' experiences, shedding light on the potential educational impacts of Service-Learning as well as the programmatic elements that facilitate positive student outcomes. As a result of this important work, we now have a good understanding of the important role that reflection, meaningfulness of service, clear learning objectives, sustained partnerships and ongoing assessment play in securing high-quality Service-Learning practice. However, more attention needs to be paid to issues concerning the faculty members who develop, implement and facilitate students' Service-Learning experiences. Their tremendous influence on the success (and failure) of Service-Learning cannot be overstated. There is much to be learned about the ways in which faculty members develop their capacity both to work effectively in community settings and to guide their students through challenging Service-Learning experiences.

Fortunately, as the Service-Learning field enters its fourth decade of development, we are seeing a broadening of the lens within the field's body of literature. Today, a greater focus is being placed on providing more critical analyses of the experiences of Service-Learning faculty members, the role and involvement of community partners, and the global advancement of Service-Learning. Recent English-language publications such as *Problematizing Service-Learning: Critical Reflections for Development and Action* (Stewart and Webster, 2011), *International Service-Learning: Conceptual Frameworks and Research* (Bringle, Hatcher and Jones, 2010), *Service-learning in Theory and Practice: The Future of Community Engagement in Higher Education* (Butin, 2010), and *The Future of Service-Learning* (Strait and Lima, 2009), just to name a few, are good examples of volumes that incorporate this new, more critical perspective on Service-Learning. These and other such volumes are emphasizing and analyzing more deeply the ways in which instructors and other faculty within and across different educational contexts approach and interpret the pedagogy of Service-Learning.

Service-Learning and Educating in Challenging Contexts: International Perspectives is one such text in this new genre of Service-Learning literature. The editors and authors of this volume, composed of scholars and practitioners from all corners of the globe, take the bold step of unpacking the inherent messiness of Service-Learning as it is applied in diverse cultural and national contexts. They dare to move beyond the typical presentations of exemplars and descriptions of models. Instead, they courageously and unapologetically explore the challenges and limitations of Service-Learning. They present the various struggles and some of the missteps that programme leaders in various national contexts have faced in implementing Service-Learning. They share their uncertainties about the true purposes and intentions of Service-Learning. They bring to the fore important insights on why particular Service-Learning practices might work in some contexts and not in others. And they offer very interesting and thoughtful analyses of the implications of these issues and challenges for securing high-quality practice. In the end, through this volume, they help bring into clearer focus the many different shades of Service-Learning.

Service-Learning and Educating in Challenging Contexts: International Perspectives stands as an important volume in the new genre of Service-Learning literature. To all who read it, this work will bring a greater and deeper understanding of the true character and essence of Service-Learning.

Acknowledgements

There are a number of people and organizations that we would like to acknowledge for helping to bring this publication to the light of day. In the first instance we would like to thank the Carnegie Research Institute at Leeds Metropolitan University for awarding us a seed-funding grant to support our initial proposal to develop the potential of the Service-Learning oriented approach within the school of education as well as across the university. This grant supported the visit of Professor Andrew Furco to Leeds Metropolitan University in January 2010. He offered faculty and university-wide seminars on the research and pedagogic possibilities of this approach. His ongoing support and advice has greatly facilitated the embedding of the Service-Learning oriented approach at this institution.

Also, we are indebted to the work of the Community Knowledge Initiative (CKI) at the National University of Ireland Galway (NUIG) which was very instrumental in initially introducing the authors to the potential of the Service-Learning oriented pedagogical approach for academic enrichment and civic engagement capacity building. The International Centre for Service-Learning in Teacher Education (ICSLTE) also had a significant impact on the development of this project. The initial idea for this publication was conceived in the wake of their Second International Conference at NUIG in July 2009. A number of the contributors to this publication were presenters at that conference, and in many ways this publication would not have come to fruition without their willingness to participate and their ongoing commitment to the project.

We would also like to acknowledge the work of Professor Furco, ably assisted by Alfonso Sintjago and Beth Dierker in supporting and translating chapter 10 of this book, and thank our commissioned editor, Iain Poole, for his steadfastness and commitment to the overall project. In a similar way, we would like to express our gratitude to Continuum for all their support and advice throughout the process which has been invaluable. And, finally, we would like to thank our respective families and colleagues for the time and support that they gave to the project. Without that support it would almost certainly have been much more daunting to complete the project in as timely a manner.

Timothy Murphy and Jon E. C. Tan
Leeds Metropolitan University, Leeds, U.K.
February 2012

Introduction

Timothy Murphy and Jon Tan

Within this volume, there are a number of key themes that resonate throughout and can be represented by many, if not all, of the authors who have contributed. What is clear is that taking a Service-Learning oriented approach offers significant opportunities for students, teachers and professionals to deepen and enrich their engagement and theorization of the contexts in which they are situated. What we have found most exciting about bringing together these authors from across the globe is that they all stand as exemplars of educators that facilitate critically reflexive learning anchored within social justice. Their commitment to working within authentic contexts speaks to the pivotal importance of the experiential dimension as integral to the learning process.

There is something significantly dispositional and transformative in the ways in which the authors present their case studies. For instance, Borrero's chapter addresses the potential of Service-Learning as a way to critically analyze classroom content within authentic settings outside of the classroom. The chapter has a particular focus on the challenges and opportunities involved in teaching in urban contexts. His local context is San Francisco which is characterized by a high degree of diversity in the schooling population. It is acknowledged that this presents a particular challenge for beginning teachers. Borrero contends that it is vitally important for these teachers to have an informed understanding of, and appreciation for, the diverse experiences that their young people bring into the classroom. He demonstrates that Service-Learning can address that prerequisite. Additionally, it can make them aware that they, too, are lifelong learners and that learning is something that happens both in the classroom and in the community.

Like Borrero's work, another chapter that clearly illustrates the commitment to social justice and diversity is that by Petersen and Dunbar-Krige. Here, they consider the educational challenges presented by the exigencies of post-apartheid society in South Africa. Resonant with other authors, the potential of education to transform human lives is very evident. Education for social justice is a hallmark of the orientation to Service-Learning that is presented here. Petersen and Dunbar-Krige also fuse the concept of care into their approach. They offer a three-tier Service-Learning model involving undergraduate pre-service teacher education, school counselling and educational psychology. The authors carefully consider the challenges involved in working with communities in a Service-Learning partnership. In this respect, the students are invited to carefully scrutinize their relationships with the community members to which they offer service. There are also important ethical considerations and these are well described. Of equal importance here is how Petersen and Dunbar-Krige also make us aware of another key characteristic of the Service-Learning oriented approach, acknowledging that it is their own students who are finding solutions to the outlined challenges. As a consequence, there is a dialogic relationship set in play here whereby students and the authors are co-constructors of knowledge.

The transactional interplay between the community and Service-Learning projects wedded to a social justice commitment is also well represented in the work of Boland and Keane, and Luna. Firstly, Boland and Keane have developed an approach to Service-Learning, which they also refer to as community-based learning, called *Learning to Teach for Social Justice* (LTSJ). The authors acknowledge that there is a considerable 'diversity gap' between the teachers and their pupils, especially in light of increasing immigration in recent years. Boland and Keane describe how service/community-based learning constitutes a potentially transformative pedagogy for diversity and social justice in challenging contexts.

Parallels can be drawn between Luna's depiction of 'from the school to the community initiative' and Boland and Keane's LTSL project. The programme's intended outcome of making the participants increasingly aware of the value of diversity and intercultural understanding has resonances with a number of the contributors. The capacity for Service-Learning oriented approaches to engage the school as a critical formative public space for citizens-in-the-making is well articulated in this chapter, as it is also in the chapter contribution from Murphy and Tan. Luna also acknowledges that the litmus test for a school in this regard is the extent to which we are able to engage with young persons who have become alienated from the schooling process. Her contribution offers an evaluation of the 'From the School to the Community' initiative along those lines.

Crucial in the conceptualization and effective development of Service-Learning approaches are the ways in which such opportunities deepen understanding through critical reflection. This is very much in evidence in all of the chapters. What is significant is that in exploring the centrality of critical reflection we are able to gain valuable insights into complex processes involved in Service-Learning oriented approaches. At the same time, such a consideration is illustrative of the ways in which critical reflection moves us beyond the expression of professionalism by means of a set of externally-configured 'standards' to being more about how we live out our professional identities within and close to practice.

As an example of this connection with professional identity, Bamber incorporates Service-Learning as part of a 'Wider Perspectives in Education' course. The participants involved in this initiative have discovered that the Service-Learning oriented approach that they have been engaging with has a significant impact on the professional identity of our future educators. They found that the development of a teaching statement alongside a community engagement project followed by a period of school-based learning (also known as teaching practice) is a potent combination that provokes deep learning.

In similar ways, Power's chapter reflects on their Professional Experience 3 Program, embedded within the Master of Teaching Secondary Course at the University of Western Sydney. It involves the student teachers in working in a Service-Learning context that encompasses social disadvantage. Power's contribution evidences that, through deep engagement with young people from diverse backgrounds and situations, beginning teachers acquire skills to work more effectively and the recognition that as teachers they can make a difference to young people's lives. This potential for the Service-Learning approach is characteristic of each of the contributors to this volume. It underscores the potential significance of this approach for the ongoing professional development of the education workforce. The alignment that Power draws between the Graduate Professional Standards and PE3 outcomes is congruent with Klopsch and Sliwka's Service-Learning programme in Germany which is also designed to meet professional standards for teachers.

Sliwka and Klopsch focus on Service-Learning in the context of German Teacher Education. They contend that the Service-Learning process makes contributions possible that individuals can make only in collaboration with others. Significantly, the authors emphasize how Service-Learning is well suited to prepare students for meeting the professional standards of the teaching profession. For instance, through such approaches teachers can develop a profound understanding of the diversity of their prospective students and their families. Sliwka and Klopsch further acknowledge that teachers need to see themselves as lifelong learners and need to collaborate professionally with their colleagues and other members of multi-professional teams.

The need for professionals to work collaboratively is also represented within our chapter (Murphy and Tan). Here we argue for the articulation of Service-Learning oriented approaches that are located within and close to practice rather than as supplementary to it. It considers the significance of critical dialogic approaches in the support and development of professional educators across the life-course of their careers. Conceptualizing schools in challenging social contexts as sites where practice and service intersect, it opens up a discussion of the ways in which equity and social justice can be anchored within the context to which it is applied. At the core of the two case studies we present is a sense of two-way learning and collaborative knowledge-building for students, practitioners and academic partners alike. Perhaps most importantly, the chapter provides examples of the close coupling of practice and the theorization of practice that fosters participants' capacity for critical thinking.

Collaborative learning also figures centrally in Gonzalez, Frumkin and Lauria's chapter that documents a collaborative inquiry approach to Service-Learning involving the use of study groups. In particular, they draw on an initiative which was comprised of seven student teachers between the ages of 21 and 24 who partnered community members from a local Head Start programme serving families and children with high needs in a discussion about poverty. It became evident from their engagement with the process that the students became active participants of the learning process by connecting theory with practice and were able to develop personal pedagogical goals that were related to their interpretation of the literature and individual experiences, as well as discussion with peers and community members.

This intersection of personal development and civic engagement is also well articulated in the contribution by Lovat. Here, he argues that effective values education is not just an academic endeavour; rather, it also needs to be deeply personal, deeply real and deeply engaging. Offering an overview of the Values Education Program in Australia, Lovat emphasizes that effective learning is inherently values-based. Specifically, he speaks about the connectedness of values education, quality teaching and Service-Learning as a 'troika' working together in the interests of student well-being.

A further constant feature of Service-Learning, represented within this collection, is the idea that such an approach requires a strong commitment to addressing 'real world' issues and making a difference. All of the contexts present in these international studies are complex environments that offer multi-dimensional challenges. Thus, in making the commitment to situating learning within such 'spaces' and, at the same time, in making a valuable civic contribution, all of the work here is cognisant of the need for strong and sustained partnerships that enable connections between academic professional learning and social engagement to occur.

The connectedness with 'real world' concerns is ably illustrated in the contribution by Strait, Londy and Panone, drawn from their work in New Orleans, following the devastation caused by Hurricane Katrina in 2005. The work involved a collaborative initiative between a university and a local high school and a high school in one of the most deprived wards in New Orleans. Strait and her colleagues show how participants benefited from enhanced interactive and interpersonal skills with communities that were different from their own.

Recognizing and working with diversity also resonates with the sense that as professionals we bring different perspectives to collaborative working. The importance of, and effort involved in, building and sustaining effective partnerships is something that is well addressed in a number of the chapters. Most importantly, in extending the potential for Service-Learning, we must recognize that opportunities for partnership exist beyond the formal sector of education. This is significantly evident within the contribution by Sáiz and Battle where they explore work with organizations that operate within non-formal, alternative sites of education.

Finally, in looking across the chapters, there is an important message about diversity and collaboration. We believe that this collection has mirrored these emphases in bringing together an international range of authors, each being able to speak with authenticity about diversity in their local and national contexts. The value of Service-Learning in addressing social justice issues through collaboration and the drawing together of the nexus between theory and practice is that it enriches the learning of all involved, both academically and in terms of civic engagement. Perhaps most importantly, such enrichment acts equally across learners, tutors as facilitators and communities. It is a true collaborative venture and it is in this spirit that we present this book.

Part I

Service-Learning and Educating in Challenging Contexts in the United States of America

1

Study Groups and Service-Learning: A Framework for Discussion to Engage Pre-Service Teachers

Katia Gonzalez, Rhoda Frumkin and Jennifer Lauria

Introduction

This chapter offers an in-depth narrative on how a framework for discussion was utilized as a pedagogical tool to provide pre-service student teachers with the opportunity to reflect on course content as they considered their Service-Learning and community engagement experiences while working in partnership with local schools and community members. Examples of how a course management system served as a tool to expand on the conversations held during face-to-face interaction is provided while the impact of utilizing a framework to organize discussion during study groups is explored.

Service-Learning and the Adult Learner: A Collaborative Endeavour

The use of Service-Learning experiences in higher education is often seen as an excellent way to provide students with opportunities to become active participants in their learning while developing meaningful relationships with members of the community (Smith, 2003). 'Service-learning promotes good deeds and academic achievement, but its greater potential lies in preparing students to be engaged citizens' (David, 2009, p. 83). Defined as 'a teaching method that involves students performing community service in order to learn knowledge and skills connected to curricular objectives' (Billig, 2002, p. 184),

Service-Learning is utilized in many colleges and universities, in particular with pre-service teachers, around the United States and 'must exist in environments that are supportive, positive, and celebratory' (Jeandron and Robinson, 2010, p. 6). Critics contend that higher education does not always emphasize skills important for success outside of academia, including real world problem-solving and critical thinking (Steinke and Fitch, 2007). With the addition of a Service-Learning component, however, higher education incorporates organized educational experiences while Service-Learning experiences hold the promise of encouraging students' involvement by linking course outcomes with community collaboration, and ensuring 'an equal focus on both the service being provided and the learning that is occurring' (Furco, 1996, p. 5). 'Intentional consideration of experiences in light of particular learning objectives' (Hatcher and Bringle, 1997, p. 153) can be a powerful way for students to critically reflect on course materials and experiences while working through any preconceived notions about the particular community need or topic being discussed.

The ability for students to have the possibility of a 'transformational experience' (Diambra et al., 2009) is exciting, especially when they are immersed in reflective and collaborative practices. One of the main challenges for faculty becomes how to organize, assess and integrate these Service-Learning experiences with course objectives and goals (Anderson et al., 2001), without losing the much needed flexibility of adapting to the specific needs of the adult learners involved. Although not all students may be transformed by an experience, studies have indicated that Service-Learning does provide opportunities to increase content knowledge and skills, while feeling a sense of responsibility toward the needs of others (Smith, 2003; Eyler et al., 2000).

Faculty members who have modified their courses to integrate a Service-Learning component need to determine what, if any, benefits students derive from participation in specific Service-Learning experiences. This information is crucial for confirming the value of Service-Learning in higher education, and for identifying any areas of the Service-Learning project which require modification. Clear, observable and measurable evidence of students' progress toward stated learning outcomes is needed to address each of these valid concerns. Anecdotal evidence of the benefits of this specific type of experiential learning is useful but appears not to be sufficient. According to Ash et al. (2005), failure to clearly demonstrate significant intellectual gains can reduce the legitimacy of Service-Learning in the eyes of administrators who decide how to allocate resources across programmes. If institutions of higher learning are to continue to encourage and fund Service-Learning efforts, evidence of positive impact on student learning is essential.

Another potential challenge for Service-Learning experiences closely tied to course content is how to sustain the engagement of all stakeholders when a common vision may not be present or clearly outlined from the beginning. Research indicates that Service-Learning experiences, in particular for pre-service teachers, can impact on civic responsibilities and instructional practices (Jenkins and Sheehey, 2009, p. 669) and that 'often, the nature of service-learning experiences diverge from more traditional field experiences as traditional placements tend to be arranged based on the needs of university personnel rather than in response to the needs of schools, teachers, or students in our communities' (Lawrence and Butler, 2010, p. 158). Although Service-Learning experiences often are developed and implemented working closely with community partners, typically a faculty/staff member and/or college develops this partnership with the community, based on specific needs, while students may not come into the process until after the connection has been established.

The lack of student participation from the beginning of the planning process, although understandably not always possible, has the potential to affect motivation when the Service-Learning experience that has been created is not fully shared or agreed upon by all adults involved. Knowles (1984) explained how adult learners are goal- and relevancy-oriented, practical and want past experiences and knowledge to be considered while being provided with a sense of autonomy and self-direction during the learning process and the development of critical thinking skills. Because Service-Learning opportunities, especially for pre-service student teachers, may not always be self-selected by students due to specific requirements imposed by a course, faculty should carefully consider how to motivate and engage adult learners in collaborative and critically reflective practices in which preconceived notions about specific topics and experiences are explored and personal goals can be developed.

The use of collaborative inquiry to engage and motivate learners with prearranged Service-Learning experiences may be helpful in alleviating the initial lack of student involvement during the planning process:

> Learning is a collaborative process. We explore and actively work on new idea constructions in a social milieu before using them independently. We try out, explore, revise, refine, and extend our knowledge through social interaction with others. When engaged with others in this way, we are capable of crafting

solutions to life problems that we could not craft on our own. (Muth and Kiser, 2008, p. 350)

With 'democratic inquiry', students can start the process of becoming engaged in the sharing of multiple perspectives, while being encouraged to review assumptions as they practise good listening skills (Brookfield and Preskill, 2005, p. 25). The use of discussion as a way to connect Service-Learning experiences with course content and goals while considering specific needs of the adult learner appears to be an important component in the development of students' critical thinking skills and motivation.

> Adult learners are life-centred (or problem-centred) in their orientation to learning. They are motivated to learn when they perceive that learning will help them address their own problems, needs, or concerns and ultimately, improve their quality of life. In addition, the most effective learning occurs when the change in behavior (i.e., knowledge, attitude, skills and practices) is presented in the context of their application to their own life. (Kistler, 2011, p. 30)

Brookfield (1995) explained how 'our most influential assumptions are too close to us to be seen clearly by an act of will' (p. 29) and that critical reflection provides opportunities for adult learners to 'probe beneath the veneer of a commonsense reading of experience. They investigate the hidden dimensions of their practice and become aware of the omnipresence of power' (Brookfield, 1995, p. 7). 'A good discussion is one that leaves issues open for further inquiry and in which as many questions are raised as are answered' (Brookfield and Preskill, 2005, p. 23). The challenge becomes how to evaluate what may be considered successful interactions, while also being able to negotiate the needs of different learners during a 'democratic discussion' balancing the amount of input and guidance being provided by a faculty member when discussions are taking place (Brookfield and Preskill, 2005, p. 42).

Study Groups as a Teaching Strategy to Have all Participants on Board

It is not uncommon for faculty to consider pedagogical techniques and tools that are collaborative and reflective in nature in order to elicit the participation of learners with different learning styles and needs. Chassels and Melville (2009) explained how twenty-first century skills 'require individuals to develop habits of inquiry and lifelong learning in their professional and personal lives' (p. 735). When students are involved in the process of inquiry, they are actively participating in the development of ongoing professional and personal goals while being able to 'experience the process of knowledge creation' (Spronken-Smith et al., 2007, p. 2). The constructivist nature of an inquiry-based approach provides adult learners with the opportunity to engage in socially constructed knowledge while being able to be motivated in the exploration of concepts (Sproken-Smith et al., 2008). The inclusion of study groups as a teaching strategy in courses for pre-service student teachers has the potential of encouraging discussion, reflection and collaborative problem-solving. These strategies are key to Service-Learning experiences and constructivist approaches which require sharing of multiple perspectives in order to explore preconceived notions about the specific needs of students and families in schools.

Study groups can 'engage students in reading, writing, and thinking critically about a topic to spur some kind of action' (Lent, 2006, p. 69). According to Wildman et al., (2000), the opportunity for participants in 'study groups' to reflect upon 'the relationship between experience and reflection, the importance of narratives of practice, and the power of collaborative learning' (p. 248) is essential. The difficulty arises when discussions in study groups are not facilitated in an organized manner; in which certain 'dispositions' to create an atmosphere that does not limit interactions are not in place. Brookfield and Preskill (2005) explained how 'learning the dispositions and practices of democratic talk takes time and effort' (p. 42) and that faculty must consider ways of 'providing plenty of space for students to speak, giving them an opportunity to learn from others, and showing them what they say has an impact on how their peers think ... asking questions that stimulate and provoke students to examine their own and other's experiences and that establish an atmosphere for critical inquiry' (p. 100). These dispositions clearly require the use of organized collaborative practices, such as the use of study groups, in order for groups to have successful interactions and fit nicely with a social constructivist model in which knowledge is seen as 'fluidly created and recreated through reflection upon accumulated experiences' that 'may only be understood from the perspectives of understanding rooted in social context' (Smith, 2003, p. 80).

When reviewing the impact of a study group on the professional development of teachers, Vandeweghe and Verney (2006) explained that teachers became more reflective about their practice, gaining a sense of their ability to contribute to discussions as experts as they increased their pedagogical knowledge through the process of collaboration and inquiry within a group setting (p. 286). Since the use of study groups has been proven effective as a strategy to increase stakeholders' process of inquiry, the selection of a framework within a study group model can only enhance the organization of the experiences faculty facilitate to meet the needs of all members involved.

Study Groups and Service-Learning for Pre-Service Teachers: A Framework for Inquiry and Action

The rationale behind the 'Study Groups and Service-Learning for Pre-Service Teachers: A Framework for Inquiry and Action' (Gonzalez-Acquaro et al., 2009) is based on social constructivist theory and an inquiry-based model focusing specifically on the needs of adult learners (Knowles, 1984) while considering the benefits of discussion as a reflective tool (Brookfield, 1995). By viewing pre-service educators 'as holding a repertoire of ideas' (Dietz and Davis, 2009, p. 221), the authors kept in mind that not all learners may be prepared or have the necessary skills to regulate their behaviour to actively engage in the process of inquiry through the use of discussion. 'Inquiry-based learning is an umbrella term that encompasses a range of approaches designed to engage students in the research process' (Spronken-Smith and Kingham, 2009, p. 242), while 'social constructivism is based on the social interactions ... along with a personal critical thinking process' (Powell and Kalina, 2009, p. 243). Key to this process of inquiry is the ability of faculty to scaffold information utilizing tools and techniques to meet the needs of a diverse group of learners (Oliver, 2007) while facilitating the exchange of perspectives between different stakeholders through experiences requiring learner engagement. Taking into consideration learning styles becomes essential when considering ways to engage student teachers that have their own needs as learners but also specific responsibilities as they engage with students, colleagues and families from the community.

Grasha (1996) defined learning styles as 'personal qualities that influence a student's ability to acquire information, to interact with peers and the teacher, and otherwise to participate in learning experiences' (p. 41). Similarly, Dunn and Dunn (1998) maintained that learners have individual learning-style strengths and preferences that affect how well they concentrate on, process, internalize and remember new and difficult information. It was noted by Dunn and Griggs (2000) that concentration occurs differently for different people as dictated by a variety of stimuli, which creates the need for educators to identify individuals' learning styles to trigger their concentration, energize their processing and increase their long-term memory. Additionally, Kolb and Kolb (2005) affirmed that 'to learn requires facing and embracing differences; whether they be differences between expert performance and one's novice status, differences between deeply held ideas and beliefs and new ideas, or differences in the life experience and values of others that can lead to understanding them' (p. 207).

Learning style research findings in higher education support the need for consideration of students' learning styles (Dunn and Stevenson, 1997; Given et al., 2000; Lenehan et al., 1994; Nelson et al., 1993). In alignment with such research, Dunn and Griggs (2000) stressed the need for a shift in focus from the *content* of what is to be learned to the individual learning style characteristics of students – which should dictate the *process* of learning. Likewise, Rundle et al., (2002) reported that when students utilized suggested learning-style responsive approaches, they gradually honed and became adept at strategies that enhanced their communication, concentration and team interactions. Further experimental research with college students documented significantly higher achievement in a variety of disciplines when learning-styles based instruction was used in comparison with traditional teaching methods, and sufficient results have been reported to convince educators that consideration of learning styles can be crucial for the diverse learners who attend institutions of higher education (Boyle et al., 2003; Dunn et al., 1990; Miller et al., 2000–1). As a natural extension of careful consideration of students' learning styles in curriculum design and pedagogy, educators need to critically reflect on their teaching styles. Honigsfeld and Schiering (2004) have documented that when teachers have the opportunity to reflect on their teaching practices, they develop (a) a better understanding of the teaching process, (b) stronger pedagogical skills, and (c) improved attitudes toward the teaching-learning process and their diverse students. Similarly, Harr et al. (2002) describe the need for both teachers and students to recognize that they perceive, process and communicate information in unique ways. Such a belief system is crucial to the establishment of an optimal instructional environment conducive to quality teaching and learning

Several models of inquiry-based learning have been developed in which the use of reflection and assessment has taken a central role in engaging students in the process of inquiry while being able to sustain engagement based on learning styles. In these models, 'learning is stimulated by a question or a problem' as participants seek out information while the instructor serves as a 'facilitator' (Spronken-Smith and Kingham, 2009, p. 242). In 'Study Groups and Service-learning for Pre-Service Teachers: A Framework for Inquiry and Action' (Gonzalez-Acquaro et al., 2009), all stakeholders participating in Service-Learning are asked to engage in the process of inquiry using discussion framed by a problem or question in order to develop goals while assessing experiences. By promoting the development of ongoing goals, students are engaged in the process of reflection about their Service-Learning experiences, considering different perspectives while getting into the habit of developing daily goals leading to action.

Brookfield (1995) explained how the process of reflecting on our own may narrow opportunities to become more 'critical' as we explore a variety of perspectives that may shed a different light on the way we perceive certain experiences. By engaging in the process of reflection utilizing discussion, learners construct and assess knowledge focusing on the development of personal and group goals while sharing experiences listening to the perspectives of others.

Key to this model is the utilization of techniques to empower learners with different needs and goals in self-directing their learning while encouraging a social construction of knowledge that focuses on ongoing reflection, connection of theory to practice and the learner's assessment of experiences in relation to their personal and group learning goal. By reflecting on the content of learning within the context of their community experiences as well as on the input of colleagues, pre-service teachers construct a fuller understanding of the meaning of the varied interactions occurring within their community placements. The process of reflection enables them to integrate what they 'have been absorbing through the course content with the community external to the college campus' (Collier and Williams, 2005, p. 83). As pre-service teachers reflect, they explore and evaluate varied perspectives in light of their own understanding, and broaden that understanding to include perspectives in addition to their own. Their newly-constructed understanding becomes the knowledge base upon which to build through future experiences.

Organizing Input: Students and Community Coming Together

Implementation phase

Special note

The next section of this chapter is the narrative description of the utilization of the framework during a three-hour discussion focusing on the topic of poverty and its effect in schools. A total of seven student teachers, between the ages of 21and 24, participated with community members from a local Head Start programme serving families and children with high needs in a discussion about poverty facilitated by one of the authors of this chapter, who also served as the faculty member for this senior course. As Davis (2009) explained, planning courses with a Service-Learning component can certainly be time consuming for faculty. However, when resources are carefully researched, opportunities for reflection incorporated and course content with student learning outcomes kept in mind, it can be an invaluable experience for faculty, students and community members. Many Service-Learning experiences incorporate the concept of 'reciprocity' among all stakeholders (Davis, 2009, p. 233), clarifying the connections between academic work and the Service-Learning experience, while considering specific needs of community members and students. This can be invaluable for the overall success of Service-Learning.

The interdisciplinary nature of this course and the need to stay abreast of changes happening in the education field created exciting opportunities for students to become more critical as they collaborated with peers and members of the community. Topics for discussion included the study and examination of the philosophical, sociological and historical foundations of education, taking into consideration current research related to school, diversity and society. After overall/overarching course content and goals were established, an extensive literature review was conducted to stay abreast of current research, and demographic needs of partner schools and the experiences of student teachers were carefully considered. Local, national and international perspectives and policies were utilized to frame readings and discussions.

Because several of the steps related to the framework for discussion required the development and assessment of individual goals, it was decided that utilizing the college's course management system (Moodle) as a medium to encourage reflection beyond the three hours scheduled for the course, could be valuable as a 'space' for students to reflect upon and organize their thinking related to their pedagogical goal. Additionally, the need to seek out more than one experience related to the goal, required students to be actively engaged with the topic while reflecting on their experiences.

Table 1.1 provides information about the first two steps of the framework which are done individually by each student. In step one, and utilizing the assigned reading, students had to identify three key words based solely on the author's perspective. In step two, students chose one of the three key words from step one and explained why that word stood out to them the most, connecting it to an experience. Table 1.2 provides information related to steps three and four. In step three, specific discussions about the topic and key word from step two (individual reflection, small and larger group discussion) is provided, while step four outlines pedagogical goals and experiences related to goals that were identified by each student. Table 1.3 relates specifically to step five in which students had to individually assess their experiences related to their pedagogical goals while peers had to provide feedback.

Table 1.1. *Using the framework to organize input and scaffold information*

1st Step: 3 Key Words from Theory	2nd Step: Theory and Practice Selecting One Key Word from Readings to Experiences
Student 1: Privilege, Poverty, Stereotyping	**Privilege** Arguments of people about the meaning of privilege.
Student 2: Income, Poverty, Socioeconomic Status	**Socio-economic Status** Language and economic barrier at school.
Student 3: Poverty, Stereotyping, Misinformed	**Poverty** Economic distress in the US and effects at school.
Student 4: Poverty, Diversity, Socioeconomic Status	**Poverty** Impact of poverty internationally and effects of good teachers.
Student 5: Stereotyping, Poverty, Technical Data	**Stereotyping** Impact of students forming groups and effects on how people classify one another.
Student 6: Poverty/Privilege, Data, Stereotyping	**Data** Central to article. Empirical research and curriculum considerations.
Student 7: Research, Disagreement, Segregation	**Segregation** Positive individual experience related to unity in schools.

Table 1.2. *Using the framework to organize input and scaffold information – Steps 3 and 4 – overall comments*

3rd Step **Discussion: Overall Comments and Key Words** **Individual** **Small Group** **Large Group**	4th Step **Individual Pedagogical Goals and Experiences Related to Goals**
Student 1: PRIVILEGE *Self:* Considering experiences growing up and impact of race. 'White privilege' – social connections/opportunities. Readings often discuss challenges of multicultural/low income community and representation/experiences of staff. *Small Group*: Empirical data to support teaching practices impacting differences in the classroom and 'privilege lifestyles' and 'diverse lifestyles' of students. Difficulty between group discussing empirical data because of variety of level of understanding related to the topic. *Whole Group Discussion*: Access to resources based on 'privilege'. Discussion related to gifted and talented programmes. Correlation between academic programmes and socioeconomic status.	*Goal: Learn about Communicating with Parents.* Discussion with cooperating teacher – impact of school administration and laws when supporting teachers working with diverse students. Impact of technology and different mediums to reach out to parents.
Student 2: SOCIO-ECONOMIC STATUS *Self:* Focus for comments. Remembrance of being able to go to school well fed daily. Impact of lack of supplies at current school and apparent lack of accessibility to good nutrition due to limited items being brought to eat. Concerned also about the lack of language skills of families which may impact the way they assist their children with homework.	*Goal: Learn how to help with the sharing of supplies and involving parents in the school life of their children.* Conversation with paraprofessional.

▶

Student 3: POVERTY
Self: Considering experiences at current school placement and the inability of students to bring in required/mandated supplies.

Small Group: Focus was a colleague's experience with another public school facing a similar situation related to lack of supplies. In addition, these students also are in conflict with students from bordering towns due to diverse backgrounds and needs.

Whole Group Discussion: Witnessing poverty in schools in different ways. Discussion of how Head Start reaches out to students of impoverished families with children with special needs. Impact of community members reaching out with limited funding.

Goal: Create a non-prejudiced classroom where money is not the focus – identification of strategies utilized. Sharing supplies as a whole, not individually. Availability of uniforms as clothing.

Ways teacher adapts class materials to provide access to all regardless of need.

Student 4: POVERTY
Self: Considering international perspectives about poverty based on travel experiences. Good teaching is what can impact learning regardless of socio-economic status or learning environment.

Small Group: Discussion related to different types of socio-economic status within placement/experiences. Lack of family support and minimal resources in some schools.

Whole Group Discussion: The benefit of hearing from community members serving the needs of students while serving as a model when a teacher grows up in a different environment.

Goal: To relate better with students – never become a teacher that thinks she is better than her students. Conversations with students.

Evaluating contact information of students provided a better understanding of family dynamic and how this may impact students' well-being.

Student 5: STEREOTYPING

Self: Impact of placing students into groups based on a personal experience of being stereotyped while attending school.

Small Group: Students placing one another in groups based on socio-economic status and the impact it is having on students with less resources being more stereotyped.

Whole Group Discussion: Community members discussing poverty and how it is impacting classrooms – a problem that needs to be addressed in order to avoid 'distance' between groups. Conversation about poverty connecting with stereotyping because of how groups are being formed.

Goal: For students being stereotyped to be involved with other students.
Observing interactions during gym/playground.

Focusing on activities that could get everyone involved.

Conversation with gym teacher about ways to encourage a more diverse group of students playing together. Coming up with strategies. Not letting students pick their own teammates.

Ensuring everyone has an opportunity to be a helper in the classroom and be involved regardless of ability.

Student 6: DATA

Self: Focusing on data due to the lack of a system at current placement. Strongly believing in the importance of standardization to ensure students are viewed the same way by all educators.

Small Group: Difficult time having a conversation about key words and trying to link them. Realized that poverty and stereotyped are linked and assessments needs to be adapted based on individual experiences of students. Group also discussed how assessments are written for a select group and can create situations in which students are stereotyped.

Whole Group Discussion: Discussion centred on how having a good financial situation can impact on resources to help students do well in tests. Also discussed ways families, regardless of resources, can help students do well in tests but are at a disadvantage.

Goal: To learn about types of assessments being utilized, focusing specifically on reading, writing and maths (individual and overall). Student preparation and teacher attitudes toward assessments.
Meeting with cooperating teacher/sharing of resources.

Reviewed with cooperating teacher individual scores and developed a plan to assist students based on needs.

With cooperating teacher, focusing on self-regulation skills to assist students with anxiety related to tests.

▶

Student 7: SEGREGATION
Self: Reflecting on the lack of opportunities for students at current placement to socialize or develop strong friendships/communicate with peers.

Small Group: Discussed how some schools border both a rich neighbourhood and poverty stricken neighbourhood. Challenges related to segregation due to socio-economic status.

Whole Group Discussion: Spoke about privilege-equity/equality and the impact of funding in relation to opportunities.

Goal: Reduce biases and prejudice and increase friendships between students. Selection of reading/discussion of classroom literature focusing on differences/similarities.

Modelling the sharing of resources and the need to complement one another. Seeing the impact of the cooperating teacher reinforcing respect and friendships in the classroom.

Adapting lessons to include more socialization between students while helping students remain on task.

Table 1.3. *Using the framework to organize input and scaffold information – Step 5 – overall comments*

Step 5: Assessing Experiences and Contributing Resources in Relation to Pedagogical Goal	Primary Focus of Peer Comments Related to Step 5
Student 1 Reported observing positive teacher–parent interactions and parent's feeling that teacher knows and differentiates for each student. Discussed teacher's successful use of range of communication options for parental communication in situations of need and for positive feedback. Noted that communication is not impeded by economic or ethnic differences.	Impact of privilege on students' access to resources. Instances of stereotyping as a result of privilege. Need for teachers to avoid judgement based on privilege. **Suggested Action Plan: None** Desire to encourage sharing and to increase involvement of parents who have difficulty understanding English.

Student 2
Reported observation of students' attempts to share materials being met with teacher disapproval. Instances of students' failure to return forms filled out by parents due to parental difficulty in understanding English.

Instances of students being reprimanded for sharing and of student not being allowed to use mechanical pencil and not having writing implement.

Positive impact of parent–teacher collaboration for improving student behaviour.

Noted difference in teachers' attitudes about parents in different schools

Suggested Action Plan:

1 Attend parent–teacher conferences (to facilitate more parental involvement with school work).

2 Run college fundraiser to buy school supplies.

3 Talk to paraprofessional about writing class notes and homework in Spanish.

Student 3
Described classroom efforts to support all students – students offering to share supplies; teacher making supplies available to all; alternate requirements for materials; laptop computers provided for activities.

Shared similar concerns about students having supplies, and beliefs that money should not interfere with education.

Suggested Action Plan:

1 Have fundraisers to create small community within classroom (school).

2 (Encourage school to) buy inexpensive supplies at local stores.

3 College class can have fundraiser to buy supplies.

Student 4
Reported that assessing pedagogical goal (to relate better to students) can be done by noting number of times students approach her with problem or conflict, leading to idea of whether or not students feel comfortable with her.

Discussed need for teachers to understand students' backgrounds and to teach students in any learning environment.

Suggested Action Plan: None

▶

Student 5

Reported efforts to facilitate involvement among students who are and are not stereotyped through joint kickball game. Efforts to make students feel as though they are a unit rather than stereotyped into groups because of athletic or academic ability. Efforts by gym teacher and self to create fair team assignments and complete participation.

Shared childhood and current student teaching experiences, and multiple suggestions for improving students' ways of relating to one another in the gym.

Suggested Action Plan:

1　With gym teacher, teach lesson unit on stereotyping.

2　Teach 'everyone's different' lessons as student teachers did in multicultural class.

3　Facilitate classroom focus on 'uniting' and 'being a community'.

Student 6

Discussed importance of using data to prove effectiveness of instruction, her own learning about specific assessments and benefits of assessment data, and plans to work with her cooperating teacher to use and assess impact of differentiated instruction.

Shared positive opinions about using data to assess student learning, including ways to involve students in self-assessment as mentioned in experiences described by Student 6.

Suggested Action Plan: None

Student 7

Observed that students realized that they are being rewarded for doing the right thing and being respectful. Cooperating teacher reinforces this behaviour. Noted need to increase socialization opportunities in class to assist some students in overcoming differences and getting along.

Discussed comments about positive reinforcement and importance of students bonding and communicating with one another.

Suggested Action Plan:

1　Do activities that encourage students' focus on how they are alike rather than different to bring the class closer together.

2　Reiterate the importance of friendships.

3　Create lessons focused on students getting to know each other to establish a better foundation for students' friendships.

Framework and Scaffolding Information: Results, Discussion and Future Research Directions

Results from the utilization of the framework to scaffold information during discussion indicated that students became active participants of the learning process by connecting theory with practice and were able to develop personal pedagogical goals that were related to their interpretation of the literature and individual experiences, as well as discussions with peers and community members. The use of collaborative tools and techniques appeared to be effective in increasing the input provided by all students while also challenging many of them to focus on specific ways to achieve goals, assess experiences, and consider specific action plans.

In step one, all but one student identified and had in common the word *poverty* among three key words from their assigned reading as a focus for discussion related to the author's perspective, while one student focused specifically on information related to issues of equity and equality when discussing research related to students from different backgrounds and needs. What is interesting to point out is that only two students chose to use the word poverty as their main focus when connecting theory to experiences (step two), choosing to focus on issues related to equity and equality that could, but not always, be influenced by poverty. As mentioned by Brookfield and Preskill (2005), engaging in critical inquiry appeared to help students broaden their thinking about the topic by specifically relating it to their experiences. The process of breaking down information during steps one and two also appeared to help students organize their thinking to focus on underlying messages from the article they were reading. For step three, in which students were asked to engage in individual reflection, small and whole group discussions prior to developing pedagogical goals, six out of seven students were able to go through this process without difficulty, while only one student focused on the individual perspective. It is interesting to point out that the one student that only considered the individual perspective identified only one experience for the self-developed pedagogical goal, while the remaining students had several experiences listed. The opportunity to have a whole group discussion with the community members appeared to shed light and broaden students' perspectives toward the topic being discussed, while all but one student connected the conversation with the community members directly to the word selected during step two.

For step four, in which students were asked to develop a pedagogical goal for the week related to the topic discussed during class, it is interesting to point out that five students opted to focus on instructional strategies and techniques while two combined techniques with increasing their self-efficacy as educators. All students chose to focus on goals that clearly related to increasing effective communication (between families, students, sharing of assessment information) and all had to do with the facilitator (teacher) making changes either personally or with instruction or with classroom environment. The conversation with community members appeared to be present for many students when developing their pedagogical goal to assist students facing challenges since the experiences pre-service teachers focused on related not only to their individual and small group reflection but also considered the perspective and experiences of the community with the topic. This process of having a dialogue between everyone involved in Service-Learning experiences can be valuable to the development of goals and the identification of experiences that will meet a particular need of a community while encouraging student teachers to consider theory and focus on areas of interest to them, while carefully considering ways to serve specific needs of the community.

Students' interest in increasing communication was aimed at creating a community within the classroom. They reported:

(a) efforts to increase interactions across ability lines:
    The thing I am working on in my class is making it (so) that everyone helps and that everyone is a unit and not stereotyped into groups based on athletic ability or how smart you are ...
(b) socio-economic differences:
    Having fundraisers is one way to continue your idea of creating a small community within the classroom;
(c) and roles, as one student expressed her desire to 'never become the teacher who thinks she is better than her students'.

After developing a pedagogical goal, students were asked to assess their experiences and contributing resources in relation to their goal (step five). Student reflections related to their assessments of experiences tied to pedagogical goals indicated that their main focus was the use of dialogue between different stakeholders in order to identify ways to achieve pedagogical goals. When students from the class were asked to provide feedback on peers' pedagogical goals, experiences and assessment of experiences, all drew clear and specific connections between the assessment and each peer's individual classroom experiences, frequently reporting experiencing similar situations as those described. All seven students validated initial ways their peers approached challenges but only four encouraged an action-oriented approach to situations which could be closely linked to their own comfort level as educators based on their knowledge about the topic or situation or previous experiences. Students providing an action-oriented approach to a pedagogical goal was viewed by the instructor as a positive indicator of students sharing ideas to reach solutions.

Pre-service student teachers mentioned how specific feedback from peers helped shed a different light or provided support in the development of new ways to approach situations that originally appeared challenging or exclusive to individual placements. The evaluation of experiences and their relevance to pedagogical goals conducted individually, but also in light of peers' perspectives, appeared to motivate students to seek out a variety of ways to approach challenges in their placements. This was apparent as one student expressed appreciation to classmates: 'Thank you everyone for the great feedback ... I especially liked your idea of a bagel sale, because those funds could definitely help mine or anyone else's classroom if they are in a financial setback.' The student making this comment was the one student that had only focused on the individual perspective during step three. Based on the response to peers, receiving other perspectives appeared to be helpful when thinking about ways to initiate possible solutions to the situation. However, it is interesting to note that feedback was overwhelmingly/consistently positive in nature. While it is possible that student teachers consistently shared one another's interpretation of classroom interactions, it is also possible that colleagues deliberately refrained from suggesting alternate interpretations because of concerns about appearing confrontational.

In addition to being helpful to the recipient, peer feedback may have been useful to the student teacher providing the feedback. Dunlap and Grabinger suggested that 'the process of reviewing someone else's work can help learners reflect on and articulate their own views and ideas, ultimately improving their own work' (Dunlap, 2005, p. 20). It is possible that generating feasible solutions to colleagues' concerns helped peers to consider whether these solutions could be applicable in their own classrooms. As one student noted, 'What was helpful about the process was that rather then just discussing our ideas casually, based on articles we read, we further reflected on our own experiences, heard other opinions from classmates, and then were forced to look within and around the elementary classroom where we were student teaching.'

Examples provided in the framework often expanded upon the initial ideas presented in the literature, while input from peers appeared to not only provide different perspectives but also impact on decisions to be made in their classrooms. The challenge of thinking 'critically and analytically' (Duch et al., 2001), while breaking down the amount of information provided by everyone involved, seemed to help with the organization and introduction of relevant pedagogical goals to tackle a variety of situations.

An essential component related to the utilization of this framework was to help students feel a sense of ownership about their pre-assigned placement experience and Service-Learning project by being able to provide their individual input while being exposed to 'multiple perspectives'. As adult learners, having the opportunity to 'respect diverse talents and ways of learning' is important since 'people bring different talents and styles of learning to college ... learning in new ways that do not come so easily' (Chickering and Gamson, 1987, p. 4). The ability of students to use the framework to break down information while examining ideas presented by the literature, colleagues and community appeared to have impacted on the way specific situations were viewed as well as the development of practical applications that could affect experiences encountered in their placements and Service-Learning projects.

Because of the results related to the specific action plans provided between peers, it is recommended for future research that teachers' knowledge, attitudes and self-efficacy skills toward a particular challenge during Service-Learning continue to be explored, while consideration is also given to how it may impact on the development, implementation, assessment and sharing of ideas and support between all stakeholders during a Service-Learning experience.

References

Anderson, J. B., Swick, K. J. and Yff, J. (2001), *Service-learning in Teacher Education: Enhancing the Growth of New Teachers, Their Students, and Communities.* Corporation for National Service. Washington, DC: Office of Educational Research and Improvement.

Ash, S. L., Clayton, P. H. and Atkinson, M. (2005), 'Integrating reflection and assessment to capture and improve student learning'. *Michigan Journal of Community Service-learning,* 11 (2): 49–60.

Billig, S. (2002), 'Support for K-12 service-learning practice: A brief review of research'. *Educational Horizons,* 80 (4): 184–9.

Boyle, R. A., Russo, K. and Lefkowitz, R. F. (2003), 'Presenting a new instructional tool for teaching law-related courses: A Contract Activity Package for motivated and independent learners'. *Gonzaga Law Review,* 38 (1): 1–31.

Brookfield, S. (1995), *Becoming a Critically Reflective Teacher.* San Francisco, CA: Jossey Bass

Brookfield, S. and Preskill, S. (2005), *Discussion as a Way of Teaching.* San Francisco, CA: Jossey Bass.

Chassels, C. and Melville, W. (2009), 'Collaborative, reflective, and iterative Japanese lesson study in an initial teacher education programme: Benefits and challenges'. *Canadian Journal of Education,* 32 (4): 734–63.

Chickering., A. W. and Gamson, Z. (1987), 'Seven principles for good practice in undergraduate education'. *American Association of Higher Education Bulletin,* 39 (7): 3–7.

Collier, P. J. and Williams, D. R. (2005), 'Reflection in action: The learning-doing relationship', in C. M. Cress, P. J. Collier and V. L. Reitenauer, *Learning Through Serving: A Student Guidebook for Service-learning Across the Disciplines*. Sterling, VA: Stylus.

David, J. L. (2009), 'Service-learning and civic participation'. *Educational Leadership*, 66 (8): 83–4.

Davis, B. (2009), *Tools for Teaching*. San Francisco, CA: Jossey Bass.

Diambra, J. F., McClam, T., Fuss, A., Burton, B. and Fudge, D. L. (2009), 'Using a focus group to analyze student's perceptions of a service-learning project'. *College Student Journal*, 43 (1): 114–22.

Dietz, C. and Davis, E. (2009), 'Preservice elementary teacher's reflection on narrative images of inquiry'. *Journal of Science of Teacher Education*, 20 (3): 219–43

Duch, B. J., Groh, S. E. and Allen, D. E. (2001), *The Power of Problem-Based Learning*. Sterling, VA: Stylus Publishing, LLC.

Dunlap, J. C. (2005), 'Workload reduction in online courses: Getting some shuteye'. *Performance Improvement*, 44: 18–25. doi: 10.1002/pfi.4140440507.

Dunn, R., Deckinger, E. L., Withers, P. and Katzenstein, H. (1990), 'Should college students be taught how to do homework? The effects of studying marketing through perceptual strengths'. *Illinois School Research and Development Journal*, 26 (3): 96–113.

Dunn, R. and Dunn K. (1998), *Practical Applications for Individualizing Staff Development for Adults*. Westport, CT: Praeger Publishers.

Dunn, R. and Griggs, S. (2000), *Practical Approaches to Using Learning Styles in Higher Education*. Westport, CT: Bergin and Garvey.

Dunn, R. and Stevenson, J. M. (1997), 'Teaching diverse college students to study with a learning styles prescription'. *College Student Journal*, 31 (3): 333–9.

Ertmer, P. A., Richardson, J. C., Belland, B., Camin, D., Connolly, P., Coulthard, G., Lei, K. and Mong, C. (2007). 'Using peer feedback to enhance the quality of student online postings: An exploratory study'. *The Journal of Computer-Mediated Communication*, 12 (2): 412–33.

Eyler, J. S., Giles, D. E., Stenson, C. M. and Gray, C. J. (2001), *At a Glance: What We Know About the Effects of Service-learning on College Students, Faculty, Institutions and Communities*. 3rd edn. Nashville, TN: Vanderbilt University.

Furco, A. (1996), *Service-learning: A balanced approach to experiential education. Expanding boundaries: service and learning*. Washington, DC: Corporation for National Service, pp. 2–6.

Given, B. K. and Tyler, E. P. with Hall, N., Johnson, W. and Wood, M. (2000), 'Tactual learning at the doctoral level: A risk worth taking', in R. Dunn and S. A. Griggs (eds), *Practical Approaches to Using Learning Styles in Higher Education*. Westport, CT: Bergin and Garvey, pp. 100–8

Gonzalez-Acquaro, K., Frumkin, R. and Rosenberg, S. (2009), *Study Groups and Service-Learning for Pre-Service Teachers: A Framework for Inquiry and Action*. Unpublished framework.

Grasha, A. F. (1996), *Teaching with Style*. Pittsburgh, PA.: Alliance.

Harr, J., Hall, G., Schoepp, P. and Smith, D. (2002). 'How teachers teach to students with different learning styles'. *The Clearing House*, 75 (3): 142–5.

Hatcher, J. A. and Bringle, R. G. (1997), 'Reflection: Bridging the gap between service and learning'. *College Teaching*, 45(4): 153–7.

Honigsfeld, A. and Schiering, M. (2004), 'Diverse approaches to the diversity of learning styles in teacher education'. *Educational Psychology*, 24 (4): 487–507.

Jeandron, C. and Robinson, G. (2010), *Creating a Climate for Service Learning Success*. Washington DC: American Association of Community Colleges.

Jenkins, A. and Sheehey, P. (2009), 'Implementing service-learning in special education coursework: What we learned'. *Education*, 129 (4): 668–82.

Kistler, M. (2011), 'Adult learners: Considerations for education and training'. *Techniques (ACTE)*, 86 (2): 28–30.

Knowles, M. (1984), *Andragogy in Action*. San Francisco: Jossey-Bass.

Kolb, A. and Kolb, G. (2005), 'Learning styles and learning spaces: Enhancing experiential learning in higher education'. *Academy of Management Learning and Education*, 4 (2): 193–212.

Lawrence, M. and Butler, M. (2010), 'Becoming aware of the challenges of helping students learn: An examination of the nature of learning during a service-learning experience'. *Teacher Education Quarterly*, 37 (1): 155–75.

Lenehan, M., Dunn, R., Ingham, J., Murray, J. B. and Signer, R. (1994), ' Effects of learning-style intervention on college students' achievement, anxiety, anger and curiosity'. *Journal of College Student Development*, 35 (6): 461–6.

Lent, R. (2006), 'In the company of critical thinkers'. *Educational Leadership*, 64 (2): 68–72.

Miller, J., Ostrow, S., Dunn, R., Beasley, M., Geisert, G. and Nelson, B. (2000–1), 'Effects of traditional versus learning-style presentation of course content in ultrasound and anatomy on the achievement and attitudes of allied-health college students'. *National Forum of Applied Educational Research Journal*, 13 (1): 50–62.

Muth, B. and Kiser, M. (2008), 'Radical conversations part two: Cultivating social constructivist learning methods in ABE classrooms'. *Journal of Correctional Education*, 59 (4): 349–64.

Nelson, B., Dunn, R., Griggs, S. A., Primavera, L., Fitzpatrick, M., Bascilious, Z. and Miller, R. (1993), 'Effects of learning style intervention on students' retention and achievement'. *Journal of College Student Development*, 34 (5): 364–9.

Oliver, R. (2007), 'Using mobile technologies to support learning in large on campus university classes' in *ICT: Providing choices for learners and learning. Proceedings ASCILITE*, Singapore 2007: Retrieved 17 August from http://www.ascilite.org.au/conferences/singapore07/procs/oliver.pdf

Powell, K. and Kalina, C. (2009), 'Cognitive and social constructivism: Developing tools for an effective classroom'. *Education*, 130 (2): 241–50.

Rundle, S., Honigsfeld, A. and Dunn, R. (2002), *An Educator's Guide to the Learning Individual*. Danbury, CT: Performance Concepts International Limited.

Smith, V. (2003), ' "You have to learn who comes with the disability": Students' reflections on service-learning experiences with peers labeled with disabilities'. *Research and Practice for Persons with Severe Disabilities*, 28 (3): 79–90.

Spronken-Smith, R. and Kingham, S. (2009), 'Strengthening teaching and research links: The case of a pollution exposure inquiry project'. *Journal of Geography in Higher Education*, 33 (2): 241–53.

Spronken-Smith, R., Angelo, T., Matthews, H., O'Steen, B. and Robertson, J. (2007), *How effective is inquiry based learning in linking teaching and research?* Paper prepared for An International Colloquium on International Policies and Practices for Academic Enquiry. Marwell, Winchester, UK, 19–21 April 2007. Available at http://portallive.solent.ac.uk/university/rtconference/colloquium_papers.aspx.

Spronken-Smith, R., Bullard, J. E., Ray, W., Roberts, C. and Keiffer, A. (2008), 'Where might sand dunes be on Mars? Engaging students through inquiry-based learning in Geography'. *Journal of Geography in Higher Education*, 32 (1): 71–86.

Steinke, P. and Fitch, P. (2007), 'Assessing service-learning'. *Research and Practice in Assessment*, 1 (2): 1–8.

Swick, K. J. and Rowls, M. (2000), 'The "Voices" of preservice teachers on the meaning and value of their service-learning'. *Education,* 120 (3): 461–9.

Vandeweghe, R. and Verney, K. (2006), 'The evolution of a school-based study group'. *Phi Delta Kappan*, 99 (4): 282–6.

Wildman, T. M., Hable, M. P., Preston, M. M. and Magliaro, S. G. (2000), 'Faculty study groups: Solving 'good problems' through study, reflection, and collaboration'. *Innovative Higher Education*, 24 (4): 247–63.

2

Service-Learning and Urban Teaching in the United States of America: Building Communities for Social Justice

Noah Borrero

Introduction

The population of students attending public schools in the United States (US) is among the most diverse in the world. For example, data show that approximately one out of every five school-aged child in the US is the child of an immigrant family (Capps et al., 2005). Further, youth from ethnic minority backgrounds are shown to make up more than half of the urban public school population in the country (Fry, 2009). In urban contexts like San Francisco, Chicago and New York, students of colour comprise the majority of the overall population under the age of 18 (Darling-Hammond, 2002). The cultural and educational diversity represented in these schools and communities proffers tremendous possibilities and tremendous challenges. Unfortunately, this diversity is all too often framed as a 'problem' to be solved or an 'obstacle' to be overcome (Borrero and Yeh, 2010; Dorner et al., 2007). In fact, current educational discourse seems to focus entirely on issues like 'drop outs' and the 'achievement gap' between students of colour and Caucasian students – presupposing the failure of students who do not fit the prototypical model of what a student is supposed to be (e.g. Camangian, 2010; Duncan-Andrade, 2007; Kozol, 2005).

Much of this deficit approach to student diversity stems from a hyper-focus on standardized testing, and teacher accountability in public education in the US Academic achievement scores are not improving, and students in the US are falling behind students from other countries (Darling-Hammond, 2007). As a result, there is an increased focus on the problems with the US school system, the failure of students and the blaming of 'underperforming' students who are bringing the system down (Camangian, 2010; Rist, 1970). These students, typically, are those from urban communities, living in poverty. Research shows that many schools in the US proliferate this deficit approach to diversity by failing to acknowledge the cultural assets and multiple learning experiences and perspectives that students of colour possess and bring with them to school (Borrero and Yeh, 2010; Moll et al., 1992; Paris, 2010). In essence, there is a cultural disconnection between the lives students experience at school and the lives they experience at home and in their communities (Tyler et al., 2008; Nasir and Saxe, 2003).

One specific way to frame this cultural disconnection is through a focus on public school teachers in the US and the students they teach. While the population of students from ethnic minority groups continues to grow (Fry, 2009), the teaching force in the US remains predominantly middle-class and Caucasian. In fact, Caucasian teachers make up over 80 per cent of the teaching force (Zumwalt and Craig, 2005) and the vast majority of these teachers come from middle-class backgrounds (Banks et al., 2005). These cultural disparities place a specific onus on the role of Teacher Education programmes to address the 'demographic divide' between teachers and students, and the need for new teachers to enter the profession with an understanding and appreciation of the diverse experiences that their youth bring into the classroom. An understanding of youth's cultural and community contexts outside of the classroom is essential for making learning possible in the classroom. In this chapter, I discuss the possibilities for Service-Learning as a conduit for such understanding, as it can help teachers and youth to build connections to their communities and their possibilities as learners. Specifically, I present two cases of Service-Learning projects developed by pre-service teachers within an Urban Education programme in California. The cases are described to show different ways that new teachers can create connections with community partners in urban areas, and in so doing begin to bridge the demographic divide between themselves and their students.

Service-Learning and Social Justice in Urban Communities

Building on the description of Service-Learning as 'a teaching and learning approach that integrates community service with academic study to enrich learning, teach civic responsibility and strengthen communities' (National

Commission on Service-learning, 2002, p. 3), the specific focus of this chapter looks into the role of Service-Learning in teacher education, and its potential to connect teachers, students and communities through learning. I pay special attention to the importance of this integration between service and learning, and draw upon Furco's (1996) work on the importance of a balanced approach to Service-Learning. This balance is in contrast to the idea of using service mainly as an avenue for practitioners to reflect on their experience of providing a service, or using service mainly as a way of providing much needed resources to communities in need. Instead, Service-Learning is framed as the connection between the service provided and the opportunity for learning and reflection. As a practice, Service-Learning must strive to achieve this balance by providing service in conjunction with in-class curriculum. Both service and learning aspects are given equal priority by teachers, students and community partners (Furco, 1996).

As a teacher educator in an urban context in the US, I feel that Service-Learning must be part of a more broadly defined social justice perspective. Romero (1988) stated that 'education must recognize that the development of the individual and of the peoples is the advancement of each and all from less-human to more human conditions' (p. 36). This humanizing, ecological approach applies to educators working with youth in urban schools. For example, social justice, as it relates to urban education can be seen as:

> ... principles of personal safety in interpersonal relationships, attention to the here and now, sensitivity to group dynamics, use of students' viewpoints to launch dialogue, and fostering social awareness and social action ... in which experience is tied to critical analyses of systemic issues and power 'of deeply embedded roots of racism, discrimination, violence and disempowerment'. (Cuban and Anderson, 2007, p. 146, quoting Leistyna and Woodrum in Brown, 2001, p. 20)

For new teachers working with youth from cultural backgrounds different from their own, there are multiple approaches towards teaching for social justice. For example, James-Wilson (2007) talks about *representative* and *redistributive* classroom work for social justice. The representative approach focuses on in-class issues of discourse and representation; that is, a critical examination of texts and other cultural media (popular and otherwise) and the ways in which these texts shape discourse and relations of power. The redistributive approach towards social justice places redistribution of wealth and privilege as the main foci for combating oppression and marginalization as found in classroom contexts (James-Wilson, 2007). Service-Learning, with a social justice perspective, helps to bring these two approaches together by connecting the curriculum of the classroom with the reality of the communities in which students live (Solomon and Sekayi, 2007).

In teacher education, this means modeling classroom practice and curricula that is validating of students' cultural lives (Valenzuela, 1999) and utilizing Service-Learning as a way to critically analyze classroom content within authentic contexts outside of the classroom (Solomon and Sekayi, 2007). Positive relationships between teachers, students and parents are prerequisites for effective teaching, and these relationships are often hard to foster when there are barriers between teachers coming from elite academic institutions and students and families from low-income communities (James-Wilson, 2007).

Service-Learning with a social justice perspective is one approach towards developing these relationships between teachers and the communities they serve. However, Service-Learning cannot generate these connections as an isolated practice. While the research has shown that relationships have developed between teachers engaged in Service-Learning projects and the communities they serve, these relationships must be reciprocal, and cannot be seen as fixed once they begin (Cuban and Anderson, 2007, p. 9). At times, even relationships developed through Service-Learning end up reproducing the power relations of privilege that we find in the broader society (Butin, 2007, p. 3). This form of social reproduction, then, leads back to the question of how to effectively utilize Service-Learning for social justice in teacher education without having it become a mere formality for teachers, or seen as a shortcut towards the goal of developing positive teacher–student–community relationships.

Positioned in this manner, teaching for social justice is a framework that can allow pre-service urban teachers engaged in Service-Learning to foster community strengths and engage in community struggles outside their classrooms, while also relating these struggles to their in-class practice and pedagogy. If this can be done in an authentic way, such that pre-service teachers are developing and transforming their day-to-day thinking about teaching in urban communities (Butin, 2007), Service-Learning with a social justice orientation can be an important first step towards developing the relationships, reflections and practices needed for effective teaching (Banks et al., 2005). The cases presented in this chapter illustrate these possibilities, demonstrating how Service-Learning can be used in a teacher preparation programme to promote values and vision of social justice (Anderson and Erickson, 2003; Villegas and Lucas, 2002). Such vision is necessary to help bridge the demographic divide between teachers and students in urban contexts.

Socio-cultural Learning and Teaching: An Asset Approach

Along with a balanced approach to Service-Learning and a social justice orientation within teacher education, one key theoretical and pedagogical perspective guides this in diverse urban contexts: a socio-cultural approach to learning. Youth learn via social interactions within, across and in between cultural contexts (Borrero and Yeh, 2010; Nieto, 2002; Vygotsky, 1978) and this learning, even when it occurs outside of school, must be acknowledged and fostered in the classroom. New teachers need to enter the profession with a clear understanding that students learn from their families, communities, peers and school experiences, and the diversity of students' cultural backgrounds in our urban schools today must be seen as a resource (Moll et al., 1992; Paris, 2010). This is far from the case, however, in many schools. Instead, students of colour are forced to assimilate traditional, largely Caucasian, cultural norms of American schooling, or they are alienated from the system entirely (Borrero and Yeh, 2010; Camangian, 2010; Darling-Hammond, 2007; Nieto, 2005). Research shows that youth must feel a part of a school community that values their cultural background so that they have the opportunity to develop their self-efficacy as learners (Bandura, 1997) while taking pride in their cultural backgrounds. Service-Learning is a tool that can help with this process (Furco, 2009; Villegas and Lucas, 2002).

This work links back to the perspective developed by Banks and colleagues (2005) who argue that in order to be prepared to teach students whose backgrounds differ from their own, teachers must learn how to learn about their students, themselves and the craft of teaching. From my experience as a high school teacher and as a teacher educator, it is vital that this learning involves critical self-reflection on the part of a new teacher so that they can see their role as one that must combine vision with practice (Borrero, 2009). Teachers need to continually spend time reflecting on their own identities, desires to teach and goals for their students as they develop their classroom practice. Learning about students, their families and their communities is a crucial part of this reflection, and the asset approach must frame this reflection because if new teachers want to teach in urban contexts, they are going to be teaching students from diverse cultural backgrounds (Banks et al., 2005).

In the section below, I briefly describe the elements of the Urban Education Programme at the University of San Francisco in California. This is a Masters programme for prospective teachers (typically between the ages of 22 and 30) to earn their California Teaching Credential so they are certified by the state to teach in K-12 public schools. Specifically, this programme is designed to prepare teachers to work with youth in urban contexts (see Borrero, 2009). I highlight aspects of the programme that support pre-service teachers in their development of a social justice perspective that can involve Service-Learning as a way to build connections with their students and school communities while also enhancing their vision and practice as new teachers.

Urban Teacher Education in San Francisco, California

Pre-service teachers in the Urban Education Programme at the University of San Francisco enter the two-year programme with a specific focus on and commitment to working with urban youth in local, community schools. All students are graduate students – in the state of California, pre-service teachers must earn a bachelors degree before acquiring their teaching credential. The district schools within which these pre-service teachers embark on their student teaching experience are both diverse (in the cultural, economic and educational backgrounds of students) and high-need.

The local K-12 district, whose schools house these prospective teachers for their student teaching experience, serves some 55,000 students. The district is urban in its make-up, serving a population that is nearly 70 per cent students of colour. Twenty-eight per cent of students are classified as English Language Learners (ELLs) and 54 per cent qualify for free or reduced lunch. The University of San Francisco is a private university with an annual tuition fee of approximately $30,000. The student body is approximately 39 per cent Caucasian, 20 per cent Asian-American, 15 per cent Latino/Hispanic, 4 per cent African American, and 2 per cent Pacific Islander/Native Hawaiian. The university has a stated commitment to be the 'city's university' and the School of Education is actively involved in collaboration with local schools.

During their second year in the Urban Education Programme, pre-service teachers take two courses – Critical Pedagogy in Urban Education and Action Research and Service-Learning for Urban Teachers – in sequence while they are completing their student teaching experience in a local school. These two courses focus specifically on the theoretical and pedagogical approaches discussed above with regard to socio-cultural learning and teaching, on cultural assets, and on community-based connections and learning (see Borrero, 2009). Additionally, students learn about Service-Learning as a pedagogical practice through course readings and assignments. For example, students are exposed to the 'Seven Elements of Effective Service-learning' (Youth Service California, 2006) – integrated learning, high quality service, collaboration, student voice, civic responsibility, reflection and evaluation – as a framework within which to examine the goals of Service-Learning.

For their culminating assignment as Masters students in the Urban Education Programme, pre-service teachers complete an action research project based on a classroom intervention that they design, implement, assess and reflect upon. A required element of this action research project is a Service-Learning component in which prospective teachers design curricula involving collaboration with local community organizations. The details of the action research project and the Service-Learning component are left up to the pre-service teacher, and projects are assessed based on a predetermined rubric for depth of inquiry, quality of innovation for the intervention, depth of critical analysis and level of critical self-reflection. The Service-Learning component is assessed on the degree to which it addresses the Seven Elements of Effective Service-Learning (Youth Service California, 2006).

In the section below, I describe two Service-Learning projects that were created by two different pre-service teachers in the Urban Education Programme. These examples are presented in an attempt to show the tangible and specific foci that students focused on in their projects. They are not intended to be representative of all students, nor are they distinctly superior or inferior in comparison to projects undertaken by other new teachers in the programme.

Service-Learning Case Studies

Developing student and community voice

Sam, a fourth-grade student teacher in a local K-6 school, was especially focused on her students' writing. She was not happy teaching the expected, scripted curriculum that she was given, and was worried that her students only wrote short, meaningless responses to prompts in a workbook in her class. She felt her students had no voice in their writing and connected their lack of investment in their writing with a general disconnection between the curriculum in class and students' lives outside of school (Valenzuela, 1999). To combat this discon-nection, she created a unit of study that focused on biography as a form of writing. However, instead of focusing on form per se, she focused on context, and designed the teaching unit in ways to get her youth to connect with their families and communities.

The unit itself had three main parts. First, students designed, conducted, recorded and transcribed interviews with a family or community member who had lived in their neighbourhood for multiple generations. This interview process was largely developed in class and then students were free to choose an interviewee of their choice. Interview questions focused on the history of the family/neighbourhood, important landmarks and key events from the last 50 years. Second, students wrote a biography of their interviewee based on the interview transcript and their experience meeting/interviewing this person. Again, much of this writing was scaffolded during classroom instruction, and students were given specific prompts about possi-bilities for connecting their interviewees' stories with key events being studied in a Social Studies unit on immigration and California state history. Third, the class went on a field trip to a local organization which was working on a project to document the history of the many different murals in the neighbourhood. The community organization was working to collect as much information as possible from long-time residents about the history of different murals, their creators and their alterations over time. Fourth graders worked as 'interviewers' one day and went (as a group) to different neigh-bourhood parks where they interviewed adults about their knowledge of the nearby murals. After the field trip, students transcribed their interviews and went back (on a second field trip) to the community organization to share their findings.

The final step of this project involved the fourth graders writing their own 'autobiography' about their life in their neighbourhood, their connections to family and community members, and their favourite murals. Sam urged students to be creative and to even tell their stories from the perspective of a person on one of the murals that they learned about or via a certain event in the neighbourhood's history.

Community interpreters

Tanya, a high school English teacher in a local school, approached Service-Learning within her action research project from a different perspective.

She was a student teaching in a ninth-grade English as a Second Language (ESL) class where over 90 per cent of her students were native Spanish speakers who had been in the US for less than one year. She had relatively little training in ESL, knew a small amount of Spanish and was (obviously) a brand new teacher. Pedagogically, she was most interested in building relationships with her students and helping them to develop their literacy skills in English. She was familiar with much of the recent research on bilingual learners, and knew that one way to potentially help her students' reading capabilities was to tap into their knowledge of Spanish (e.g. Dorner et al., 2007; Padilla, 2006).

One of the first tasks she undertook, in an attempt to build a rapport with her students and to begin making connections with parents, was to have her students help her write a letter (in English and Spanish) to parents inviting them to a 'back to school night' (an event where parents come to school and meet their children's teachers). After having some success with the letter writing (and a good turnout of parents on back to school night), she decided to develop a unit of study around students' bilingual skills.

Tanya found a local non-profit organization that provided English tutoring to parents, and made a connection with the director. The two shared resources and realized that the agency drastically needed student volunteers to help as translators/interpreters during some of the tutoring sessions. Together, Tanya and the director decided to create a curriculum manual for student volunteers who could serve as translators/interpreters at the organization. Tanya used the opportunity to involve her students in the creation of the curriculum by asking them about their experiences as interpreters and by involving them in the creation of the readings/materials. Along with specific readings and references (in Spanish and English), the curriculum focused on a number of key literacy strategies for bilingual learners. These strategies were essential tools for translating and interpreting – namely active listening, vocabulary development, questioning and paraphrasing – and also key strategies for students to develop in English. In place of weekly homework assignments, students were required to volunteer at the community organization for three hours per week.

Further, because of the success of the collaboration between Tanya, the organization and the students, Tanya was able to start a Translation Club at school, where students could come and 'work' as translators and interpreters at school when monolingual teachers and parents needed support.

Discussion: Learning in the Community and in the Classroom

New teachers with vision and practice

As new teachers, Sam and Tanya's learning via these Service-Learning experiences is important on many different levels. Not only did they learn about their students and their school communities, but they learned about themselves. Like many of their classmates in the Urban Education Programme, the Service-Learning component of their curricula enhanced their teaching and their learning. Specifically, these aspects of their teaching enabled them to apply theory to practice, build community connections and engage in learning alongside their students.

Applying theory to practice

As graduate students training to become teachers, Sam and Tanya spent plenty of time reading about and discussing educational theory. Their Service-Learning projects embodied the application of theory to their classroom practice. Specifically, these projects reflected knowledge of and belief in the importance of a socio-cultural approach to learning and the value of the multiple contextual learning experiences of students. For example, Tanya valued the bilingual interpreting experiences that her students were engaged in outside of class (Borrero, 2008; Dorner et al., 2007) and wanted to harness it to help her students become better readers. Even the small assignment/decision to have students help her craft a bilingual letter home to parents sent a strong message to her students – she cared about them, cared about their language and wanted their parents to be a part of school. This is an important message for students (especially students labelled ELL) to receive, as all too often the only messages they receive at school are about their deficits as learners and their imminent failure (Borrero and Yeh, 2010; Camangian, 2010; Paris, 2010).

From this perspective, both Tanya and Sam enacted curriculum and teaching that tapped into the learning experiences that students were engaged in outside of class to enhance their classroom learning. The fact that they saw such learning experiences from an asset approach made the cultural diversity of their students a powerful force in their classrooms and brought out the true potential of Service-Learning for social justice. The combination of belief in a socio-cultural approach to learning and a vision for student success that embraced students' strengths showed these new teachers that cultural difference is not a problem to be overcome, but a resource to be fostered.

Making community connections

Through connecting theory with practice, these new teachers were not only able to enhance their abilities to engage more learners in their curricula, but also extended the learning environment beyond the walls of the classroom. For example, Sam, through making connections with the community organization interested in the neighbourhood's murals, made her classroom a place that directly related to her students' lives. Her curriculum became relevant, timely and culturally aware (Camangian, 2010; Duncan-Andrade, 2007). Her students were able to see themselves in the curriculum and make connections to their own families, neighbourhoods and histories. In reflecting on the unit, Sam commented on how students who typically only wrote one- or two-sentence responses in workbooks, wrote full-page biographies by the end of the unit. She reflected on how important it was to create a curriculum that offered students opportunities to write about themselves.

Through creating community connections, these two new teachers also began to develop professional relationships with community partners who could help them create and enact a meaningful curriculum. These relationships were formative for both teachers. These relationships took time to create, but led to important advancements in these teachers' growth and development. They were able to see that teaching did not have to be a solitary act (Borrero and Bird, 2009) and that they were building connections in the community that would serve them (and their students) for years into the future. This type of networking and community development is crucial for new teachers but it is also elusive. Most new teachers spend all of their time focused on planning lessons for their students within their classrooms from day to day (Banks et al., 2005). There is little breathing room for long-term community and relationship-building. This Service-Learning project forced teachers to seek out community partners and begin to build connections with organizations in the community that could enhance student learning. Through engaging in this process, Sam, Tanya and many of their colleagues formed relationships that will continue to reap benefits – not just for student learning, but for their own professional support and growth.

Engaging in learning alongside students

Ultimately, Sam, Tanya and their students engaged in learning together. They learned about each other and their communities, and they grew as teachers and learners with learning that was definitely 'value added'. In this respect, Service-Learning provided an avenue for these new teachers to show their students that they too are lifelong learners, and that learning is something that happens in the classroom and in the community. This explicit, transparent, collaborative approach to learning is something that can benefit all teachers, but is especially powerful for new teachers, as it brings out the very best parts about teaching, namely building relationships and authentic learning.

Involving youth in their communities

Although not the particular focus of this chapter, the learning of these fourth and ninth graders cannot be overlooked. Sam was focused on her students' writing and their ability to connect with and provide more voice in their writing. In her own writing about the project, not only did she reflect on students' improvement and increased interest in writing, but she noted how much pride they began to take in their writing (and speaking) about their neighbourhood and the murals. They were able to make connections with real people in the community and see that the murals really meant something to a lot of people – not just because they were pretty and tourists were always taking pictures of them, but because they were a part of the history of the neighbourhood and each mural had a story. This personalization of history was something that most of these (primarily Latino and East Asian) students had not experienced. It was this personalization of history and community that brought out students' voices in the writing, and, perhaps more importantly, showed students that learning about their personal histories was valuable and valued at school.

Tanya's ninth graders also learned a lot about themselves via their service. Many of them stayed on as volunteers long after the project ended, and they all learned to become better translators and interpreters through the process of making the curriculum. They saw that translating and interpreting were skills that they could improve upon, and in the process of doing so, they learned key literacy strategies in Spanish and English. Also, they experienced being 'smart' at school when they were the interpreter for someone who only spoke one language. This experience showed students that they could succeed at school, and that being bilingual was an important strength they possessed.

Conclusions and Implications: Acknowledging and Promoting Cultural and Community Assets through Service-Learning

As with other chapters in this book, Service-Learning in this chapter is positioned as 'value added' for educators in challenging contexts. Specifically, for the pre-service urban teachers in the Urban Education Programme at the University of San Francisco, Service-Learning is a required component of their Masters Degree work. More important than this requirement in their culminating project as student teachers, however, is their vision for entering the teaching profession with a desire to connect to the communities in which they teach. This vision is paramount for overcoming the demographic divide between the teaching force in the US and the student population in urban schools (Banks et al., 2005; Capps et al., 2005).

As discussed earlier in this chapter, Service-Learning can provide an avenue through which teachers can connect with communities and make learning authentic for urban youth (Villegas and Lucas, 2002). These two outcomes are crucial for students and teachers alike, but it is important that Service-Learning is not seen as a silver bullet. As a pedagogical tool it can foster benefits for both students and teachers, but it must be part of a larger agenda in a teacher's pedagogy. In the cases of Sam and Tanya, both new teachers believed in their students' success, acknowledged their cultural backgrounds as important resources and found ways to make classroom learning applicable and meaningful to their lives outside of school. In these ways, Service-Learning was a powerful tool to connect classroom teaching with community organizations. Without this synergy between the classroom and the community, Service-Learning cannot reap its full potential (Furco, 1996; James-Wilson, 2007). This is why I see teacher education playing an important role in the development of balanced Service-Learning (Furco, 1996) and a social justice orientation to teaching. New teachers need to find ways to connect their classrooms to the community, and they need support in doing so.

When Service-Learning can be effectively developed within a broader social justice orientation, it holds the potential to powerfully impact on teachers, students and communities. When operating within an asset approach to cultural diversity, Service-Learning is both theoretically and practically valid – it provides an outlet for new teachers to show that they believe in their youth and want to be engaged in their learning outside of the classroom. It is this authentic learning that makes the socio-cultural (Nieto, 2002; Vygotsky, 1978), asset-based approach (Borrero, 2008; Borrero and Yeh, 2010; Moll et al., 1992) that frames this chapter a pedagogical reality. Without the community-based learning embedded in Service-Learning, this theoretical framework is removed from actual classroom practice, and therefore less realistic for new teachers to enact.

The balanced approach to Service-Learning (Furco, 1996) also complements the asset approach to diversity in school as it draws an important distinction between learning in the community and the classroom versus the notion of the 'haves' saving the 'have-nots'. In the context of teacher education, this means that new teachers are not going into students' communities and saving youth and their families. Instead, they are learning with their students about the strengths and challenges of their school communities. This learning (by both student and teacher) is what makes Service-Learning meaningful and sustainable.

This approach to learning and teacher education provides a much needed response to changes in urban schooling in the US. The demographic of the teaching workforce is now less representative of the student population in US schools than ever before (Capps et al., 2005; Fry, 2009; Zumwalt and Craig, 2005). Further, the myopic focus on standardized test scores and academic achievement in current educational discourse occludes teachers from embracing the diversity of their youth and utilizing the cultural resources that all students bring into the classroom. Service-Learning is needed in our schools and it is needed in our teacher education programmes as now, more than ever, we as educators must strive to make connections between classroom learning and community learning.

References

Anderson, J. and Erickson, J. (2003), 'Service-learning in preservice teacher education'. *Academic Exchange Quarterly*, 7: 111–15.

Bandura, A. (1997), *Self-Efficacy: the Exercise of Control*. New York, NY: W. H. Freeman and Company.

Banks, J., Cochran-Smith, M., Moll, L., Richert, A., Zeichner, K., LePage, P., Darling Hammond, L., Duffy, H. and McDonald, M. (2005), 'Teaching diverse learners', in L. Darling-Hammond and J. Bransford (eds), *Preparing Teachers for a Changing World: What Teachers Should Learn and be Able to do*. San Francisco: Jossey-Bass, pp. 232–74.

Borrero, N. E. (2008). 'What students see, hear, and do: linguistic assets at the Bay School'. *English Leadership Quarterly*, 30 (3): 2–5.

—(2009), 'Social justice for new teachers: bringing a sense of community to teacher education'. *Multicultural Perspectives*, 11 (4): 221–26.

Borrero, N. E. and Bird, S. (2009), *Closing the Achievement Gap: How to Pinpoint Student Strengths to Differentiate Instruction and Help Your Striving Readers Succeed.* New York, NY: Scholastic.

Borrero, N. E. and Yeh, C. J. (2010), 'Ecological language learning among ethnic minority youth'. *Educational Researcher*, 39 (8).

Brown, D. (2001), *Pulling it all together: A method for developing service-learning and community partnerships based in critical pedagogy.* Washington, DC: Corporation for National Service. National Service Fellowship Program.

Butin, D. (2007), 'Justice-Learning: Service-learning as Justice-Oriented Education'. *Equity and Excellence in Education*, 40: 177–83.

Camangian, P. (2010), 'Starting with self: Teaching auto ethnography to foster critically caring literacies'. *Research in the Teaching of English*, 45 (2): 179–204.

Capps, R., Fix, M., Murray, J., Ost, J., Passel, J. and Herwantoro S. (2005), *The New Demography of America's Schools: Immigration and the No Child Left Behind Act.* Washington, DC: Urban Institute.

Cuban, S. and Anderson, J. (2007), 'Where's the Justice in Service-learning? Institutionalizing Service-learning from a Social Justice Perspective at a Jesuit University'. *Equity and Excellence in Education*, 40: 144–55.

Darling-Hammond, L. (2002), 'Educating a profession for equitable practice', in L. Darling Hammond, J. French and S. P. Garcia-Lopez (eds), *Learning to Teach for Social Justice.* New York: Teacher College, pp. 201–12.

—(2007), 'The Flat Earth and Education: How America's Commitment to Equity will Determine Our Future'. *Educational Researcher*, 36 (6): 318–34.

Dorner, L., Orellana, M. and Li-Grining, C. (2007), ' "I helped my mom" and it helped me: Translating the skills of language brokers into improved standardized test scores'. *The American Journal of Education*.

Duncan-Andrade, J. (2007), 'Gangstas, Wankstas, and Ridas: defining, developing, and supporting effective teachers in urban schools'. *International Journal of Qualitative Studies in Education*, 20 (6): 617–38.

Fry, R. (2009), The Rapid *Growth and Changing Complexion of Suburban Public Schools.* Washington, DC: Pew Hispanic Center.

Furco, A. (1996), 'Service-learning: A balanced approach to experiential education'. *Expanding Boundaries: Serving and Learning.* Washington DC: Corporation for National Service. Reprinted in Campus Compact's (2000) *Introduction to Service-learning Toolkit.*

—(2009), 'Research for the future: charting the next phase of service-learning in Teacher Education'. *Paper presented at the International Conference on Service-learning in Teacher Education.* Galway, Ireland.

James-Wilson, S. (2007), 'Using representation to conceptualize a social justice approach to urban teacher preparation', in R. P. Solomon and D. Sekayi (eds), *Urban*

Teacher Education and Teaching: Innovative Practices for Diversity and Social Justice. Mahwah, NJ: Lawrence Earlbaum.

Kozol, J. (2005), *The Shame of the Nation: The Restoration of Apartheid Schooling in America.* New York, NY: Three Rivers Press.

Leistyna, P. and Woodrum, A. (1996), 'Context and culture: what is critical pedagogy?', in P. Leistyna, A. Woodrum and S. A. Sherlbom (eds), *Breaking Free: the Transformative Power of Critical Pedagogy.* Cambridge, MA: Harvard Educational Review, pp. 1–11.

Moll, L. C., Amanti, C., Neff, D. and González, N. (1992), 'Funds of knowledge for teaching: Using a qualitative approach to connect homes and classrooms'. *Theory into Practice,* 31 (2): 132–41.

Nasir, N. and Saxe, G. B. (2003), 'Ethnic and academic identities: A cultural practice perspective on emerging tensions and their management in the lives of minority students'. *Educational Researcher,* 32 (5): 14–18.

National Commission on Service-learning (2002), Learning in Deed: The Power of Service-learning for American Schools. Accessed 31 October 2010 from: http://www.servicelearning.org/what-service-learning.

Nieto, S. (2002), *Language, Culture, and Teaching: Critical Perspectives For a New Century.* Mahwah, NJ: Lawrence Erlbaum Associates, Inc.

—(2005), 'Social Justice in Hard Times: Celebrating the Vision of Dr. Martin Luther King, Jr.'. *Multicultural Perspectives,* 7 (1): 3–7.

Padilla, A. (2006), 'Second language learning: Issues in research and teaching', in P. A. Alexander, P. R. Pintrich and P. H. Winne (eds), *Handbook of Educational Psychology.* New York: Erlbaum Association.

Paris, D. (2010), '"The second language of the united states": Youth perspectives on Spanish in a changing multiethnic community'. *Journal of Language, Identity and Education,* 9 (2): 139–55.

Rist, R. (1970), 'Student social class and teacher expectations: the self-fulfilling prophecy in ghetto education'. *Harvard Education Review,* 40 (3): 411–51.

Romero, O. (1988), *The Violence of Love: The Pastoral Wisdom of Archbishop Oscar Romero.* New York: Harper and Row.

Sigmon, R. (1979), 'Service-learning: three principles'. *Synergist,* 8 (1): 9–11.

Solomon, R. P. and Sekayi, D. (2007), *Urban Teacher Education and Teaching: Innovative Practices for Diversity and Social Justice.* Mahwah, NJ: Lawrence Earlbaum.

Stanton, T. (1987), 'Service-learning: groping toward a definition'. *Experiential Education.* National Society for Experiential Education, 12 (1): 2–4.

Tyler, K. M., Uqdah, A. L., Dillihunt, M. L., Beatty-Hazelbaker, R., Conner, T., Gadson, N. C., Henchy, A. M., Hughes, T., Mulder, S., Owens, E., Roan-Belle, C., Smith, L. and Stevens, R. (2008), 'Cultural discontinuity: Towards the empirical inquiry of a major hypothesis in education'. *Educational Researcher,* 37 (5) 280–97.

Valenzuela, A. (1999), *Subtractive Schooling.* Albany, NY: SUNY Press.

Villegas, A. M. and Lucas, T. (2002), *Educating Culturally Responsive Teachers: A Coherent Approach.* Albany, NY: State University of New York Press.

Vygotsky, L. (1978), *Mind in Society: The Development of Higher Psychological Processes*. Cambridge, MA: Harvard University Press.

Youth Service California (2006), *The Seven Elements of High Quality Service*. Accessed 9 November 2009 from: http://yscal.org/cm/Service-learning/Downloads.html.

Zumwalt, K. and Craig, E. (2005), 'Teachers' characteristics: Research on the demographic profile', in M. Cochran-Smith and K. Zeichner (eds), *Studying Teacher Education: The Report of the AERA Panel on Research and Teacher Education*. Mahwah, NJ: Lawrence Erlbaum Associates, pp. 111–56.

3

Service-Learning in Challenging Contexts: Online and in the Disaster Zone

Jean Strait, Jenna Londy and Ana Panone

Abstract

In an attempt to create a disaster response model of service using college students and middle school students, this chapter presents how online Service-Learning and face-to-face (ftf) Service-Learning were integrated to create a model for addressing immediate needs for schools, teachers, students and the community after disaster strikes. In this case the disaster was a hurricane and the aftermath of rebuilding a community. College students were taught levels of community service, including project development, design, grant writing and mentoring online with students and community groups. College students report that the life skills they learned in this process are skills they will use and continue to develop in their career choice. Skills are highlighted and compared in this narrative.

Hurricane Katrina smashed the coast of New Orleans in 2005, quickly establishing itself as one of the top three deadliest hurricanes and the costliest natural disaster to occur in the United States. Over 80 per cent of the city became flooded and flood waters remained for several weeks. The worst damage occurred in the seventh and ninth wards of New Orleans, also the poorest areas of the city. Nearly five years later, residents were still living in temporary housing and a high school had yet to open in the ninth ward. Currently, 80 per cent of eighth graders do not continue to ninth grade. This is not because of lack of desire; rather it is because of lack of access to a local school.

Background

Hamline University, a mid-sized college in St Paul, Minnesota, dedicated resources and time to New Orleans, Louisiana, in its efforts to rebuild and reclaim the city. Days after Hurricane Katrina hit, Hamline sent students, faculty and staff to help with recovery efforts. The Education Club adopted Martin Luther King Science and Technology School (MLK) soon after to help in cleaning and rebuilding the school and sent over $20,000 in books, supplies, merchandise gift cards, food and water to help with this effort. Still fuelled by the great need in New Orleans for assistance, the group's leader, Dr. Jean Strait, worked with Traveler's Insurance Company and received a grant of $30,000 to start an online tutoring and mentoring programme that would be staffed by Hamline University and Avalon High School students in St Paul. Students travelled to New Orleans in March of 2008 to meet their MLK student mentees, help with self-esteem programming and create relationships of trust and respect with the mentees. The first phase of the project ended in June of 2008.

Hamline Students who were part of the initial trip accompanied Dr. Strait and Dr. Rob Schumer (University of Minnesota) to New Orleans in July of 2008, continuing to volunteer service in the clean-up and remodelling of the Depot House, a historic landmark in the warehouse district on O'Keefe Avenue.

According to a report compiled by the Cowen Institute for Public Education Initiatives in 2008, a post-Katrina school system is vastly different from the previous public system. Changes include:

1 The expansion of the state's Recovery School District (RSD) to take control of over 100 Orleans Parish School Board (OPSB) schools performing below the state average.
2 The RSD reopened schools initially only as charters: schools run by non-profit organizations that receive public money and provide free education.
3 In November 2005, the first OPSB-run school reopened. A number of OPSB charter schools opened soon after.
4 In the spring of 2006, the RSD opened its first district-run schools.

In all cases, opening schools in the 2005–6 school years after Katrina was a difficult and chaotic ordeal. In addition, the public education landscape in New Orleans has several new and, in some cases, unique features:

1 Eighty public schools in New Orleans are run by 29 different operators, including the OPSB, the RSD and 27 charter school operators.

2 Fifty-seven per cent of public school students now attend charter schools, more than any other urban school district in the country.

3 In most cases, parents now have the choice to send their children to any public school in New Orleans where they can gain admission, regardless of where they live (The Second Annual State of Education in New Orleans Report, 2008).

It has been five years since the storm and there are several successes for the schools. Strong leadership has emerged at the state and local levels, school buildings have been brought up to basic standards and schools have significantly more supplies. A sufficient number of teachers was hired for the 2007–8 school year. The community is much more involved in schools than before Katrina. For example, the Broadmoor Community was able to save Wilson Elementary as a neighbourhood school. Without their efforts, the school would have been destroyed and not rebuilt. Overall, there is a sense among students, teachers, school leaders and community members that there have been significant improvements in most schools since last year.

However, there are still significant challenges that exist in New Orleans. Many teachers do not have the skills or support they need to teach a diverse student population with very high needs. Current levels of school spending cannot be sustained. Both the RSD and the OPSB are spending more per student than they will be able to receive from regular per-pupil funding in the coming years. Special education and mental health services are severely lacking. Post traumatic stress disorder (PTSD) tops the list of mental health issues. Never before has society seen this level of PTSD in children. There is poor cooperation among schools and districts. There is a lack of timely and accessible school information for parents, students and the public. The current retention rate of seventh/eighth graders into ninth grade is 38 per cent in New Orleans (The Second Annual State of Public Education in New Orleans Report, 2008, pp. 2–3).

Project Design

The Project's long-term goal was to create a national-disaster-related education response model that could be replicated in any city in the US. The programme consisted of a joint online Service-Learning tutoring/mentoring programme between Hamline University, Avalon High School and grades five to nine

New Orleans students. Hamline students served as tutors/mentors to both the Avalon High School students and the grades five to nine students. Hamline students and Avalon students were paired together to lead pods or groups of New Orleans students as a team. Each pod had from five to six participants. Prior to the March 2008 trip, both Avalon and Hamline students took part in weekly training sessions for mentoring, PTSD, the history and culture of New Orleans, working with online technology, and building a culture of trust and respect with their pods.

Martin Luther King Science and Technology Magnet was chosen as a partner because of its great need and location in the ninth ward, which was essentially wiped off the map during Hurricane Katrina. The faculty, staff and administration for MLK knew that this school was an essential link for community survival and that it had to be back up and running as soon as possible. Many children were already behind one to two years in academic skills, and closure of the schools would make the situation worse. The Education Club at Hamline University adopted the school and began sending students to help clean up, supplies to help with the clean-up, and as the school began to re-emerge, Hamline sent over $12,000 in donated supplies, gift cards from Target (to help students buy clothes) and cash to help rebuild the structure.

In December of 2007, Dr. Strait was able to receive a $30,000 grant from Traveler's Insurance to help implement the first phase of 'Each One, Teach One'. The training of the project required dialogue between university and high school students around the following questions:

- *What constitutes citizenship skills?*
- *How should we teach and involve students in a community project to reinforce their learning?*
- *How can we measure student achievement of those skills?*

The seemingly simple concept of asking the questions and engaging in dialogue and decision-making around teaching about disaster and assessing citizenship had not been done before. The action component of this work was to create a tutor/mentor system with the high school students and seventh and eighth graders via the internet to assist with reading and study skills. In turn, these skills should increase their success in high school classrooms. Other goals of this programme included:

1 Improving the quality of education for New Orleans students and increasing their academic achievement by at least one grade level per academic year,

encouraging students to finish high school, teaching students and teachers how to use technology, and teaching students how to become civically engaged through Service-Learning projects in New Orleans with Hamline students.

2 Using technology to create a long-standing partnership with the New Orleans schools to help students gain the mentoring, tutoring and support they need to be successful while also creating a much needed home to school connection for parents.

3 Helping Hamline students meet a graduation requirement for community engagement, known as LEAD (Leadership Education and Development) and helping Avalon students meet a similar graduation requirement in Service-Learning.

The Project Implementation Team included the Field Director and Project lead Dr. Jean Strait, who had been working with the community and schools for two years; Avalon Lead Mentor Dr. Walter Enloe, public policy and charter school expert; and two Hamline student coordinators, Tony Wilson and Joyce Jones, trained extensively for leadership in the project. The major partners included Hamline University, Avalon High School (a St Paul Public Charter School), MLK Science and Technology and The Depot House.

Methodology

The process for creating this programme emerged by doing an informal needs assessment of MLK once the building was inhabitable. Coupled with the low academic achievement rates, dropout rates of eighth graders in New Orleans are three times that of the rest of the United States (Cowen Institute, 2008). The United States high school completion rate has dropped from 77.1 per cent in 1969 to 69.9 per cent in 2000, and 2007 reports estimated around 63 per cent (Azzam, 2007). What is happening to cause such a drop? It is also reported that the retention rate varies by culture: 93 per cent of white students finish high school while only 43 per cent of their peers of colour do; and the lower the socio-economic status, the less likely a student is to complete high school. Students report that they are lacking self-esteem and skilled teachers in their subject areas. They also note that group size conducive to their learning is not available, and that the learning they are doing is neither relevant nor fun.

Service-Learning is reciprocal in nature. The student group providing the service and the agency receiving the service gain equally from their interactions.

A key component of Service-Learning is critical reflection. Students must have the opportunity to mentally process the service they are providing and learn to integrate these essential skills into their strategy banks through practice. *Hard skills* refer to academic skills. *Soft skills* are more interpersonal in nature. Listening and oral communication are considered soft skills (Strait, 2008). Many students access hard skills through soft skills. For example, it is much easier for a student to work on content if they can discuss it with a friend, or work in a small group. The development of interpersonal skills creates cognitive pathways in the brain, which, when used on a frequent basis, make it easier for students to then access the academic skills. *Soft skills* are often referred to as civic skills or civic competencies, which are commonly developed through Service-Learning. The idea behind this pedagogy is to develop civic professionals through these new basic skills (Basttistoni and Longo, 2007).

Quality Service-Learning teaches students problem-solving, critical thinking, decision-making, public speaking, teamwork and how to interact with communities that are different from their own cultural membership (Basttistoni and Longo, 2007). Service-Learning also teaches moral reasoning skills. Like character education, Service-Learning experiences help focus the responsibilities of the individual and community by integrating the cognitive, affective and behavioural dimensions in moral reasoning skill development. In a recent study done by Skaggs and Bodenhorn (2006), students who were involved in moral reasoning skill curriculum were less likely to drop out of school. *Each One, Teach One* (see Figure 3.1) sought to strengthen student skills through a long-term, high quality Service-Learning experience.

The Process Emerges

Students were involved on the ground level of the development of the programme. Four months before the training was to begin, the leadership team began to convene on a weekly basis constructing the process of the project. Six major stages emerged:

1 *Identifying issues.*
2 *Forming relationships with partners.*
3 *Identifying and training mentors.*
4 *Face to face work in New Orleans.*
5 *Reflections, surveys and summations.*
6 *Evaluation/feedback (to lead back into stage 1 in the second year).*

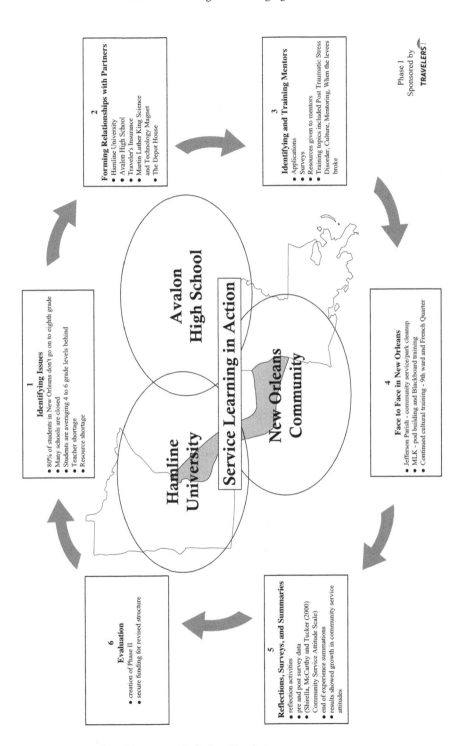

Figure 3.1: Hamline University Each One Teach 1

Identifying issues

To prepare for the training sessions, the leadership team read *Come Hell or High Water* by Eric Dyson and watched a documentary done by Spike Lee called *When the Levees Broke*. The team also spent a great deal of time discussing issues with the Principal of MLK, Doris Hicks, and the curriculum director, Steven Martin. Throughout these investigations the following pressing issues continued to emerge:

- Eighty per cent of students in the ninth ward of New Orleans don't go on to eighth grade.
- Many schools are closed.
- Students are averaging four to six grade levels behind.
- There is a teacher shortage in charters that have reopened.
- There is a resource shortage in these same schools and districts.

The team was dedicated to finding ways to begin to address these issues as a part of the project. Through continued research and discussion, we found that many students didn't go on to eighth grade because at the time of writing this chapter, schools housing grades eight to twelve were either torn down, condemned for demolition, or not yet open in the ninth ward, and this was three years after the storm! Because of the building closures and the socio-economic status of the students (unable to travel to other areas), the option to continue education had been essentially eliminated. Students who were averaging two years behind academically were now falling four to six grade levels behind, with no hope of ever catching up. In addition, job opportunities for students at that level were limited or non-existent.

Forming relationships with partners

As the lead partner in this initiative, Hamline University was very determined about asking MLK what they needed, and what the programme could provide to help address or meet these needs. Having these dialogues helped to form good relationships and build trust with the partners and made it much easier for the participants to understand each other's culture.

Avalon High School student levels ranged from ninth to twelfth grade. These students served as role models and peers for New Orleans students, showing them what they could expect from a high school education and could relate to them on their equal developmental levels. After joint research from the Hamline and Avalon students, The Depot House became a service partner. Owned by Denis Hilton, The Depot House is a historic landmark that was severely damaged by the hurricane and in need of renovation. A partnership was created where students would stay at The Depot while in New Orleans, working to clean and renovate the property so it could be used by other groups for lodging and service. The other service partner in this project was Jefferson parish, which was in desperate need of a park and open space clean-up. Traveler's Insurance, the funding partner of the team, also contributed several New Orleans employees to the clean-up portion of the programme while in New Orleans.

Identifying and training mentors

Applications were distributed during information sessions held at Hamline and Avalon. Students were required to have two letters of recommendation submitted and have evidence of their academic standing and teamwork skills. The leadership team interviewed the applicants and accepted 15 Avalon and 10 Hamline students for participation in the pilot year. Training of the group began at the end of January 2008 and continued for eight weeks, covering topics such as the culture and history of New Orleans, mentoring, tutoring, PTSD, relational trust, blackboard training (online format) and building community. Avalon and Hamline students each received their own copy of *Come Hell or High Water*. The Hamline students also received *The Mentor's Guide: Facilitating Effective Learning Relationships* by Lois Zachary. All students were required to fill out medical forms, pre-surveys, and keep a journal throughout the process. The group travelled to New Orleans via bus and used the bus time to watch *As the Levees Broke*, giving them the first-hand experiences of Katrina victim stories and tragedies, many of which would be in the ninth ward.

Face to face in New Orleans

The face-to-face component of the project was a ten-day experience in New Orleans, staying and working at The Depot. The first two days of the trip continued on the ground training, by participating in a tour of the ninth ward given by Common Ground, a non-profit group trying to educate about and advocate for citizens of the ward. Students were put into teams doing things like scavenger hunts of the French Quarter and wisdom circles at the end of the day to help focus reflection on what they were learning. Starting the school week, students worked in Jefferson parish doing a clean-up of various parks with Traveler's Insurance volunteers in the mornings, took a break for lunch and then spent the afternoons at MLK doing team building, skills building and blackboard training in the pods. After dinner, the entire group would gather at The Depot for an end-of-the-day reflection discussion.

Reflections, surveys and summaries

Both pre- and post-survey data was collected using the Shiarella, McCarthy and Tucker (1999) Community Service Attitude Scale. Both Hamline and Avalon students were given the scale on the first day of training and again on the bus trip back to Minnesota. The team was asked not to use the surveys with MLK students as they were trying to focus students on preparation for the spring Louisiana standardized tests.

The pod groups worked on continued practice of student skills for the test instead. Students were asked to complete an end of experience questionnaire in May and blackboard interactions were collected and analyzed for comments.

Evaluation

Once all data were collected, they were analyzed by the leadership team. Results were used to revise the programme, enhance learning opportunities and investigate a larger-scale version of the project by identifying future partners, continued service work and finding ways to secure larger funding to accommodate more participants. It was hoped that the leaders could identify best practices, areas for growth and ways to strengthen areas of the programme that showed limitations. This phase was carried out in June and July, which included a second trip by project lead Jean Strait and eight of the Hamline students who participated in the March project. Dr. Robert Shumer from the University of Minnesota joined this group in New Orleans in July to teach students about student-led evaluation and begin to identify ways in which next year's pods could capture evaluation. Phase II began in January of 2009.

Data Collection

Data were collected from different sources for the purpose of triangulation of themes. A mixed method approach was used, gathering pre- and post-survey information, end of trip questionnaires, end of trip final summative reflections and three-month post questionnaires. The initial Shiarella, McCarthy and Tucker (1999) Community Service Attitude Scale was compared for quantitative data including descriptive statistics, a paired sample t-test and paired correlations for significance (see Table 3.1). Qualitative data was collected from the end of trip summative reflection, three months post-survey and videotaped interviews of participants on the July trip. Of the 25 student participants from Avalon and Hamline, 18 completed both the pre- and post-surveys. One of the biggest challenges of using quantitative analysis is having a large enough sample size. Our sample was small to begin with but even smaller with survey returns. Although having pre- and post-data on a pilot project is recommended, using small groups for Service-Learning that involves travel is a limitation.

Quantitative Data Analysis

The mean response on the paired samples showed that 15 of the 18 respondents increased their mean average response to the Shiarella, McCarthy and Tucker (1999) Community Service Attitude Scale. This may indicate a growth in the students' attitudes. Two of the 18 paired respondents' means decreased. When asked if they could tell why they thought their mean decreased, both students said that once the project was finished they realized how vital their answers were and so tended to be far more authentic in their answers than they were in the pre-survey. One set of pre- and post-pairs stayed the same. When interviewed, this student said that their experience in New Orleans only solidified their previous beliefs so they weren't surprised that they showed little change in response. It is also interesting to note that all three of the students mentioned above were Avalon High School students and all three were seniors. Again, when looking at the quantitative data, paired correlations do not show significance (see Table 3.2). However, 66 per cent of the two-tailed t-test results do reveal significance (see Table 3.3).

Qualitative Data Analysis: Post-Trip Surveys and Summative Pieces

Unlike the pre- and post-surveys, we did manage to collect data from the New Orleans community. We collected information from the MLK student online responses, the Traveler's Insurance volunteer workers, the Jefferson parish workers and leaders, and The Depot House owner and staff. Below are some of the comments that were transformative. We divided comments by Hamline, Avalon and New Orleans community. Here are some of the quotes we captured:

Table 3.1. *Quantitative results*

		Mean	N	Std. Deviation	Std. Error Mean
Pair 1	F2	5.4043	47	1.97440	.28800
	F3	5.7021	47	1.92145	.28027
Pair 2	F5	5.4043	47	1.83753	.26803
	F6	5.8298	47	1.57865	.23027
Pair 3	F8	5.9787	47	2.00531	.29250
	F9	6.3191	47	1.90087	.27727
Pair 4	F11	6.1489	47	2.06396	.30106
	F12	5.4043	47	2.28092	.33271
Pair 5	F14	5.7021	47	2.15603	.31449
	F15	6.1915	47	1.94085	.28310
Pair 6	F17	5.7234	47	2.09245	.30522
	F18	6.1277	47	2.16310	.31552
Pair 7	F20	5.7872	47	1.84080	.26851
	F21	5.2553	47	1.96123	.28608
Pair 8	F23	6.6596	47	1.84481	.26909
	F24	6.7021	47	1.97721	.28841
Pair 9	F26	5.4419	43	2.35334	.35888
	F27	5.3721	43	2.35051	.35845
Pair 10	F29	6.3617	47	1.59722	23298
	F30	6.6596	47	1.52196	.22200
Pair 11	F32	6.6596	47	1.84481	.26909
	F33	6.8511	47	1.75671	.25624
Pair 12	F35	6.3191	47	2.46811	.36001
	F36	7.0213	47	2.29829	.33524
Pair 13	F38	6.8723	47	2.17313	.31698
	F39	6.8723	47	2.06015	.30050
Pair 14	F41	6.2128	47	2.77360	.40457
	F42	6.2553	47	2.50624	.36557
Pair 15	F44	6.0319	47	2.27081	.33123
	F45	6.0638	47	2.21069	.32246
Pair 16	F47	6.5000	47	2.35907	.34411
	F48	6.8298	47	2.11947	.30916
Pair 17	F50	5.7234	47	3.15334	.45996
	F51	5.8723	47	3.22097	.46983
Pair 18	F53	5.7872	47	2.96308	.43221
	F54	6.1489	47	2.93390	.42795

Hamline student

This experience really made me aware of my self-concept and how important being able to express empathy is to me. It seems that people in the United States tended [sic] to sympathize with what happened in New Orleans rather than actually engaging in empathy. People will say that they can't even imagine what it was like to live through such a traumatic experience and so they don't even

Table 3.2. *Paired sample correlations*

		N	Correlation	Sig.
Pair 1	F2 & F3	47	.886	.000
Pair 2	F5 & F6	47	.684	.000
Pair 3	F8 & F9	47	.834	.000
Pair 4	F11 & F12	47	.767	.000
Pair 5	F14 & F15	47	.850	.000
Pair 6	F17 & F18	47	.863	.000
Pair 7	F20 & F21	47	.961	.000
Pair 8	F23 & F24	47	.901	.000
Pair 9	F26 & F27	43	.895	.000
Pair 10	F29 & F30	47	.830	.000
Pair 11	F32 & F33	47	.963	.000
Pair 12	F35 & F36	47	.926	.000
Pair 13	F38 & F39	47	.895	.000
Pair 14	F41 & F42	47	.874	.000
Pair 15	F44 & F45	47	.913	.000
Pair 16	F47 & F48	47	.920	.000
Pair 17	F50 & F51	47	.891	.000
Pair 18	F53 & F54	47	.936	.000

try to put themselves in the same situation. If these people were to actually go to New Orleans they would see that their sympathetic understanding could never capture the severity of the effects produced by Katrina. Being in New Orleans really shocked me by seeing the damage still lingering after three years, which made me realize how one can't rely on the media for actual representation. It made me upset to see that the United States has shifted attention and resources away from New Orleans when help is still needed. This project just confirmed that I want to spend my life helping others. – Ana

Avalon students

I've learned my different learning styles, evaluated how I deal with new people and how service work helps me grow so much as an individual because it gives me so much prospective [sic]. – Sarah

I think I've learned to care for not only myself [sic], but other people and places all over because it affects the overall well-being of the global community, which affects me and every other human on earth. – Kayla

I am really interested in investing in the community and to learn about the major issues in a different way than I am used to doing. I can make the positive impacts on people that we all talk about doing, if I apply myself and put in effort to find a way to do so. – Ben

Table 3.3. Paired sample two-tailed results

		Paired Differences							
					95% Confidence Interval of the Difference				
		Mean	Std. Deviation	Std. Error Mean	Lower	Upper	t	df	Sig. (2-tailed)
Pair 1	F2–F3	−.29787	.93052	.13573	−.57108	−.02466	−2.195	46	.033
Pair 2	F5–F6	−.42553	1.37911	.20116	−.83045	−.02061	−2.115	46	.040
Pair 3	F8–F9	−.34043	1.12823	.16457	−.67169	−.00917	−2.069	46	.044
Pair 4	F11–F12	.74468	1.49591	.21820	.30547	1.18390	3.413	46	.001
Pair 5	F14–F15	−.48936	1.13965	.16623	−.82397	−.15475	−2.944	46	.005
Pair 6	F17–F18	−.40426	1.11627	.16283	−.73201	−.07650	−2.483	46	.017
Pair 7	F20–F21	.53191	.54578	.07961	.37167	.69216	6.682	46	.000
Pair 8	F23–F24	−.04255	.85865	.12525	−.29466	.20956	−.340	46	.736
Pair 9	F26–F27	.06977	1.07781	.16437	−.26193	.40147	.424	42	.673
Pair 10	F29–F30	−.29787	.91283	.13315	−.56589	−.02986	−2.237	46	.030
Pair 11	F32–F33	−.19149	.49512	.07222	−.33686	−.04612	−2.651	46	.011
Pair 12	F35–F36	−.70213	.93052	.13573	−.97534	−.42892	−5.173	46	.000
Pair 13	F38–F39	.00000	.97802	.14266	−.28716	.28716	.000	46	1.000
Pair 14	F41–F42	−.04255	1.35064	.19701	−.43912	.35401	−.216	46	.830
Pair 15	F44–F45	−.03191	.93486	.13636	−.30640	.24257	−.234	46	.816
Pair 16	F47–F48	−.32979	.92828	.13540	−.60234	−.05723	−2.436	46	.019
Pair 17	F50–F51	−.14894	1.48878	.21716	−.58606	.28819	−.686	46	.496
Pair 18	F53–F54	−.36170	1.05141	.15336	−.67041	−.05300	−2.358	46	.023

New Orleans partners and community members

The most important thing is our health – you keep up the good work. Your heart is so strong and your spirit is unmatched – we need more people in this world like you Jean. – The Depot House

I hope your return home went well and all are safe and sound. The Depot looks so much better and we truly appreciate your contributions to our 'Journey House'. – The Depot House

I just want to let you know that these were the best volunteers I have ever worked with IN MY LIFE, they were dedicated and mature. – Jim, Travelers Insurance volunteer, New Orleans

My favourite thing about the E.O.T.O visiting is that I get to meet new people, learn about new places, and learn new things. – Daraun, MLK school student

Thank God people have not forgotten us like our government. – Staff member, MLK school

In all of the comments above, some themes emerge. Students commented about self-concept, and a sense of empowerment and control. They realized that they can make a difference and that they can enter careers that are focused on attaining such differences. There also appears to be a conscious sense of awareness outside of their common community and a sense that communities are interconnected and global. The MLK students had initially been overwhelmed after Katrina as all the strangers rushed to help with 'fly-by' service. Their trust levels were low and building a community of learners was essential to helping them feel comfortable with the Minnesota students. Once the relational trust was built, the students continued to converse about many things. The New Orleans students wanted to come to Minnesota to experience snow. The community members expressed much sincere appreciation. Everywhere the group went, sales clerks, waiters, staff at school would pull us aside to personally thank us for our commitment when 'everyone else forgot' them. There is an overwhelming sense that the federal and state governments failed to protect the citizenry and are refusing to rebuild the community. For example, although the federal government has set aside billions of dollars to help schools and communities in New Orleans, the process is so difficult to find and follow: many schools, agencies and businesses cannot gain access to it.

Limitations

Even with all of the preparation for our project, we still faced limitations. The age differences between the Hamline students and Avalon students sometimes created friction in the group. The developmental levels of students aged 14 to 25 are very different, and for the 2009 project we planned on narrowing the age range and providing more training about and for those differences. Contact with the community partners in New Orleans was difficult. Because so few people are responsible for so many things, it is difficult to communicate within business hours. Leaders from MLK and Hamline held most of their communications at the weekend. Computer access was also an issue at MLK. The computer lab was small and difficult to gain access to. Internet connections were difficult to maintain and the network would crash from time to time, leaving students without access to their mentors for days. The leadership team hoped to have *Best Buy* involved in year two of the project, by providing both technology and technicians to assist partnering schools. Hamline was also able to get MLK another computer station through the Traveler's Insurance grant to add to the lab.

Future Development in the Ninth Ward

Over the life of the project, many organizations have followed Hamline's lead, partnering with MLK school to help maintain its success. It was a natural progression for EOTO to begin to seek a high school partner, a place where MLK students could complete their high school education. Our School at Blair Grocery (OSGB) was initiating its charter to use environmental and business curriculum and was located just three blocks from MLK. This became a seamless partnership. Using a sustainable farming model, volunteers helped to renovate the building, obtain empty lots, build greenhouses, set up rain water systems and clean empty lots. As of this writing, the school has three buildings (school and dorms) and 22 lots. In July 2010 they received a three-year, $100,000 grant from the United States Department of Agriculture. OSGB is in need of community partners and funding which EOTO will aid in developing. EOTO will continue to be a presence in years to come as the school gets up and running.

Conclusion

The government has used the storm as an excuse, demolishing much needed public housing that never received any damage in Katrina. Schools have been bulldozed with no plans to rebuild them. After three years, there is still not a high school open in the ninth ward. Levee walls are still to be repaired. Stores and businesses remain closed, sitting vacant in waste, so citizens can't even get supplies and food they need in the area and have to travel several miles to get them. Jobs are gone. Houses sit in waste with no one to claim them and no one to clean them up. Families have been scattered over the southern states after the storm. Still, a resilience in the community remains. It may seem like too large a problem to solve or that according to media representation, everything is back to normal. It is not, and estimates say that the area won't even begin to reach 2005 (before the storm) standards in the next ten years. Citizens have to be creative and inventive in finding solutions for New Orleans. These solutions will be the ones we turn to when disaster strikes anywhere on the globe. We need the next generation to be empowered and encouraged. Service-Learning shows participants that they can and do make a difference, a transformative difference in themselves and in those they help. 'Each One, Teach One' will continue to bring students and community together, empowering them to teach each other.

'Each One, Teach One' hopes to use our resources in the future to support another ninth-ward school. Our School at Blair Grocery is an agricultural-based school for students to learn techniques for urban farming and building a self-sustained community. At the school, students gain their academic knowledge through plotting land, growing crops, taking care of animals and selling their produce to the community. The school also has an active after-school programme for students of MLK and other children in the area. In pursuit of building a better New Orleans, 'Each One, Teach One' hopes to support our friends and family in the south while bettering our plan for a general urban rehabilitation programme post-disaster.

References

Azzam, A. (2007), 'Why do Students drop out?' *Educational Leadership*, 64: 91–3.

Battistoni, R. M. and Longo, N. V. (2007), *Connecting Workforce Development and Civic Engagement: Higher Education as Public Good and Private Gain*. North Shore Community College Public Policy Institute, Danvers, Massachusetts.

Shiarella, A. H., McCarthy, A. M. and Tucker, M. L. (1999), *Refinement of a Community Service Attitude Scale.* Paper presented at the Annual Meeting of the Southwest Educational Research Association, San Antonio, TX, 21–23 January 1999.

Skaggs, G. and Bodenhorn, N. (2006), 'Relationships between implementing character education, student behaviour and student achievement'. *Journal of Advanced Economics*, Vol. 18, No. 1: 82–114.

Strait, J. R. (2008a), 'Constructing experiential learning for on-line courses: The growth and development of service-e-learning', in A. Dailey-Hebert, E. Donnelli and L. Stocks (eds), *Service-e-Learning: Educating for Citizenship in a Technology-Rich World.* Greenwich, CT: Information Age Publishing.

—(2008b), 'Deepening community-based learning through collaboration and assessment'. *The International Journal of School Disaffection*, 6 (1).

Tulane University, Cowen Institute for Public Initiatives (2008), *The Second Annual State of Public Education in New Orleans Report, 2008*, pp. 2–3.

Zachary, L. J. (2000), *The Mentor's Guide: Facilitating Effective Learning Relationships.* San Francisco, CA: Jossey-Bass.

Part II

Service-Learning and Educating in Challenging Contexts in Europe, South Africa and Australia

4

Educating Educational Practitioners for a Post-Apartheid South Africa: Using Service-Learning to Integrate School Communities and University Students

Nadine Petersen and Helen Dunbar-Krige

Introduction

Community engagement is one of the three legs which support and underpin a restructured and transformed post-apartheid higher education system in South Africa (SA) (along with teaching and research). Many universities see community engagement as an overarching strategy for the transformation of both higher education and society, given the country's history of legislated discrimination and exclusion, through the promotion of academic programmes that are responsive to social, political, economic and cultural needs (Hall, 2010). At the University of Johannesburg (UJ), the policy agenda encourages academic staff to demonstrate social responsibility and commitment to the public good through their community engagement activities. Within this broad framework, Service-Learning (SL) as a form of community engagement has been recognized for its potential for diversifying the social purpose and research agenda of higher education (Nxonga, 2010; Subotsky, 1999).

In this chapter we present a South African Faculty's integrated Service-Learning model built over a five year period (2005–10) for educating educational practitioners for the demands of a post-apartheid society. The SL model is grounded in a theoretical framework of care and social justice, and establishes an interdependent form of working with a number of schools and communities to address identified educational and social challenges. Both the theoretical framework and the reciprocity of the service exchange with partners is meant to help students at three levels (at pre-service, honours and masters) learn what the task of teaching young people in a world of 'social interdependence' (Johnson and Johnson, 2009, p. 365) and 'moral interdependence' (Noddings, 1998) comprises. School and community partners are specifically chosen for the diversity of issues and population groups they serve and include a school for learners with special educational needs, one for street children, one for the physically disabled, and an organization that caters for HIV and AIDS orphans.

Background and Contextualization to Service-Learning in the Faculty of Education

The South African government has recorded significant achievements in education since independence in 1994, with increased access to primary and secondary school, improved participation of children in early childhood development and one of the highest participation rates of girl children in the world. Despite attaining these milestones, the South African public education sector still faces numerous challenges, such as huge infrastructure backlogs, the dubious quality of teaching and learning in many schools, an inability to produce the skills required for the economy and employment creation, a lack of poverty combating measures that improve the environment for teaching and learning (such as nutrition programmes) and inadequate social support for children.

In particular, reading literacy, mathematics and science scores are exceptionally poor. Numerous cross-national tests attest to this: SA children show lower levels of literacy than other developing countries and even lower scores than neighbouring poorer African countries (JET, 2006). In the latest Progress in International Reading Literacy Study (PIRLS), a comparative reading literacy study with 32 participating education systems, South African learners' reading literacy scores at Grade 4 and 5 levels are among the lowest of all the participating countries (Howie et al., 2008). For the important areas of mathematics and science, the picture is not much better. The results of the comparative Trends in International Mathematics and Science Studies (TIMMS) reveal consistently low performance for South African learners in the grades tested.

Some of the contributing factors are that many learners learn in a second or third language, have little access to books and computers in the home, and that most come from homes where the highest educational level of parents is primary school (http://www.hsrc.ac.za). In addition, more than 59 per cent of public ordinary schools are classified as 'no-fee' schools which means that they fall within the lowest two of five categories (or quintiles) of schools. Those schools in the lowest two quintiles are deemed poor and allow learners to enrol without paying fees, with the government funding expenses that would have been covered by fees. This is reflective of the scale of economic disadvantage in the county and has an impact on educational resourcing and provisioning. When taken in conjunction with the high proportion of the population infected and affected by HIV and AIDS, it has serious implications for the economy, the provision of health care and for the schooling sector.

This combination of a troubled education system, a largely uneducated and unskilled workforce and insufficient economic growth has turned SA into a country with a large economic and socially disadvantaged population which directly impacts on the state of public schooling.

As a Faculty of Education (FoE) operating in such a complex environment, we are concerned about finding a way of preparing our students for the demands of the profession, who are equipped with the skills sets and attitudes to work effectively in challenging contexts. Key to our deliberations about how we could achieve this purpose was defining a way of working collaboratively with other role players in the school and broader community. Such a relationship needed to be mutually supportive of meeting our various needs and which could draw on our respective strengths and resources. This meant establishing an interdependent relationship between the FoE and our partners (a number of communities and schools), and it is within this context that the multi-tiered service and support model we use was founded.

A Framework of Social Justice and Care for Service-Learning

Our main concern as a FoE in our education and training of students for diverse professions within the schooling sector (teachers, school counsellors, educational psychologists) was to give expression to the idea of education, and educational practitioners, in service of society. We argued that to be accountable as higher education teachers we had to work together with communities to design learning environments for higher education students in which they could learn this both academically and experientially. Service-Learning, with its long history as liberatory pedagogy (Stanton et al., 1999) seemed a viable pedagogy for this purpose. Implicit in this purpose, however, was the idea that the overarching frame for SL would move beyond isolated rendering of 'service' to needy communities in philanthropic mode by well-meaning staff and students. We wanted a frame for SL that would be capable of helping students become 'active agents in constructing new kinds of knowledge and relationships' (Hayes and Cuban, 1997, p. 78) and in which students could learn how to move from operating mainly as users of knowledge to a position as creators and co-creators of knowledge in conjunction with others (Dewey, 1924; Moore, 1990; Shor, 1992).This orientation would in our view allow participants (teachers, students and community members) both the opportunities and the leverage to define and produce knowledge according to the social, historical and cultural contexts in which they find themselves (Tierney, 1993).

In crafting a SL model for this purpose we had to carefully choose a theoretical frame that fitted this philosophical orientation and which would support curriculum development in three broad areas (teacher education, counselling and educational psychology) while also creating an agenda and framework for service and support by our students in schools/communities. We thus had to consider a theoretical frame for SL that fitted our wider commitment and purpose as a Faculty of Education while also establishing a usable, adaptable and practical structure for our activities that would respond to the challenges presented by our intended partners.

In this quest we looked firstly to the Faculty conceptual framework for teaching and learning. This framework indicates that 'we are committed to the preparation of caring, accountable and critical reflective educational practitioners who are able to support and nurture learning and development in diverse educational contexts'. It then became a type of 'blueprint' for crafting and defining the streams of our inter-departmental collaboration and working relationship with outside partners. Most importantly, the framework crystallized our ideological ideas about the potential of education to transform human lives, with our practical efforts to craft educational curricula and programmes that would also address the *how to* of building a more humane and just society.

Consequently, we decided these purposes would best be served with a focus on care and social justice. To us the ethos of care and social justice was in line with the Faculty conceptual framework and could thus also be infused in our teaching, learning and community engagement activities, which included SL. In deliberating about the reciprocity of care and social justice in our work, we proposed that these concepts were not just topics of study but were also a way of being and doing and that students could learn these experientially in the service relationship. We thus focused specifically on social justice (see, for instance, McDonald and Zeichner, 2009) and care as essential elements in our deliberations, practices and decisions and drew heavily on the work of Noddings (1984, p. 72) in this respect. She for example says the following on care in education:

> The primary aim of every educational institution and of every educational effort must be the maintenance and enhancement of caring. It functions as an end means, and criterion for judging suggested means. We cannot separate means and ends in education because the desired result is part of the process and the process carries with it the notion of persons undergoing it becoming somehow 'better'.

Noddings' work influenced our view of the process of student learning about care and social justice and was instrumental in influencing our pedagogical practices through SL. We argued that to be accountable as higher education teachers preparing students for diverse professions within the schooling sector (teachers, school counsellors, educational psychologists), we had to work together to design learning environments for students in which they could encounter care in a responsible and moral way (Tronto, 1993) so that they would be able to recognize, face and (begin to) address issues of social injustice in the communities where they worked. On the flip side, our understanding of social justice was influenced by views such as those of Boyles et al. (2009) and Adams et al. (1997, p. 3), who argue that it includes:

> ... the full and equal participation of all groups in a society that is mutually shaped to meet their needs. Social justice includes a vision of society in which the distribution of resources is equitable and all members are physically and psychologically safe and secure ... social justice involves social actors who have a sense of their own agency as well as a sense of social responsibility toward and with others and the society as a whole.

Our aim was thus to teach students that 'moral interdependence' (Noddings, 1998) and 'social interdependence' (Johnson and Johnson, 2009) came together in the SL enterprise. According to Johnson and Johnson (2009), social interdependence is possible when the outcomes for individuals are affected by their own and others' actions. This meant that students would become interdependent with community members through the establishment of common goals in SL. In this way, care and social justice could be infused in the *process* of student learning (both in the classroom context and through learning from experience such as in SL). For our students, SL provided opportunities in which they could learn to practise care and social justice in a manner other than the more skills-based and technique-oriented opportunities already included in their curriculum. Service-Learning, defined in this way, enabled us to enrich student learning in care and social justice by providing the opportunities for them to cross the traditional 'borders' (Giroux, 1992, 1993; Torres, 2009) of the higher education classroom. Our aim was to transform the process of student learning, the situation in which they learned and the nature of their learning experience.

We also drew on the ideas of Baer (2006, p. 207) in our quest to heighten students' awareness of how offering educational and psychological services can facilitate social justice and at the same time expand the repertoire of our own pedagogies. We firmly believe that in order to understand the needs of those being offered service requires active involvement and commitment to them, their needs and projects. Through this process we strove to develop 'new lenses' for understanding social conditions (O'Grady and Johnston, 2006, p. 9) in the communities in which we work and how these social conditions influenced the individuals in it, as well as us and our students. It was our vision that this agenda would also inform, enrich and transform our collaboration across various departments in the SL model. In order for the academic coordinators of each of the three tiers of service to achieve this, we believed that it was important to consult widely with school communities where our students would be placed. We wanted to foster the conditions for engagement with our community which would be reciprocally beneficial and which enabled long-term partnership development and investment. We were guided by the idea of investing in a true partnership with the community as underlined among others in the work of Radebe (2007) and the Service-Learning clearinghouse (http://servicelearning. org).

This conceptual and philosophical orientation and our interactions with community partners led to the development of three specific SL courses, in pre-service teacher education, school counselling and educational psychology, which were designed to operate in an integrated and collaborative manner in each of the service sites. The intention was also to create connections between students at the three levels so that they would form a referral and support system for each other and for the schools at which they were placed.

An Integrated Three-Tier Service-Learning Model

The resultant integrated SL model comprises the following three levels and is presented in Figure 4.1.

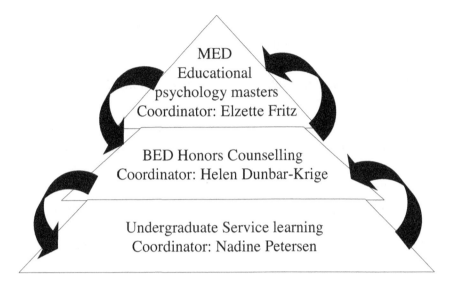

MED
Educational
psychology masters
Coordinator: Elzette Fritz

BED Honors Counselling
Coordinator: Helen Dunbar-Krige

Undergraduate Service learning
Coordinator: Nadine Petersen

Figure 4.1: An integrated three-tier service-learning model

Level 1: Undergraduate pre-service teacher education

Approximately 400 pre-service teacher education students in two programmes (Bachelor of Education and Post Graduate Certificate in Education) offer between three and five hours of educational service per week over a year. The educational services comprise individual and/or group tutoring, homework and learning support (outside of the classroom), teacher support (with learners in the classroom and/or crafting teaching aids such as charts, worksheets, etc.) and the establishment of reading pairs.

Level 2: School counselling by BEd (Hons) Educational Psychology students

Approximately 15 school counsellors within the BEd Honours Educational Psychology programme are placed at participating schools for a period of six months during which students work a full school day, five days per week. This practicum of 720 hours is a requirement of the Health Professional Council of South Africa for graduation as school counsellors and is an attempt by the HPCSA to make available more counsellors with the requisite skills to serve a broader disadvantaged community. During this period, students are expected to assess and counsel learners and provide teacher, learner, parent and community support. This experience provides the school counsellor with authentic education and training situations and students work under the supervision of a site supervisor as well as a registered educational psychologist who is an academic staff member of the university.

Level 3: Educational psychology services by MEd educational psychology students

Masters educational psychology students are subject to the stipulations of the Health Professions Council of South Africa in which a requirement of 200 practical hours is indicated for registration as an intern educational psychologist. We interpret these practical hours within a Service-Learning framework and students are required to complete the hours at the partner schools over a period of two years. These students provide a more nuanced level of support than the counsellors, and the service they provide includes family therapy as well as workshops for parents, staff and the wider community on issues such as single parenting and drug and sexual abuse. They also provide liaison services with external support services, such as the optometry department at the university so that school children can have their eyes tested.

Administration and Partnership

The administration of the model in the various school communities is facilitated by a community engagement officer (CEO) who forms part of Faculty administration and operates within the broader structure of a faculty-wide community engagement team (CET) under the leadership of the executive dean of the faculty. This team is responsible for initiating and sustaining contact with partners, for facilitating academic coordination and for structuring community engagement initiatives (including SL and other CE activities). We are aware that the financial and administrative support for a community engagement initiative is vital to its success, as is evident from much of the Service-Learning literature (Bringle and Hatcher, 2000; Driscoll et al., 2001; Erasmus, 2007; Furco, and

Holland, 2004; Mouton and Wildschut, 2005), and we are thankful that we have the necessary infrastructure to support it.

Partner schools are chosen partly on the basis of their proximity to the university. However, most are chosen because the schools face a number of challenges owing to the composition of the learner body; these include a linguistically diverse learner population, the majority of whom do not have English as a first language. Our partner schools also cater for learners with special educational needs (learning difficulties and cognitive and physical challenges), learners from challenging socio-economic circumstances (especially learners from the school for street children and refugee children) and children living in a facility which cares for those infected and affected by HIV and AIDS.

By 2010, the Faculty had signed a memorandum of understanding with 14 community partners of which the main purpose is to:

1 Advance the mutual interests of the Faculty of Education and the participating schools and community organisation in such a way that they both serve and respond to the needs of students, teachers, the Faculty of Education, the city and its citizenry.
2 Provide Service-Learning opportunities to students in order to promote a sense of social responsibility and foster an ethos of care for the community; and also to prepare students to become caring, accountable and critical-reflective educational practitioners who are able to support and nurture learning and development in diverse educational contexts.
3 Enable research that could lead to the improvement of education practice and build a 'scholarship of engagement' in the Faculty.

In addition to the services offered as part of the three-tier Service-Learning model, Faculty of Education staff also offer additional support by, for example, presenting workshops and seminars to staff and parents as needs are identified. For instance, many schoolteachers struggle with the identification of learning difficulties and how to support these in the classroom, and this became a focus for a number of years. Other issues included dealing with discipline and implementing 'shoestring' approaches for teaching science using everyday, common household materials.

Challenges in Working with Communities in a Service-Learning Partnership

Although we believe that we have made great strides in the education and training of teachers, counsellors and educational psychologists with this initiative, we also acknowledge that it is fraught with a number of challenges. The challenges present themselves on a number of levels. In this section we will briefly outline these and illustrate by way of example how we address them.

One of the most challenging aspects for the authors is how we deal with issues of power in SL. Working within a social justice frame implies that we have to be cognisant of how issues of power pervade the teaching, training and supervision contexts within which we work. This means that we have to constantly examine our relationships with students and the community and encourage our students to scrutinize their relationships with the community members to which they offer service. Given the unequal power dynamic which usually exists in higher education, and with which most students and staff are familiar, this is an aspect which requires constant interrogation and addressing. It is also an aspect which requires due attention if we are to truly have a shared understanding of care and social justice in our move towards more collaborative relationships characterized by participation, engagement and critical dialogue with the school community. For instance, power in schools tends to be vested within the school management team (the principal, head of department, etc.). The school counsellor, offering her service at a school, is not a permanent member of staff like a teacher, and thus does not have the authority to take decisions related to school learners with respect to serious issues such as abuse. School counsellors are taught by university staff that it is their ethical and legal responsibility to report abuse and this can be at odds with the views of the school management if they do not want to, or do not know how to, deal with such matters. The tension such situations create impacts on the training of the students and the relationship with the school and will require the intervention of the UJ faculty to resolve. We have had two such cases this year. Fortunately the nature of our relationship with schools built up over many years allows for intervention towards resolving the issue.

A second challenge we identified in the course of our work with student school counsellors and educational psychology Masters students in disadvantaged and special needs schools, is that students have to work with situations that they had initially not been trained to address. For example, students found that the majority of the children they were expected to counsel had been exposed to either physical or sexual abuse. Neither they, nor we, were experienced enough to provide all their training needs and so we had to establish further partnerships with other organizations that had the necessary expertise to assist us. This has had a positive spin-off, with the establishment of an additional partnership with the Teddy Bear Clinic, a non-governmental organization (NGO) that deals with child abuse. Their counsellors helped train our students to recognize signs and symptoms of abuse and how to manage such in its various forms. Broadened partnerships with NGOs such as these in turn not only extend our growing network of service and support in the community but also led to further curriculum innovation and adaptation. However, working with an extended network also has its downside. For instance, during the FIFA World Cup in 2010, there was growing concern nationally about the increased risks of human trafficking, especially for children from disadvantaged backgrounds (such as those in our partner schools). As faculty we had extensive meetings with national and international stakeholders, including private corporations and NGOs, but found that their individual interests and branding concerns were clouding cooperation. We were forced to terminate widely consultative workshops and instead incorporated ideas from the initial meetings into students' curricula at the three levels in order to formulate a Faculty response.

Third, as our partnership schools comprise different types of schools – we have full service, special and mainstream schools – this creates a further challenge in terms of the supervision of school counsellors and educational psychologists. For lecturers supervising the BEd (Hons) and MEd students, these varied circumstances proved difficult to manage; we have to constantly update our own expertise in terms of addressing various learning barriers in order to provide the necessary supervision and support to our students. Ethics also becomes another challenging area. In many of the schools, parents cannot be contacted for permission to work with their children. This is especially worrying when parents are semi-literate or have little understanding of the work of tutors, counsellors and educational psychologists. We then have to find creative ways around such obstacles and often work through trusted community leaders to gain access and/or permission for treatment. This has meant that accepted university protocols for ethical clearance have had to be adapted and readapted to suit the circumstances of the schools. This is sometimes time consuming and difficult for university administrators to appreciate. At another level, we often have to re-evaluate our own procedures for working with schools. For instance, when students tell us about problematic disciplinary measures implemented by teachers (such as striking misbehaving learners), it demands a response, without attacking schools for breaking the law. This has meant that we have to update and rework our Service-Learning guidelines and agreements with schools each year to find constructive ways of addressing issues such as these without endangering our partnership.

Fourth, we sometimes find ourselves being called upon to solve *other* problems schools are experiencing (often with individual learners) which falls outside of our SL memorandum of understanding. We work within a framework that advocates a systemic approach rather than assisting with individualized problems, so that schools can take responsibility for their own issues. So for us, the individual cannot be understood outside of the social context and we encourage solutions that look to interventions from a multi-levelled perspective (Visser, 2007; see also Billig and Furco, 2002). This stance sometimes brings us into conflict with the school that wants an immediate response to or assistance with the individual problem. However, these instances are not wasted opportunities; it is when we gain insight into these factors in the school that the quality of the supervision of the school counsellor or the educational psychology students is informed. The SL students are then able (under supervision) to put into place interventions that deal with more than simply giving attention to the individual but which help address systemic issues. One such example is the response to bullying in a school context: instead of only engaging with the individual in a therapy session, a systemic intervention is implemented. This includes the participatory development of a policy for bullying in the school, workshops for learners, parents and teachers about bullying and the creation of links to organizations such as The South African Society for Depression and Anxiety.

One of our greatest challenges thus far has been forging and solidifying the referral system between each tier of service offered in every school. Students at the various levels are not always clear about the parameters of their influence, the correct procedures for referral and the circumstances under which referral to a more experienced service provider is possible. Most importantly, the service and support initiative has to work within the existing systems such as the School-based Support Team of each school, which in many cases are very different and present unique circumstances, posing unique problems for the training and supervision of SL students. Nevertheless, we recognize that these challenges, some of which may be unique to our context, are in essence not different from the general challenges identified in the Service-Learning literature internationally (see, for example, Billig and Furco, 2001; Kahne et al.,

2000; McTighe Musil, 2003; and nationally, Mitchell and Humphries, 2007, and Osman and Atwood, 2007). We constantly strive to address these collaboratively and constructively with our community partners so as to maintain our working relationship in the spirit of 'social interdependence' referred to by Johnson and Johnson (2009).

Discussion and Reflection

In order to improve the system, we solicit feedback annually on the Service-Learning partnership from the schools through the Faculty's Community Engagement Officer. A large part of the feedback is very positive, which is a great encouragement to us and helps us refine the initiative accordingly. Some of the positive feedback about the pre-service teachers is that 'It has been really helpful and added value to our children's day' and 'staff is assisted by having another adult in the classroom to *lengthen the reach* of the teacher'. Also, pre-service students, through exposure to the learners' curriculum themes, often take it upon themselves to assist in expanded opportunities for learning; one student arranged for a selection of farm animals to be brought to a school in a disadvantaged community as many of the children had not seen these animals live before.

The Masters students and the school counsellors spend an extended time in the schools and the feedback about their input is often more comprehensive and again largely positive. Schools have indicated that 'they make a huge contribution to the welfare of the learners', 'they are involved in the daily discussions/meetings and become part of our staff', 'they provide learners with counselling in terms of physical, emotional, scholastic and behavioural barriers' and 'they are also willing to extend their services to teacher support and provision of workshops/training to staff'.

Schools do highlight real challenges in their feedback which we then try to address in a consultative workshop with them at the end of each year. Some of the more problematic aspects include organization and managing large numbers of students in the absence of suitable processes and organizational structures. The large number of undergraduate students who arrive and depart from the school at different times can sometimes be chaotic. It is also hard for the schoolteachers to deal with the negative attitudes of some pre-service students: a few are unmotivated and uninterested and do not make a valuable contribution to the school. Unfortunately, we have found this out too late in the year to address it in time. In response, the CEO has begun to make more regular checks on students in the early months at the schools to identify and deal with such cases.

Despite these problems, we have found that in many respects it is our students themselves who are finding solutions to the challenges we have encountered and who are teaching us in the process. For instance, students have been innovative in assisting us with the links between theory and practice. In addition, their superior experience and knowledge of the sites and their insight into traditional counselling and psychological practices have informed the curriculum and the procedures for our work with such diverse communities. Also, over time, we found that as the school counsellors are at the different partnership schools for a longer, more sustained period of time, they have broader insight into the needs and operations of the placement school. These insights enhance our overall understanding of the levels of care and support needed at each particular school and are a vital early part of structuring the service and support system for the following year. A pertinent example hereof is how a counsellor is able to gain an in-depth understanding of the manner in which a school deals with HIV and AIDS, and how this informs the subsequent measures to develop circles of care within such a school.

Conclusion

The aim of this chapter was to describe a Faculty of Education's use of Service-Learning in the education and training of educational practitioners for the challenges of a post-apartheid South Africa. The process of building and sustaining a SL partnership with schools and community has been a humbling experience for us and our students. As academics who believe in the notion of higher education serving the needs of a developing country, we are extremely pleased at the success of this initiative which continues to grow and expand each year. Addressing the many challenges associated with working in such a collaborative manner has been fraught with difficulties. Together with our students, we have found solutions to these challenges and have begun by encouraging all stakeholders to move away from looking to the traditional 'expert' for a solution. As academics we have also had to learn how to approach communities without focusing firstly on their needs but from a perspective in which we acknowledge their assets and strengths. In the process we are also learning to re-evaluate our view of ourselves as 'providers of a service' and the community as 'recipients of service' and to examine the inequitable social systems within which we work.

Most importantly, the recognition of the importance of community engagement within South Africa Higher Education, and within the UJ structures itself, is promising. In a recent national audit, the Faculty of Education's three-tier service and support model was singled out as an example of best practice in community engagement at the institution. The recognition of our integrated approaches for teaching for a world of 'social interdependence' and 'moral interdependence' through Service-Learning and community engagement is encouraging. Our next goal is to focus more closely on the research associated with this initiative in order to achieve the successful cross-articulation between teaching, research and community engagement referred to by Boyer (1990, 1996) as the 'synthesis' dimension of scholarship.

References

Adams, M., Bell, L. A. and Griffin, P. (eds) (1997), *Teaching for Diversity and Social Justice: A Sourcebook*. New York: Routledge.

Baer, E. R. (2006), 'Service-Learning for social justice: Moving Faculty from personal to pedagogical commitment through faculty development', in B. T. Johnston and C. R. O'Grady (eds), *The Spirit of Service. Exploring Faith, Service and Social Justice in Higher Education*. Bolton: Anker Publishing.

Billig, S. H. and Furco, A. (eds) (2001), *Service-learning: The Essence of the Pedagogy*. Greenwich, CT: Information Age Publishing

—(2002), *Service-learning Through a Multidisciplinary Lens*. Greenwich, CT: Information Age Publishing.

Boyer, E. (1990), *Scholarship reconsidered: priorities of the professoriate*. Princeton, NJ: Carnegie Foundation for the Advancement of Teaching, 39 (1): pp. 11–13.

Boyer, E. (1996), 'The scholarship of engagement'. *Journal of Public Service and Outreach*, 1 (1): 11–20.

Boyles, D., Carusi, T. and Attick, A. (2009), 'Historical and critical interpretations of social justice', in W. Ayers, T. Quinn, T. and D. Stovall (eds), *Handbook of Social Justice in Education*. New York: Routledge.

Bringle, R. G., and Hatcher, J. A. (2000), 'Institutionalization of service learning in higher education'. *Journal of Higher Education*, 71 (3): 273–90.

Dewey, J. (1924), *School and Society*. Chicago: University of Chicago Press.

Driscoll, A., Sandmann, L. and Rosean, C. (2001), 'Documenting and reviewing the scholarship of engagement: Support for faculty and institutional commitments'. *AAHE 2001 Forum of Faculty Roles and Rewards.* Tampa, Florida.

Erasmus, M. (2007), 'Supporting academic staff as champions of service-learning'. *Education as Change, Special Issue.* (11) 3: 109–25.

Furco, A. and Holland, B. (2004), 'Institutionalizing service-learning in higher education: Issues and strategies for chief academic officers', in M. Langseth and S. Dillon (eds), *Public Work and the Academy.* Bolton, MA: Anker Publishing Company.

Giroux, H. (1992), *Border crossings and the politics of education.* New York: Routledge.

—(1993), *Living dangerously: multiculturalism and the politics of difference.* New York: Peter Lang.

Hall, M. (2010), *Community engagement in South African Higher Education.* Pretoria: Jacana Media.

Hayes, E., and Cuban, S. (1997), 'Border pedagogy: A critical framework for service learning'. *Michigan Journal of Community Service-learning,* 4: 72–80.

Howie, S., Venter, E., Van Staden, S., Zimmerman, L., Long, C., Du Toit, C., Scherman, V. and Archer, E. (2008), *PIRLS 2006. Progress in International Reading literacy Study 2006. Summary Report. South African Children's Reading Literacy Achievement.* University of Pretoria: Centre for Evaluation and Assessment. Retrieved on 10 October 2010 from http://www.hsrc.ac.za, TIMMS Report.

JET Education Services, *JET Bulletin,* No. 14, April 2006.

Johnson, D. W. and Johnson, R. T. (2009), 'An educational psychology success story: social interdependence theory and co-operative learning'. *Educational Researcher,* 38 (5): 365–79.

Johnston, B. T. and O'Grady, C. R. (eds) (2006), *The Spirit of Service. Exploring Faith, Service and Social Justice in Higher Education.* Bolton: Anker Publishing.

Kahne, J., Westheimer, J. and Rogers. B. (2000), 'Service-learning and citizenship. Directions for research'. *Michigan Journal of Community Service-learning,* 7: 42–51.

McDonald, M. and Zeichner, K. (2009), 'Social justice teacher education', in W. Ayers, T. Quinn and D. Stovall (eds), *Handbook of Social Justice in Education.* New York: Routledge.

McTighe Musil, S. (2003), 'Educating for citizenship'. *Peer Review,* 5 (3): 5–19.

Mitchell, C. and Humphries, H. (2007), 'From notions of charity to social justice in service-learning: the complex experiences of communities'. *Education as Change. Special Issue.* Vol. 11 (3): 47–58.

Moore, D. T. (1990), 'Experiential discourse as critical education', in J. C. Kendall (ed.), *Combining Service and Learning: A Resource Guide for Community and Public Service.* Raleigh, NC: NSIEE, pp. 273–83.

Mouton, J., and Wildschut, L. (2005), 'Service-learning in South Africa: Lessons learned through systematic evaluation'. *Acta Academica. Supplementum,* 3: 116–50

National Service-Learning Clearinghouse, 2008. Accessed on 6 July 2010 from http://www.servicelearning.org/

Noddings, N. (1984), *Caring. A Feminist Approach to Ethics and Moral Education.* Berkeley: University of California Press.

—(1994), 'Caring. A feminist perspective', in K. Strike and P. Ternasky (eds), *Ethics for professionals in education: Perspectives for preparation and practice.* New York: Teachers College Press, pp. 45–53.

—(1998), 'An ethic of caring and its implications for instructional arrangements'. *American Journal of Education*, 96 (2): 215–30.

Nxonga, L. (2010), *An (engaged) response to Hall's paper: Community engagement in South African Higher Education.* Pretoria: Jacana Media.

Osman, R. and Atwood, G. (2007), 'Power and participation in and through service learning'. *Education as Change, Special Issue.* Vol. 11 (3): 15–21.

Radebe, B. (2007), 'Prevention and Empowerment', in M. Visser, *Contextualising Community Psychology in South Africa.* Johannesburg. Van Schaik, pp. 134–46, *http://servicelearning.org*, Building Effective Partnerships in Service-Learning.

Shor, I. (1992), *Empowering Education. Critical Teaching for Social Change.* Chicago: The University of Chicago Press.

Stanton, T. K., Giles Jr, D. E. and Cruz, N. I. (1999), *A Movement's Pioneers Reflection its Origins, Practice and Future.* San Francisco: Jossey-Bass.

Subotzky, G. (1999), *Addressing the social purpose of higher education: enhancing postgraduate teaching, research and outreach through service-learning in community partnerships.* Paper presented at the Second Postgraduate Experience Conference, Cape Town, 28–30 March 1999.

Tierney, W. G. (1993), 'Academic freedom and the parameters of knowledge'. *Harvard Educational Review*, Vol. 63 (2): 129–48.

Torres, C. A. (2009), *Paulo Freire and Social Justice Education: An Introduction.* The Hague: Sense Publishers.

Tronto, J. C. (1993), *Moral Boundaries. A Political Argument for an Ethic of Care.* New York: Routledge.

Visser, M. (2007), 'Systems Theory', in M. Visser., *Contextualising Community Psychology in South Africa.* Johannesburg: Van Schaik, pp. 22–36,

Zlotkowski, E. (1998), *Successful Service-learning Programs. New Models of Excellence in Higher Education.* Bolton: Anker Publishing.

5

Service-Learning and School Development in German Teacher Education

Anne Sliwka and Britta Klopsch

Although Service-Learning has a long tradition in the English-speaking world and has shown itself to be highly effective for the achievement of certain educational aims, it has only recently been introduced into the German higher education system. This chapter describes the establishment of Service-Learning in German higher education and its implementation in teacher education programmes. It then discusses the advantages of Service-Learning in teacher education and the potential links with professional standards guiding teacher education. To exemplify Service-Learning in German teacher education, two specific projects are analyzed to elucidate its practical realization.

The Development of Service-Learning

Service-Learning as a pedagogical approach developed in the USA. As early as in the nineteenth century, Alexis de Tocqueville (1805–59) stated in his *Democracy in America* that doing voluntary service was an American trait. He saw voluntary work as crucial for the development of a civil society (De Tocqueville, 1988). In the twentieth century the tradition of community service turned out to be a huge benefit, especially during the Great Depression, after World War Two, and in times of widespread unemployment in the 1960s. Many different associations and programmes to propagate and support voluntary work have since been set up in the United States. The pragmatist educational philosopher John Dewey (1859–1952) argued that education is a social and interactive process that required experiential learning in an authentic and interactive environment. The pragmatist tradition of the United States of America provided a fertile ground for 'experiential learning' and 'voluntary service' to be merged into the idea of 'Service-Learning' (see Figure 5.1 below). In 1966 this term was used for the first time and has by now developed into a broad pedagogical movement surpassing the borders of the United States to be found in schools and universities on all continents. The 1990s saw the beginning of more formal research on Service-Learning. The first academic Service-Learning magazine, the *Michigan Journal for Community Service and Service-learning*, was started in 1994, followed by the first 'International Conference on Service-learning Research', which took place in 2001 and has been held annually since then (Reinmuth et al, 2007). It was at these conferences that researchers from Germany, who were initially interested in Service-Learning in K-12 schools, started to learn about the positive impact of Service-Learning in higher education.

Service-Learning in Germany

Service-Learning does not have a long tradition in Germany. Traditionally, schools and universities did not see themselves as active, contributing members of their community. They did not reach out beyond their own boundaries

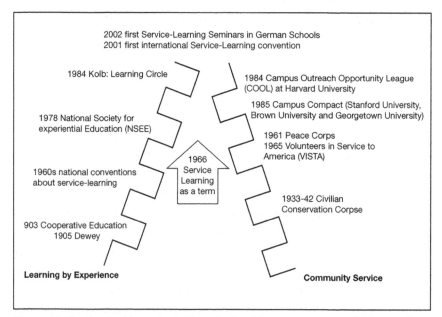

Figure 5.1: Synthesis of 'experiential learning' and 'community service' (Reinmuth et al., 2007, p. 16)

and tended to consider the circulation of knowledge among academics across universities the only fruitful way of collaboration. Reasons for this isolation are deeply rooted in German society and academic tradition. The welfare state emerging with the Bismarckian welfare reforms in the late nineteenth century and continuously expanding over the twentieth century was seen as taking almost complete care of its citizens, so that volunteering was not seen so much as a social necessity to provide needed relief against social hardship but more as a charity pursued by some Christian organizations for religious reasons.

The twenty-first century has seen significant changes with regard to charity and volunteering in Germany. Since the 1980s, governments have made serious efforts to encourage volunteering. In the economic downturn following German unification it turned out to be difficult for governments to sustain the policy of total care for its citizens. Services had to be cut. With high unemployment up to 2005 and the post-Programme for International Student Assessment (PISA) education crisis revealing that many students left the German school system as functional illiterates, volunteering saw a huge rise. More and more privileged adolescents and adults wanted to contribute to a more just and equitable society and to support those in need of help. The necessity of voluntary commitment to tackle social challenges was now clearly seen by many.

Service-Learning in Schools

Schools were the first educational institutions to make volunteering a component of their understanding of education. In 2001 and 2002, Service-Learning pilot projects were introduced in ten different German schools to test whether Service-Learning could become an appropriate method for German education (Sliwka et al., 2004). Even though Service-Learning proved to have various positive effects, its dissemination proceeded slowly. Around the same time PISA was accomplished for the first time. Due to the so called PISA shock[1] in Germany, the whole school system was fundamentally modified. Up to then all curricula were input-oriented. They stated the exact content that had to be taught in every single class level and subject. The input-based teaching was transformed into an outcome-oriented way of teaching. Content to be taught has been replaced by more complex competencies which every student should have achieved by the end of a two-year period. The shift to outcome-based learning was a great push for Service-Learning. A network of Service-Learning schools (www.lernen-durch-engagement.de) was founded in 2002 and has since been increasing in number and outreach. In 2004, the German state of Baden-Württemberg established a new curriculum that did more than determine purpose-built competencies. It embraced Service-Learning for the first time as a core feature of schooling. Its specific realization is left to the schools themselves. They can decide in what way and what range they add Service-Learning to their everyday life. To facilitate the process of implementing these new structures, there is a federal network (Netzwerk Service-learning), consisting of experienced schools and different partners, who support inexperienced schools at every stage of their project (Seifert and Zentner, 2010).

Service-Learning in Higher Education

Since 2005, universities have slowly begun to adopt the idea of Service-Learning. This coincided with a paradigm shift to more active and engaged forms of learning in higher education. A strict separation between 'town' and 'gown' was not seen as suitable any more to achieve certain motivational and cognitive aims in higher learning. Effective learning was not any longer seen as a one-way street, with one part giving and the other one taking, but rather as a complex setting in which partners 'will teach, learn, exchange resources and reap mutual benefits' (Torres, 2000, p. 3). Within teacher education, Service-Learning is still the exception rather than the norm and not used in all university training for future teachers. Nonetheless, there are several exemplary projects that already serve as role models for future Service-Learning in schools and teacher education.

German Research on Service-Learning

Furco (2004) showed that students who took part in Service-Learning processes are more content, more caring, more sensitive and more motivated than peers who don't have any experience in Service-Learning. It could easily be assumed that individuals with high interpersonal skills choose Service-Learning classes. On first sight, it seems obvious that students who do not choose those courses voluntarily won't get a lot out of them and might even do damage to the people they serve. German research, however, highlighted a paradox: high school students who did not want to take part in Service-Learning projects in the first place benefited the most in their personal development. One German secondary school student, who was described as an 'extremely difficult person' by his teacher, said: 'I would never have done this voluntarily – but now I'd be happy to do it again any time!'(Sliwka et al., 2004).

Pre- and post-test research showed that Service-Learning significantly improves political literacy, communicative skills, tolerance, critical thinking, self efficacy, commitment to community, and understanding different points of view. Even if Service-Learning students do not perform better on tests of information recall, they gain a greater depth of understanding and a greater ability to apply what they learn (Reinmuth et al., 2007). In addition to cognitive skills, social and communication skills have also been shown to be important outcomes of German Service-Learning projects. Bartsch (2009, p. 15) emphasizes two key socio-emotional outcomes: (a) the capability to establish relationships and to maintain social networks; and (b) the ability to bear differences and to cope with conflicts.

Characteristics of Service-Learning in Germany

In Germany, Service-Learning has developed on the basis of quality standards developed in the US. The connection between the real world and hands-on elements in Service-Learning should always consider the following elements (Furco, 2009):

- Learning, not teaching should be the focus.
- Learners should be active participants, making decisions about their own learning process.
- Every phase of the teaching process should be student-oriented.
- Higher-order thinking skills and reflection should be intentionally supported.
- Students should have opportunities to make interdisciplinary connections.
- Learners should be able to connect their new experience to their former experiences.
- The issues/projects should be interesting and meaningful for learners.
- The project should develop social skills.
- Students should be familiar with the Service-Learning setting.

Service-Learning places the student at the centre of the learning process. The role of a teacher shifts to being more of a coach. When playing a stronger role in their own learning process, students have to be aware of their learning styles, their aims and their steps toward achieving their aims. They should be able to reflect appropriately upon their learning process and work cooperatively with others to enhance their learning as well as their service. All this requires a deliberate focus on meta cognition and reflection.

Reflection as a Key to Learning

Not every educational experience is a positive one. Negative experiences can profoundly influence motivation and interest in learning. According to educational philosopher John Dewey, however, any experience – no matter whether learners feel comfortable or bad about it – can have a positive educational impact if it is reflected upon appropriately. Service-Learning can be defined as learning through and learning from experience. However, it is only effective when the practical experience (service) is linked to broader and deeper questions going beyond 'just the action'. In Germany, we have been using David Kolb's learning cycle as a process model to structure reflection (Figure 5.2). The following four steps are crucial for this process (Sliwka, 2009):

- Thinking about what one has observed, felt and noticed.
- Connecting the experience with former experiences.
- Thinking about the experience within a bigger picture.
- Thinking about the experience and its meaning for future life and society.

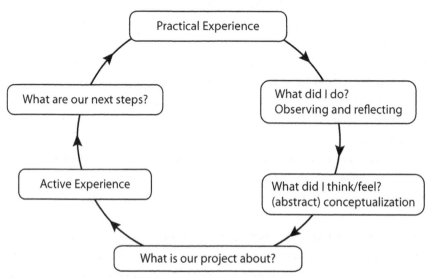

Figure 5.2: Learning circle (Sliwka, 2009, based on Kolb, 1984)

In order to help students to reflect on their experiences in Service-Learning, this circle can be transferred into a questionnaire or an interview as part of formative assessment. One possible arrangement of getting students to think about their own learning process could be based on the following questions (Sliwka, 2009):

Questions at the beginning of the enquiry

- What did the students learn while working on the project?
- How can the outcome be transferred into other situations?
- Did the students learn what they expected or did they learn something unexpected?
- What part of the learning experience did the students consider to be most important?
- What kind of professional or academic knowledge did the students need to work successfully?

Questions concerning the context

- How did the project influence the perception of a certain reality (e.g., poverty, old age, childhood)?
- How is it connected to broader social issues?
- What did the students consider to be their most important contribution within the project?
- How were the students able to impact the context they worked in?

Questions about the role and tasks of students within the project

- What exactly were the tasks of individual students within the project?
- What challenges did they encounter and how did they deal with them?
- What has been the biggest challenge?

Questions concerning the work in teams and interdependent groups

- What has been the common aim of the group?
- How did the group collaborate as a team?
- What have been the most positive and the most negative experiences within the team setting?
- What did the group members learn about themselves and about others in the team setting?
- What did they learn about teams while facing challenges?
- What would the students do differently in a future project?

In Service-Learning projects, students always work in teams, so that the ability to be able to work cooperatively with other people is crucial for achieving success.

Learning to Collaborate Successfully

The skill of working in teams does not always come easily to students. In the past, German university students tended to get only assignments on which they worked individually. Learning to work in teams is an important component in German Service-Learning courses. It is widely known that teams go through difficult phases before they begin to function effectively. According to Winer and Ray (1994), the process of collaboration is a journey from cooperation to collaboration that also involves coordination. The three implied steps are the natural way of development no matter whether the partnership is between a school and an agency, between students and community members or among the students themselves.

Although facilitating this journey can be exhausting for university lecturers at times, true collaborative Service-Learning can be extremely rewarding and revitalizing for all team members (Harwood and Lawson, 2001). Depending on what kind of projects and partnerships are in place, different compositions of teams might be needed (Winer and Ray, 1994):

- a group of students working together actively with community partners who take rather small roles or are completely passive;
- an active group of engaged community partners which includes some students;
- a group of students and active community partners which forms a real team and work mutually as collaborators.

Service-Learning is at its best, when collaboration – from the initial planning through to implementation, celebration and evaluation of the project – enhances the individual team members' skills and makes a result possible that no individual could have achieved on his or her own (Harwood and Lawson, 2001). To achieve such a successful collaboration there are certain standards we have been using in the German context.

The first standard is clear communication, that is, that everyone involved knows what his or her role is as well as what the others are responsible for. Frequent face-to-face communications about the project advancement strengthen the ongoing process. A second hallmark of collaboration is a shared goal concerning the project. A clearly communicated aim that is developed as a joint enterprise can support the process from cooperation to collaboration as well.

Effective Service-Learning should not be entered through assessing, measuring and planning programmes around needs. A shift from this 'needs-based approach' to a focus on mapping resources and building capacity instead strengthens the work in the project and facilitates a rich collaborative approach.

In working with partners like schools and social agencies, it is essential to understand the expected behaviour in order not to break implicit rules and regulations. We therefore take significant amounts of time to learn about and reflect on the organizational and psychological logic of the partner agencies we work with. Sensitivity to community partners in the sense of gaining knowledge about what they need and how they live can help in supporting Service-Learning. By carefully examining issues of trust, respect, confidentiality, liability, dignity, and sometimes even legal and regulatory issues, students can be prepared to meet the expectations. Different learning activities, from discussions of current events up to extended research, can prepare students to work on projects in which they face real-world challenges.

We found that collaboration and reflection mutually reinforce each other. 'Dealing with issues that arise during reflection in a timely manner can help to guide the Service-Learning experience for students and community partners in ways that will strengthen rather than destroy collaborative efforts' (Harwood and Lawson, 2001, p. 244). Celebration of success is an element that we have found difficult initially, but now see as crucial for the success of projects. We do not have a strong tradition of celebrating achievement in our academic culture. Celebrations help to reconnect to partners and projects, to highlight learning outcomes and to inform others about successful work. We've now added a final element of celebration to any Service-Learning project. Last but not least, any team should evaluate its work to identify things that worked out well and suggest improvements for the next project (Harwood and Lawson, 2001).

Service-Learning in German Teacher Education

Service-Learning is often seen as a methodology suitable for turning university students into 'engaged citizens'. In German teacher education, however, the main aim of Service-Learning is not to develop engaged citizens, valuable as this might be for society, but rather to prepare future teachers for the professional life as a teacher in a twenty-first-century school. Service-Learning, as we understand it, is not geared towards society in general but strongly focused on schools and their needs. The learning that occurs while fulfilling the service is supposed to benefit the students' in their future lives as teachers. Our experience in recent years has been that Service-Learning is well suited to prepare students for meeting the professional standards of the teaching practice. This will now be exemplified for five core standards of the teaching profession.

Teachers are committed to students and their learning.

The first standard carries an undeniable logic in itself. Any teacher should be committed to students and their learning. But what does it actually mean? Teachers must appreciate 'the range of interests, needs, levels, cultures, background experiences, and learning styles that children bring to the classroom … They must design instruction that not only addresses academic need but also meets social, personal, and civic needs and responsibilities' (Callahan et al., 2001, p. 55f). Service-Learning in teacher education allows students to broaden their horizons when working with individuals from different age groups and different ethnic and religious backgrounds. Through Service-Learning, future teachers can develop a profound understanding of the diversity of their prospective students and their families.

Teachers know the subjects they teach and how to teach those subjects to students

Knowing a subject and knowing how to teach it implies that teachers know the structure of a topic and can connect it to a variety of different student realities. Only if a teacher can deal flexibly with a subject can he or she find ways to make connections to an individual student's previous knowledge. Service-Learning projects in schools provide rich contexts in which teacher training students can learn how to help individual learners to experience a learning process based on their needs and interests. The practical experience helps to connect the theory of a subject with the real-world application of tools, methods and concepts that work for different kinds of learners.

Teachers are responsible for managing and monitoring student's learning

The third standard – responsibility for managing and monitoring student's learning – clarifies that pedagogical skills and strategies in organizing and managing are an important part of a teacher's repertoire. According to current learning research, twenty-first-century teachers are more facilitators and partners than instructors. Their challenge is to transform schools into learning communities and to actively involve students in their own learning processes. Service-Learning projects in teacher education take place in complex learning communities and provide excellent settings for developing student-oriented learning environments.

Teachers think systematically about their practice and learn from experience

Linking practical experience to systematic reflection is a key feature of Service-Learning. Reflection is also seen as a key skill on the way to becoming an expert teacher. A reflective practitioner is able to observe himself or herself in the school and classroom setting and to reflect consciously and continuously on his or her own practice and ways to improve it over time. Service-Learning provides an ideal learning environment for future teachers to practise systematic reflection and adaptive behaviour in a real-world context.

Teachers are members of learning communities

Professional teachers need to see themselves as lifelong learners and need to collaborate professionally with their colleagues and other members of multi-professional teams. Service-Learning in teacher education provides them with a learning environment in which they can practise and reflect upon the collaboration process with co-students and professional staff in the schools they work in. Service-Learning provides a structured environment, in which teacher-training students get opportunities and methodological support for reflecting on their team learning experience.

Service-Learning projects provide rich learning contexts in which teacher trainees can practise a whole range of professional competences in a structured and supported yet complex and authentic setting. We have come to understand Service-Learning as an almost ideal methodology for teacher education as we understand it in the twenty-first century.

Projects in teacher education can generally be split into two different types of projects: enhancing individual learning processes at school, and supporting school development and improvement.

Enhancing Individual Learning Processes at School

Service-Learning in German teacher education is driven by the needs of schools and educational practice. Kindergarten and schools, both primary and secondary, are the typical community partners in Service-Learning. The following table (Table 5.1) provides an insight into service projects which have been pursued within teacher education at the University of Mannheim.

Supporting School Development

Another type of project is Service-Learning activities directly linked to more complex processes of school improvement/school development, such as quality management, organizational development or staff development. In these kinds

Table 5.1: Combination of projects and their scientific background (Hofer, 2007)

Work at school (SERVICE)	Academic background (LEARNING)
Training peer mediators	• social psychology • violence prevention • development and training of interpersonal skills
Training students to be 'personal reading tutors'	• reading literacy • linguistics • phonological awareness • concepts of reading literacy enhancement
Training high school students to be 'homework tutors'	• peer education • self-regulated learning • concepts of homework
Training primary school parents to support their child's learning	• meso-system family-school • theory of motivation, self-determination • educational styles • learning strategies • feedback and formative assessment

of projects, teacher-training students typically provide active service to the school leadership team. University students, for example, support staff at school in evaluating and improving particular areas of the school's practice. Teams of students work like 'consultancy firms' to help the school achieve certain aims or solve specific problems. The following two projects were accomplished in two Service-Learning seminars at Heidelberg University of Education. Both seminars were open to all students no matter what number of terms or focus of school[2] they have been enrolled in.

Example 1: Primary school students as book authors (literacy)

The first project was established in a primary school to enhance reading and writing literacy. This project was arranged to support a school in implementing a new focus in its curriculum. So the basic need was to transform and establish a unit of teaching German. First of all, teacher-training students acquired a scientific framework in reading competence, reading motivation and research on reading interests of primary school students. On this theoretical basis, teacher-training students spend time in classrooms observing primary students to understand their interests and learning needs. Children aged 8–10 were encouraged to plan, write, illustrate and bind a book of their own on a self-chosen topic. The teacher-training students structured their learning process and developed material to be used in the teaching process. The books were not only presented at parents' night but also exhibited in a local book store. The project was subsequently institutionalized in the school's curriculum to become a sustainable part of the school's culture.

Example 2: Supporting quality management of a small, rural school

The second Service-Learning project was set up to support a school's process of quality management and help the staff to create a vision statement and pedagogical principles for this particular school. This project took place in a course called 'Developing and Assuring Quality at School'. In the first phase, teacher-training students worked out a theoretical basis on quality, quality management and how schools could be involved in their own quality development. Then students established contact with a small rural school which wanted to launch a vision statement and pedagogical principles to be applied in the school's everyday life. The staff's problem was that they had no idea how to start and what kind of work or research could help them. University students developed questionnaires for students and teachers to learn more about their feelings towards school, the school's strengths and weaknesses and the school's culture. On the basis of those data, the students developed a draft vision statement. Through reviewing all items and summing them up into categories, they managed to draft pedagogical principles for the school. All results were presented to a school's representative and fed into the school's improvement circle. An evaluation of the seminar and its outcome showed that students did learn more about theory than in other seminars because they had to skim through it repeatedly to assure the project's appropriate progress. The practical implementation of theory was considered to be even more valuable. Not only did students stress that they got an idea of what might be their task when working at a school in the future, but also understood how theoretical knowledge and concrete school improvement can be brought together. Problem-solving strategies, the understanding of complex interrelations, abstract thinking skills, and changing perspectives were parts of the cognitive learning process that the students had to deal with thoroughly. The improvement of their personal development was encouraged through self-reflection within the process, setting targets, planning, managing and controlling their progress and reconsidering their strategies (meta-cognition; Klopsch and Sliwka, 2011).

Service-Learning has become an important strategy for training teachers at Heidelberg University of Education. Beside the positive student evaluations we have been receiving for those courses, the readiness of students to commit to the projects far beyond the actual requirements of those courses, has shown us the positive impact of Service-Learning on teacher-training students' motivation and learning.

Conclusion

The benefits of Service-Learning go beyond the service provided to beneficiaries or the active learning of university students. Service-Learning enables students to experience self-efficacy, competent action and social integration. These three basic mental needs enhance students' intrinsic motivation and therefore lead to better learning outcomes (Deci and Ryan, 1993). We see Service-Learning as a form of leadership training, in which individuals can learn how to act in complex real-life settings and can develop the habits of a reflective practitioner. This development of individual reasoning powers, interpersonal skills and a sense of responsibility clearly meet our modern understanding of what a university should be about. It is almost an ideal training for future teachers, who are supposed to educate future generations for problem-solving and competent activity in complex settings. It is a widely known truth that 'teachers teach as they were taught and not as they were taught to teach'. Service-Learning in teacher education goes a long way towards combating this. It not only influences the values, skills and habits of individual university students but also the way primary and secondary school students will learn in the future.

References

Bartsch, G. (2009), 'Service-learning im kontext von zivilgesellschaft', in K. Altenschmidt, J. Miller and W. Stark (eds). *Raus aus dem Elfenbeinturm? Entwicklungen in Service-learning und bürgerschaftlichem Engagement an deutschen Hochschulen*. Weinheim, Basel: Beltz, pp. 102–11.

Callahan, J. P., Diez, M. E. and Ryan, L. B. (2001), 'Service-Learning and standards-based teacher education', in J. B. Anderson, K. J. Swick, J. Yff (eds), *Service-Learning in Teacher Education*. Washington, DC: AACTE Publications, pp. 53–68.

Deci, E. L. and Ryan, R. M. (1993), 'Die selbstbestimmungstheorie der motivation und ihre bedeutung für die pädagogik', *Zeitschrift für Pädagogik*, 39: 223–38.

De Tocqueville, A. (1988), *Democracy in America*. New York: Harper Collins.

Furco, A. (2004), 'Zufriedener, sozialer, sensibler und motivierter. Hoffnungsvolle Ergebnisse in den USA', in A. Sliwka, C. Petry and P. Kalb (eds) (2004), *Durch Verantwortung lernen. Service-learning in Schule und Gemeinde*. Weinheim/Basel: Beltz.

—(2009), 'Die rolle von service-learning im aufbau einer gesellschaftlich engagierten Universität', in K. Altenschmidt, J. Miller and W. Stark (eds), *Raus aus dem Elfenbeinturm? Entwicklungen in Service-learning und bürgerschaftlichem Engagement an deutschen Hochschulen*. Weinheim, Basel: Beltz, pp. 47–59.

Harwood, A. M. and Lawson, R. (2001), 'Developing rich collaborations between schools, universities, and community partners', in J. B. Anderson, K. J. Swick and J. Yff (eds), *Service-Learning in Teacher Education*. Washington, DC: AACTE Publications, pp. 234–47.

Hofer, M. (2007), 'Ein neuer weg in der Hochschuldidaktik', in A. M. Baltes, M. Hofer and A. Sliwka (eds), *Studierende übernehmen Verantwortung. Service-learning an deutschen Universitäten*. Weinheim, Basel: Beltz, pp. 35–48.

Klopsch, B. and Sliwka, A. (2011), 'Reflexion – eine zentrale lernkompetenz', in *SchulVerwaltung. Zeitschrift für Schulleitung und Schulaufsicht*. 1/2011: 8–10.

Kolb D. (1984), *Experiential learning: experience as the source of learning and development*. Englewood Cliffs, NJ: Prentice Hall.

National Board for Professional Teaching Standards (1989). *What teachers should know and be able to do*. Detroit, MI.

National Campus Compact (2005). *President's statement of principles* [online]. *www. compact.org/aboutcc/principles.html* (accessed 29 November 2005)

Reinmuth, S. I., Saß, C. and Lauble, S. (2007), 'Die idee des service-learning', in A. M. Baltes, M. Hofer and A. Sliwka (eds), *Studierende übernehmen Verantwortung. Service-learning an deutschen Universitäten*. Weinheim, Basel: Beltz, pp. 13–28.

Seifert, A. and Zentner, S. (2010), *Service-Learning – Lernen durch Engagement. Methode, Qualität, Beispiele und ausgewählte Schwerpunkte. Netzwerk Lernen durch Engagement*. Weinheim: Freudenberg Stiftung.

Sliwka, A. (2007), 'Giving back to the community – service-learning als universitäre pädagogik für gesellschaftliches problemlösen', in A. M. Baltes, M. Hofer and A. Sliwka (eds), *Studierende Ubernehmen Verantwortung. Service-learning an Deutschen Universitäten*. Weinheim, Basel: Beltz, pp. 29–34.

—(2008), *Bürgerbildung. Demokratie Beginnt in der Schule*. Weinheim/Basel: Beltz.

—(2009), 'Reflexion: Das Bindeglied zwischen Service und Lernen', in K. Altenschmidt, J. Miller and W. Stark (eds), *Raus aus dem Elfenbeinturm? Entwicklungen in Service-learning und Bürgerschaftlichem Engagement an Deutschen Hochschulen*. Weinheim/ Basel: Beltz, pp. 85–90.

Sliwka, A. Petry, C. and Kalb, P. (eds) (2004), *Durch Verantwortung Lernen. Service Learning in Schule und Gemeinde*. Weinheim, Basel: Beltz.

Torres, J. (ed.) (2000), *Benchmarks for Campus/ Community Partnerships*. Providence, RI: Campus Compact.

Winer, M. and Ray, K. (1994), *Collaboration Handbook: Creating, Sustaining, and Enjoying the Journey*. St Paul, MN: Amherst H. Wilder Foundation.

Notes

1 The first PISA study in 2001 turned out to be a shock, as Germans expected their school system to be at the top and not to reach average results.

2 There are different types of schools in the German education system. At Heidelberg University of Education there are degree programmes for primary school teachers, two kinds of secondary school teachers and teachers for handicapped children.

6

Empowering Educational Practice Through Service-Learning in the UK: Case Studies from Leeds Metropolitan University, UK

Timothy Murphy and Jon E. C. Tan

Abstract

This chapter argues for the articulation of Service-Learning (SL) oriented approaches that are located within and close to practice rather than as supplementary to it. Drawing from developing work in the Carnegie Faculty of Education at Leeds Metropolitan University, this chapter considers the significance of critical dialogic approaches in the support and development of professional educators across the life-course of their careers. Conceptualizing schools in challenging social contexts as sites where practice and service intersect, it opens up a discussion of the ways in which equity and social justice can be anchored within the context to which it is applied. Two case studies are presented: the first involved a cohort of Education Studies students who were intending to work in the broad field of education. The second initiative involved a partnership between the university and a local school in a socially disadvantaged setting. At the core of these studies is a sense of two-way learning and collaborative knowledge-building for students, practitioners and academic partners alike. Most importantly, this chapter provides examples of the close coupling of practice and the theorization of practice that fosters participants' capacity for critical thinking.

Introduction

The orientation to Service-Learning that informs the pedagogical approach of both case studies as developed below is referred to throughout as directed experiential learning (DEL). It is our contention that the DEL oriented pedagogical approach is congruent with the Service-Learning approach on several levels. It is consistent with the latter approach in its potential to deepen and enrich the learner's understanding of designated course content. It is also consistent for the manner in which it affords them opportunities to recognize the equity and justice aspects involved in the project of education. Both approaches are also framed in a dialogic approach that recognizes and validates the contribution of the learner as being pivotally important to the learning process. Such an orientation to learning is consistent with the Freirean conception that 'the teacher-of-the-students and the students-of-the-teacher cease to exist and a new term emerges: teacher-student with student-teachers' (Freire, 1970, 1996, p. 61). And, additionally, both the DEL and SL approaches are experiential for the manner in which they integrate field experiences into classroom learning, drawing in particular from the progressive approach of Dewey (1938, 1963).

It is also evident that the characteristics of DEL – directed (purposeful learning intent), experiential, dialogic and constructivist – align with the Community of Practice (CoP) orientation to teaching and learning as developed for example by Lave and Wenger (1991, p. 51), where they contend that 'knowledge of the socially constituted world is socially mediated and open ended. Its meanings to given actors, its furnishings, and the relations of humans within it, are produced, reproduced, and changed in the course of activity.' The above characteristics are also in clear alignment with Hodkinson's (2004) depiction of the CoP dimensions as mutual engagement, joint enterprise and a shared repertoire of actions and discourses, all of which are encapsulated in both of the case studies being presented in this chapter. In the initial case study, for example, the students participate in Integrated Learning Projects (ILP). They constitute the final summative assessments for the two combined Level 6 modules referred to below. In the process of developing their ILPs, the students self-select themselves into collaborative working teams which are framed around intersecting topics of interest. Each of the teams presents their final products as part of a conference-type format, for which the students truly become 'student-teachers', as depicted by Freire above, for the attending course tutors. The overall learning process that the students engage with is encapsulated by

Chapman's (2008, p. 40) comment that 'people learn best in actively designing and building artefacts to share with and for critique by others'. The second case study explores the experiences of university academics partnering school practitioners, operating to deepen considerations of education and practice in the interests of building collective knowledge in the service of the school's community. In its use of critical reflection and dialogic pedagogies for practitioner learning within this socio-educational context, it illustrates (and perhaps extends) our thinking about Service-Learning.

Case Study 1: Directed Experiential Learning and the Development of Pre-service Professional Educators

Case study 1: background

The initial case study focuses on a cohort of Level 6 (Year 3) BA Education Studies students who fulfilled their course requirements in the academic year 2009–10. In particular, it is intended that their engagement with DEL will afford them opportunities to develop their critical inquiry skills as they relate to equity and social justice issues in the broad field of education. It is also intended to evidence that engagement with this particular pedagogical approach will also afford the students opportunities to develop and enrich their understanding of related academic content, as well as developing their understanding about what it means to be an educator in the twenty-first century.

In their final year (Year 3) of the course, the students are challenged to reflect and to synthesise their accrued learning over the three years of the degree. The curricular and pedagogical input in the final year is designed with that intent, and the DEL oriented approach is pivotal for it to happen. The data upon which this initial case study is based is drawn principally from two combined modules: 'Current Educational Issues' and 'Effective Educational Placements'. Combined, they provide a very good exemplar of the DEL/Service-Learning oriented approach that is being outlined in this initial study.

Case study 1: process

In this particular case study, the field experience takes place in the second semester and is embedded in the module called 'Effective Educational Placements'. It is of three weeks duration and the students are responsible for sourcing the sites that will be optimally suited for meeting their particular learning goals. In the first semester, each student, as part of the 'Current Educational Issues' module, is invited to nominate an area of particular educational interest for further exploration and investigation. Each student prepares a critical review of literature assignment on their nominated issue. In the course of its construction, they are invited to identify some specific aspects of the issue which they would like to investigate further while they are out on placement.

Each student chooses the particular issue that they would like to investigate. They are required, however, to consider how their individually chosen issues can be responded to in the context of integrated working, an approach to professional working for children and young persons that came out of the Every Child Matters (ECM) agenda (DfES, 2004). Such a way of working, however, also has implications for leadership. Previous to ECM, professionals tended to be trained individually, trainee teachers with trainee teachers, social workers with fellow social workers, and so on. With this more recent policy direction, different professionals are required to work across professional boundaries in the interests of the child and young person.

The authors felt it was incumbent upon them to prepare the students for the integrated working context that they will encounter as future working professionals. While out on their respective placements, then, they were invited to be cognisant about how the practices of integrated working were being engaged with or not, particularly in response to the particular issue that each of the students was responding to. In order to develop and expand their thinking around integrated and multi-agency working, a number of experts and practitioners in that field were invited to speak to the students.

Case study 1: data collection and analysis

The data upon which this case study is based comes largely from end-of-year reflection sheets which each student was invited to complete. It inquired as to what aspect or issue in education each of them decided to focus on. It also invited them to specify the key questions/issues that emerged from their critical engagement with the literature on their individually chosen topic, which they then decided to investigate further through the effective educational placement opportunity. In particular, they were invited to reflect on whether or not the effective educational placement enabled them to extend their understanding about the issues that emerged as being significant for them in the context of their engagement with the critical review of literature. And, critically, the reflection prompt sheet also invited them to consider whether or not the effective placement opportunity allowed them to develop their thinking about what it means to be an educator in the context of integrated and multi-agency working. Additional data for the case study emerged from an extended interview with one of the participating students, as well as from electronic correspondence with three of the faculty who delivered specific sessions for the combined 'Current Educational Issues' and 'Effective Educational Placements' modules which drew on their particular areas of expertise.

Findings from participating lecturers

In the subsequent sections, there will be a particular focus on analyzing the data in order to assess the effectiveness or otherwise of the directed experiential approach (DEL). We would like to begin by drawing your attention to some of the comments provided by the participating lecturers which was obtained via electronic correspondence in response to specific queries. For example, in response to a query that probed their thoughts about the value of providing student placement-type experiences as a conduit for deepening and extending understanding about aspect(s) of education that the students were engaging with and discussing in the classroom, one of the lecturers commented that:

> The present workforce is struggling and changing from professionally and organisationally based thinking to one which is child and family centred. And hopefully moving towards community centred work, putting schools back as central to the community ... The placement could give them the opportunity to understand how the workforce is changing, and in some cases not! I think that will help their learning. (Lecturer 1)

This lecturer is drawing attention to an important facet of the directed experiential learning approach which not only potentially enriches learning but also equips learners with essential skills and knowledge for entering the workforce. The career enhancing attribute of the DEL approach is also evident in the data that is offered by the participating students which will be considered below.

The lecturers also commented on the potential of this approach to underpin the connection between theory and practice. Such a connection is vital for enriching the overall learning experience and for making it relevant. One of the lecturers explicitly states that he thinks the placement-type learning is invaluable in this regard as it allows the students 'to link theory with practice, and to see how some of the ideas and issues they discuss in the classroom are "played out" in the "real" world' (Lecturer 2). The same point is also emphasised by Lecturer 1 where he acknowledges that:

> My research demonstrates how the children's workforce (traditionally non-school based) and school based staff are learning what they do, what their targets are, how they work ... I think exposure to this will help them understand and underpin what is happening in the workforce in England today. Therefore they become better educators.

It is apparent that the real-life connections that the DEL approach offers helps to make the theory more relevant for the learners, enabling them to see how it fits into the potential life-world contexts that they will be engaging with as future practitioners. In order for this to happen, however, it is very important for the overall DEL experience to be underpinned by critical reflection. This is a theme that is emphasized by each of the participating lecturers. One of them even contended that an understanding that the student can critically reflect on the placement experience should be embedded as part of the learning process and 'this ought to be perceived not as a criticism of the setting per se but rather an analysis of the processes and systems within it' (Lecturer 2).

Findings from the students

An analysis of the data provided by the students' reflections for the academic year 2009–10, which were obtained from their in-class written responses to specified queries, of a nature similar to those presented to the contributing lecturers above, drew attention to themes that had also been emphasized by the latter.

In analyzing the data, it was noticeable that about half of the students who responded (N = 11) stated that they completed their placements in a primary school setting. This is not too surprising given that 50–60 per cent of graduates from Education Studies typically enrol in PGCE primary education courses. What is interesting, however, is the range and diversity of topics that they elected to investigate while they were out on placement. Approximately 40 per cent (N = 4) focused on educational challenges presented by English as an Additional Language (EAL), while 20 per cent focused on issues pertaining to truancy and multi-agency working respectively. In addition, other students elected to concentrate on inclusion of traveller children, as well as Special Educational Needs (SEN). The important area of relationship education was chosen by another student.

In addition to the primary level school placement contexts, children's centres accounted for a third of the total placement options taken up by the students

(N = 7). Issues surrounding diversity and inclusion, as well as multi-agency working, were identified as important focus areas for these students. Such topics were also significant for the students who opted to complete their placements at pupil referral units and extended service provision organizations such as Education Leeds.

In response to the reflection query as to whether or not the effective educational placement provided the students with opportunities to extend and develop their understanding of specific issues that emerged as being significant for them from their initial engagement with the literature, they all responded affirmatively. The majority of the students stated that the placement experience provided them with a greater insight into the realities and workings of integrated and multi-agency working.

There was evidence to suggest that the students stepped up to the plate in their willingness to engage with a critical appraisal of their respective placement experiences. For example, a student who had completed her placement at a primary school in a heavily deprived area had no qualms about displaying her surprise at the inadequate policy provision at that site to address the issue of truancy which pervaded the school (Student Reflection: SR 8). And, there was additional evidence for the degree of alignment between the comments from both the lecturers and the students on the extent to which placement-type experiences helped to narrow the traditional divide between theory and practice. On that issue, one of the students acknowledged that the experience 'helped to put theory into practice, although it was interesting to see how the theory was failing in some parts of the practice. In other parts of my placement it was working very well' (Student Reflection: SR 11). While another stated that 'it was extremely beneficial to further clarify the concept of integrated working, by witnessing it as a reality and applying the theoretical framework to a practical experience' (Student Reflection: SR 9).

The same student also recognized the valuable opportunity that the placement offered to interrogate the literature, especially the extent of its connectedness to what is actually happening on the ground. We can also see it in the following student's comment in which she states that through the placement experience 'I was able to ask a range of professional's questions surrounding my engagement with the critical review. Through this I was able to compare the answers with the literature and obtain a wider knowledge of the subject that I had questioned' (Student Reflection: SR 12).

It was also discernible from the data provided by the student reflections that the placement opportunity gave the students access to a range of opinions and perspectives on a variety of important educational issues. This is in evidence in the previous comment and can also be observed in the following comment from another student:

> Opportunities arose to speak with individual practitioners about their roles, their perspectives of the previous issues mentioned in relation to integrated teams with particular reference to practitioners who work on the ground with families: outreach workers, intensive support work, health visitors etc. (Student Reflection: SR 13)

In the words of one of the previously mentioned lecturers, opportunities such as this help the students to understand that 'being a good teacher, or a good social worker, is no longer valid in terms of how services will be delivered in future. It is working with both school based staff, the family and other services in a rounded holistic way' (Lecturer 1). And, this comment aligns with another critical dimension of the service-directed experiential learning oriented approach which is also acknowledged in the comments of the participating lecturers, namely its capacity to prepare students for their post-studies professional roles, especially in the context of multi-agency and integrated working.

The following comment from one of the students is quite typical of the manner in which they felt that the placement opportunity has prepared them for their future professional roles as educators: 'This placement has enabled me to understand that it is important for teachers to be actively part of other external agencies as well as parents to be able to provide better support for pupils' (Student Reflection: SR 15). There was also a general consensus in the students' comments that multi-agency working was the optimum strategy to put in place at the ground level. The students also reflected on the value of witnessing such practice first-hand. One student, for example, commented that 'with everyone working together schooling can be improved for everyone' (Student Reflection: SR 4).

Case study 1: toward critical engagement

Notwithstanding the positive insights that are evident from the student reflections about multi-agency (MA) and integrated working, there is evidence to suggest that they are also aware of the difficulties and challenges involved with such forms of working. In the course of her placement, one student became 'more intrigued by the roles, particularly the family outreach worker'. Whatever setbacks might occur with MA working, the positives were also noticeable (Student Reflection: SR 13). And, there was recognition that the multi-agency and integrated approach could offer more of a challenge for experienced teachers as they may be unaccustomed to such styles of working:

> The placement helped me to understand that multi-agency working was quite a new thing that was being more elaborated, some of the older teachers could not understand why it was being taught at university so heavily, however the younger teachers and professionals did understand why it was quite a popular topic (Student Reflection: SR 11)

It is interesting to note, however, that the same student was also beginning to discern the processes that could be put in place at the school level to respond to such a dilemma. This is evidenced, for example, in her statement that: 'The head teacher also believed it was important to learn about why people work together for the best interest of the child. He believed that maybe some training will be carried out within schools.'

We would like to conclude this section on the data analysis from the initial case study with an extract from an extended interview with one of the students. It is in response to a query about the degree to which the student's engagement with the combined modules that are the focus of this initial case study may have impacted on her understanding about what it means to be an educator:

> Massively ... And even if, even if I wanted to be a certain educator and have value ... be who I wanted to be, I think that I might not be able to achieve it because of everything that goes on around you within, within the system. It's definitely made me more open minded ... erm ... to the realities of practice because you read it and you think oh, they're just being cynical, you know, they're just ... they're just authors writing this, they don't know when actually they're probably basing it on their practice. And then you go out into the field and you see oh yeah, okay, oh yeah and then when you ask the people in the field, they say the same thing and you think it's, it's a big ... it's a big complex. (Student Interview)

One of the participating lecturers acknowledged that 'placements add depth of understanding of some of the complexities of being an educator (e.g., what some of the constraints are, and perhaps some of the opportunities for being creative within these constraints)'. In the above extract, it is clearly evident that the student is acutely aware of this complexity, to the extent that she is struggling to articulate a response to the question, one that is able to factor in all the complexities and nuances involved. She astutely observes that on account of all this complexity, it might not be possible to be the kind of educator you want to be 'because of everything that goes on around you within the system'. There is evidence to suggest, however, that notwithstanding the 'complex' habitus that surrounded this student, she still managed to take stock of the theory–practice divide that can exist. This is a facet of the placement experience that both the lecturers and the student reflections above also acknowledged.

Case study 1: the nature of the educational project

In the opening paragraphs of this initial case study, we mentioned that in their final year (Year 3) of the Education Studies course, the students are expected to reflect on and to synthesize their accrued learning over the three years of the course. There is strong evidence to indicate that the above student managed to achieve this desired learning outcome. She states explicitly that 'going throughout the courses in your like philosophy of education and things like that, all those little things start coming into your head and it opens up a huge ... there's so much more to it to what is an educator?' This closing comment is a very good insight into the cyclical nature of the learning process, one that summons up Greene's existentialist understanding that 'I am who I am not yet' (Pinar, 1998).

Case Study 2: The School in the Community – A Site for Collaborative Knowledge-Building

Case study 2: background

The idea of universities engaged in teacher education working within schools as sites of practice has a long history as a model of both initial teacher training and in-service professional development. Indeed, at Leeds Metropolitan University, the connectedness of school practice, students' inquiry based-learning and the facilitative role of teacher educators was emergent in the work of Winfred Mercier at the then City of Leeds Training College over 100 years ago (Beckett and Tan, 2007).

Whilst an approach to teacher education that connects theorization and practice together is thus not new, perhaps less obvious has been the recognition that such sites of practice have a referential position to the communities in which they are situated. In this sense there are, perhaps, unrecognized 'service' and 'community' elements to teacher education. If we then close-couple these aspects of practice with opportunities for critical reflection, there emerges a significant parallel between teacher education that adopts such a conceptualization and traditional notions of Service-Learning.

Within the UK context, it may also be argued that over the past ten years, further policy-related factors have drawn closer together education, child welfare and health agendas (Moss and Petrie, 2002; Anning, 2005). Similarly, directives from the former Labour central government, such as the Children's Plan (DfES, 2007), emphasized the importance of schools working with parents and the need for a more outward-facing approach by school practitioners that extended the role of educators to be at the centre of the provision that addressed children's welfare and rights. As a consequence, the relationship between teachers and the communities that their schools serve has become more visible. For teachers working with communities that experience social and economic disadvantage, the coincidence of these socio-economic and cultural factors with learning is played out in their practice on a daily basis. Thus, their practice and their 'service' within the community become inseparable.

In the second case study, we explore the experiences of university academics partnering school practitioners, operating to deepen considerations of education and practice in the interests of building collective knowledge in the service of the school's community. In its use of critical reflection and dialogic pedagogies for practitioner learning within this socio-educational context, it illustrates (and perhaps extends) our thinking about Service-Learning. At the same time, its emphasis on the purposeful interrogation of experiences as productive learning pedagogies resonates with the core principles of directed experiential learning as explored in case study 1.

The case study that follows draws from a number of related school-based partnerships that focus on practitioner learning within challenging school contexts. In the interests of confidentiality, the identities of these schools will not be revealed but it is useful to understand in brief the social and educational contexts in which they are situated. All of the partnership work took place in urban school settings in the north of England. These schools served communities where high levels of unemployment, long-term unemployment and general economic deprivation were common. At the same time, the communities from where they drew their pupils were significantly culturally diverse, with many children having English as an additional language. Furthermore, some schools exhibited higher than average intake from displaced families or of pupils deemed unaccompanied refugees. School inspection reports made reference to such formal indicators of poverty and low socio-economic status (e.g., the incidence of free school meals). Characteristically of those schools involved, one primary/ elementary school was summarized in a recent government inspectors' report as having:

> ... about a fifth of pupils ... from White British backgrounds. Other pupils come from a wide range of ethnic backgrounds with Black African and any other Asian backgrounds being the next largest groups. Nearly two thirds of pupils speak English as an additional language and this is high; a significant number of new arrivals are at an early stage of speaking English. The proportion of pupils with special educational needs and/or disabilities is above average. The nature of these difficulties lies mainly in the areas of emotional, and speech, language and communication difficulties. The proportion of pupils eligible for free school meals is much higher than is normally found. The proportion of pupils who leave and join the school at different times is high. (Ofsted, School Inspection Report, Primary School, 2010)

The above extract came from one of the area's primary schools, serving children aged 5–11. For those involved in secondary, high school education, the social and demographic make-up exhibited a similar pattern. Again, an example drawn from a local high school's Ofsted report typifies the sort of factors that impact upon educational provision in this area:

> Most students come from ... where there is very high social and economic disadvantage. Almost half of all students are eligible for free school meals, which is more than three times the national average. A significant number of students join the school mid-year: many are either new to this country or have been excluded from their previous school. Around two thirds of students are from minority ethnic backgrounds and over 40 languages are spoken in the school. The number of students for whom English is not their first language is very high and rising. Attainment on entry in Year 7 is low and a very high proportion of students have learning difficulties and/or disabilities. (Ofsted, School Inspection Report, High School, 2009)

In the following discussion of the critical, reflective and inquiry-based approaches used to support the schools, we have taken care not to identify any one school, nor draw comparisons between them. Arguably, whilst there are similar social and demographic contexts present in the sample, at the same time there are many other complexities (e.g., of staffing, leadership, institutional and community history, local and national political decision-making) that make each school have a unique story. Our role as academics working with such schools was to support and enrich practitioners' conceptualization of the community which they served and of their contributions as professionals working in the field. Through the use of exemplars from reflective journals, school newsletters and participant responses, we will now explore the key issues for consideration in utilizing Service-Learning pedagogies in partnership work between academic and school-based practice.

Case study 2: preparing the ground – stereotypes, hierarchies and uncertainty

Perhaps most challenging in our endeavours to work as academics within schools was the need to be in a position to ask critical questions of pedagogy and conceptions of learners and communities. We were mindful of the perceived separation of academic and school practitioner domains and, indeed, its representation in the research community as *academic* and *practitioner* research having different status. Scholarly work on school improvement and inquiry-based approaches also suggested how the field was challenging inasmuch that getting teachers to focus critically on their professional practice, represents high stakes within a performative environment (Goodson, 1992; Zeichner, 1993, 2008; Ball, 2003). For academics, in 'ivory towers', perhaps we also needed to recognize our 'outside view'.

From the start of our professional learning work with partner schools, we were careful to recognize these challenges. Like Mockler and Sachs (2006), at the core of the collaboration has been a focusing on practitioner concerns, on the day-to-day manifestations of 'real work'. Recognizing the autobiographical in the ways in which practitioners represent their work and make sense of their role has been important in the journey towards finding places to interrupt any dominant external discourse on professionalism. Important, too, has been our own willingness to turn the lens on our own practice and challenges, and to equally confront stereotypical 'identities' of 'ivory tower' academics. The following extract from our school-university newsletter is indicative of this reciprocity:

Pedagogies on Display:
The skit was a dinner table conversation about the school-university partnership, intended to share our thoughts about coming together with new teacher partners

to work on school improvement. We likened the experience to a blind date with all the attendant anxieties like nerves, not knowing what the other party would be like, and whether we would like each other. We continued the commentary on our week's work at the office, to show that the concerns of academics in their place of work are not unlike teachers' and para-professionals' concerns, given Ofsted inspections, pressures and demands on time, students, conferences and meetings, teaching preparation, national curriculum, pedagogies, and assessment, as well as the stress and tiredness involved. We also wanted to share our thoughts about [school name], as far as we know, and compare and contrast our respective concerns with students (both in primary school and in higher education). We concluded with recognition, in unison, of the tough work teachers do at [school name]. (school-university newsletter, 2007)

The notion of finding 'border crossings' and 'trading points' has been taken forward by a number of authors as a way of representing, in the field of teacher professional learning, points for the intersection between academics and practitioners, between research, theory and practice (Zeichner, 1993, 2008; Goodson, 1992). Perhaps implicit in some of these discussions (in particular, Zeichner's work) has been the sense that engaging in critical considerations of practice should constitute a two-way street. By that we mean that for university academics working in teacher education, the reflective gaze we ask teachers to cast upon practice should also be applied to our own university classrooms. Equally so, in asking teachers to unravel the awkward questions (e.g., of persistent underachievement of working-class students, and middle-class advantage) as part of a more socially and politically transparent project, we have to set out our own pedagogical and political store. In the process of working with one school, where our discussions with teachers had a strong sense of their own social locations and heritage, one of us began to reflect upon his own use of his social educational autobiography in his work with first year undergraduates:

This week I have started a new year group in Social Perspectives. I used my own educational autobiography ... as a way of illustrating how different social factors can impact upon educational experiences. One of my colleagues said 'you're brave', when I told them that I had turned the sociological lens on my own life – photos of me as a babe in arms at the door of our extended family home (council estate in Wolverhampton); problematising indicators of social class; talking about activism through my great-grandfather's involvement in the Independent Labour movement in the 20's and how it politically oriented my studies and later education; my mixed Chinese-English-Welsh heritage and why bullying turned me off school in my teens. Difficult, often awkward stuff, but it generated many discussions with students about expectations, privilege, disadvantage and agency ... it was like opening a different door through which to view what happens in schools and its consequences ... now to get them reading! (Extract from personal research diary, 2007)

In this sense, personal practice was attempting to find border crossings between students' experiences of compulsory education and ways to theorize educational progressions using sociological concepts of social class, race and gender. At the same time, in the work in other modules the author was leading he was getting the students to interrogate the National Literacy Strategy using research from academic researchers such as Kathy Hall and Greg Brooks. Here, the act of bringing critical lenses to bear on government strategy within a teacher education class seemed one of legitimizing the process of re-visioning the taken-for-granted. This feeling of gaining legitimacy for certain areas for debate was mirrored in the professional learning work we were doing in schools. As one teacher reflected:

Well, just giving the teachers that permission to find out about something for themselves. Something that they were personally interested in. Giving them the professional confidence that they knew that they were doing but they wanted to find out something more; it really did improve their confidence and they came back from that first session two feet taller. (Teacher interview response)

Part of preparing the ground, then, was to try to equalize the perceived hierarchies between those of us involved in university academic work and teacher education, and those whose connectedness to school practice and work with children was more immediate. Such efforts attempted to provide a more democratic environment for critical, reflective work around our 'service', conceptualizing the purpose of our collective practice (either in teacher education or in children and young people's education) as being mutual. This approach and, in particular, the shared critical reflections from both sides was sometimes unsettling and drew forth uncertainties about our professional work and conceptualization of learners. As some of our newsletter extracts illustrate, these were also opportunities to ask difficult questions of our field and our professional role:

The [stories] raised a number of concerns, such as what such incidents mean for the rest of the class, the demarcation of responsibility for one child, and external expectations for achievement and better exam results ... Staff are also concerned about the distribution of educational and social advantage by post-code, and the capacity of educational policy to address social issues, like family dysfunction, mental health, etc, which simultaneously requires appropriate social policy. (school-university newsletter, 2008)

Case study 2: critical reflection, connectedness and the community school

At the heart of our work with the schools was a commitment to generate a collective knowledge through the partnership. In this sense, the approach adopted a pedagogical approach to professional learning that was synchronous with key elements of Service-Learning. Perhaps most evident were the emphasis on real-world experiences and concerns, particularly those that considered social inequalities, as a focus for the learning, and the placing of critical reflection at the core of our approach.

As we have documented so far, the idea of setting in motion critical conversations about teachers' work was uppermost in the thinking behind such partnerships with schools. The role of the university academics in this was necessarily dialogic in that it sought to level down any sense of hierarchies related to the production of knowledge and the theorization of professional practice. As Loughran (2006) has documented, such approaches can be a powerful means to illuminate pedagogies that would otherwise remain hidden, or taken for granted. Foregrounding such criticality in the examination of beliefs and presupposition, as writers such as Zeichner and Tabachnick (1981) and Villegas (2007) say, is crucial. As Villegas (2007) summarizes: 'Unexamined beliefs, especially those that are contradicted by new ideas about teaching introduced in teacher education courses, tend to remain latent throughout a candidate's formal preparation, only to resurface once they are placed in a classroom to teach' (pp. 373–4).

With a concurrent focus on social inequalities, we would then argue that such critical reflection operates to enable practitioners to interrogate their 'service' in relation to the learners and the communities in which they are situated. This is, however, difficult business, that often involves visiting previously unexamined conceptualizations of their learners, abilities and futures. Perhaps most important was the reconsideration of children's engagement, not to be about some individual response, but about the ways in which the teachers' role needed to operate to decipher standardized national curriculum and to connect it to children's real world. As one school principal reported:

Well my project was really a project that was ... looking at a strand across our whole community. I was looking at the underachievement of poor white boys within the city schools. The impact of the research I've done to-date has already changed the way we're doing things in school. We now introduced this 'Working on Wednesdays'; well, 'World of Work' on Wednesdays and it's trying to make a connectedness between what we do in school to what the world of work is about because one of the things I noticed about some of my disaffected boys is that they see no connection between what they do in here now and what they will do in the future. So, although I've got a list of speakers coming in and different firms and local business coming in, I've also actually been able to get, so far, two working parents, they've booked slots to come in and talk about what they do for a job. I think that for our school particularly, just the fact that two parents feel that they can come and contribute personally ... (Primary School Principal, interview, 2008)

Others talked about how pedagogically they were changing their practices and interpretation of the curriculum, based upon a reconsideration of their community of learners.

... one of our big issues in the school was the children not engaging with the science curriculum with very poor results ... continuously over a period of time. We couldn't get to grips as to why that was because we were covering the curriculum, the children were getting enough time, but they weren't getting the science. She had come from a school that had done a lot of work in developing the science curriculum, what she wanted to do was pilot delivering science within a context to her class to see if it had an impact on their learning so it was very much looking at the actual curriculum she was delivering, how to deliver it so it made sense to the children in a contextual way. (Teacher, interview, 2008)

Interesting here, then, is the idea that the curriculum, although externally prescribed, may be one that practitioners have to interpret, make sense of with an appreciation of the shifting constituency of learners and their communities. Furthermore, there was also a sense that practitioners as part of a learning community stood at the crossing-point, not just between the curriculum and their learners, but also between pre-existing negative experiences of schooling of 'their' communities (i.e. parents) and the possibilities of more positive future orientations.

Since we settled to this different way of working in our school we've had different responses from our parents. We now have more parents working in our classrooms as volunteers than we've ever had before; who themselves are becoming interested in 'Why is this happening? Why isn't this happening?' ... I think that we recognise in our schools that to truly improve outcomes for children it's about having an impact on the community as a whole and if that means putting the school at the centre of being the professional learning environment, so, in our professional learning environment we run a lot of courses for parents and they see themselves as learners now whereas they didn't see themselves as learners before. Many of them had had not very good experiences at school and felt quite degraded by school really. (Primary School Principal, interview, 2008)

Dialogic approaches to professional learning thus created spaces for practitioners to revisit and reconceptualize their work as practitioners and their connectedness with the community that they served. This involved examining pedagogy, curriculum and their professional stance. In doing so, arguably it drew closer their relationship with learners, parents and other professionals and made this a collective endeavour for the improvement of children's experiences.

Conclusion

This chapter has argued for the articulation of Service-Learning oriented approaches, as expressed in our conceptualization of 'directed experiential learning', that are located within and close to practice rather than supplementary to it. The two case studies illustrate the significance of critical dialogic approaches in the support and development of professional educators across the life-course of their careers. Conceptualizing sites of education in challenging social contexts as places where practice and service intersect, opens up a discussion of the ways in which an awareness of equity and social justice can be anchored within the context in which it is applied. At the core of these studies is a sense of two-way learning and collaborative knowledge-building for students, practitioners and academic partners alike. Most importantly, this chapter has provided examples of the close coupling of practice and the theorization of practice that fosters participants' capacity for critical thinking.

References

Anning, A. (2005), *New Forms of Professional Knowledge in Multi-Agency Delivery of Services for Children. End of Award Report*. Swindon: Economic & Social Research Council.

Ball, S. (2003), 'The teachers' soul and the terrors of performativity'. *Journal of Education Policy*, 18, 2: 215–28.

Beckett, L. and Tan, J. E. C. (2007), 'Teaching methods, pedagogies and professional learning', in L. Beckett (ed.) (2007), *City of Leeds Training College: Continuity & Change, 1907–2007*. Leeds: Leeds Metropolitan University.

Chapman, R. N. (2008), 'The reflective mentor model: growing communities of practice for teacher development in informal learning environments', in C. Kimble, P. Hildreth and I. Bourdon (eds), *Communities of Practice: Creating Learning Environments for Educators*. Charlotte, NC: Information Age Publishing, pp. 39–64.

Dewey, J. (1938, 1963), *Experience and Education*. London: Collier MacMillan Publishers.

DfES, (2004), *Every Child Matters: Change for Children*. London: DfES.

—(2007), *The Children's Plan – Building Brighter Futures*. London: TSO.

Freire, P. (1970, 1996), *Pedagogy of the Oppressed*. New York: Continuum.

Goodson, I. F. (1992), 'Sponsoring the teacher's voice: teachers' lives and teacher development', in A. Hargreaves, and M. G. Fullan (eds), *Understanding Teacher Development*. London: Cassell, pp. 110–21.

Hodkinson, P. (2004), 'Research as a form of work: expertise, community and methodological objectivity'. *British Educational Research Journal*, 30 (1): 9–26.

Lave, J. and Wenger, E. (1991), *Situated Learning: Legitimate Peripheral Participation*. Cambridge: Cambridge University Press.

Loughran, J. (2006), *Developing a Pedagogy of Teacher Education. Understanding Teaching & Learning about Teaching*. London: Routledge.

Mockler, N. and Sachs, J. (2006), *More than identity: Tools for the teaching profession in troubled times*. Paper presented at Australian Association of Educational Research.

Moss, P. and Petrie, P. (2002), *From Children's Services to Children's Spaces: Public Policy, Children and Childhood*. London: Routledge Falmer.

Ofsted (2009), School Inspection Report, High School.

—(2010), School Inspection Report, Primary School.

Pinar, W. (1998), *The Passionate Mind of Maxine Greene 'I am...not yet'*. London: Falmer Press.

Villegas, A.-M. (2007), 'Dispositions in teacher education: a look at social justice'. *Journal of Teacher Education*, 58, 5: 370–80.

Wenger, E. (1998), *Communities of Practice: Learning, Meaning and Identity*. Cambridge: Cambridge University Press.

Zeichner, K. (1993), *Educating Teachers for Cultural Diversity*. East Lansing, MI: National Center for Research on Teacher Learning Special Report.

—(2008), *Keynote address to the British Educational Research Association annual conference*. Edinburgh, September 2008.

Zeichner, K. and Tabachnick, B. R. (1981), 'Are the effects of university teacher education "washed out" by school experience?' *Journal of Teacher Education*, 32 (3): 7–11.

7

Wider Perspectives in Education: A Case Study of Transformative Global Learning from the UK

Phil Bamber

The Wider Perspectives in Education module is a compulsory 30-credit module that was recently embedded in the Primary Bachelor of Arts Qualified Teacher Status (BAQTS) four-year degree at Liverpool Hope University. As part of their third year of study, rather than complete a seven-week placement in schools, students now complete a five-week school placement and ten days of community engagement. The period of community engagement runs alongside the 'Wider Perspectives in Education' module (WPE). The overall aim of the module is to provide students with a broader experience of education beyond traditional school-based learning, develop their understanding of education for global citizenship with respect to their role as teachers, and promote a sense of themselves as active global citizens (OXFAM, 2006). The module aims to achieve this by transforming student perspectives on the role of education and their own philosophy of teaching. Drawing on transformative learning theory (Mezirow, 1991, 2000, 2009), this module challenges students in initial teacher education to rethink their underlying assumptions and begin to think and act against social injustice. The module is grounded in the rationale that a genuine worldwide horizon does not necessarily demand international experiences and must be grounded in a concern for the local as much as the global (Bamber and Hankin, 2011). 'Wider Perspectives in Education' fuses problem-based learning and reflective practice with a period of community engagement to broaden and deepen the impact of the BAQTS course. This chapter presents evidence of the ways in which these aims are being achieved. Following a brief contextual description and exploration of the rationale for this curriculum development, data will be presented that illustrates the ways in which learning in this context has transformative and global dimensions. This includes three case studies, selected to highlight the diversity of community engagement experiences that can lead to these outcomes and impact upon the professional identity of our future educators.

Context and Rationale

Liverpool Hope University (LHU) has a rich tradition of local and global community engagement initiatives (Bamber et al., 2008) that have provided a form of education for global citizenship although until recently these have not been accredited or linked into the formal curriculum. For example, the Faculty of Education has for a number of years facilitated international experiences for some students in teacher education as an additional course component. The evolution of the Primary BAQTS course from three to four years was driven in part by a desire to provide a space to incorporate these activities within the curriculum and draw on the learning and experience of members of the faculty with considerable expertise in this field. This programme deeply reflects the guiding vision and orientation of the faculty: to develop educational thought and practices which promote education as a humanizing influence on each person and on society locally, nationally and internationally. It also accords well with the university's mission to educate the whole person in mind, body and spirit as well as its strategic goal of increasing opportunities for all students to have an international experience during their time at Hope.

Although a crowded curriculum and pressures to increase standards of numeracy and literacy have taken centre stage in recent years, a Development Education Association (DEA) survey (DEA, 2009) provides further evidence that students in teacher education are receptive to course content that incorporates education for global citizenship. For example, 'thinking about the potential contribution of teaching to making the world a better place' is a significant factor in retaining teachers, particularly among recently qualified teachers: 85 per cent of young less-established teachers identified this as a reason for remaining in teaching. This provides further rationale for the initiative described here.

Community engagement outside of school-based learning affords numerous opportunities for students in teacher education (Tellez, 2000) and is more widely practised in the USA. Barr (2005) highlights the power of personal experience to encourage and educate advocates of global education. In this case it is envisaged that student placements and development of a select number of meaningful partnerships will also enhance staff engagement through collaborative research activity. Barr suggests structured opportunities such as international exchanges and linking programme (Barr, 2005, p. 12) are particularly successful in changing attitudes among teacher educators and their students. This module team contest the commonly held view that immersion in local settings cannot provoke similar outcomes. As such, the WPE module can be seen to promote 'global learning', education that puts learning in a global context, fostering:

- critical and creative thinking;
- self-awareness and open-mindedness towards difference;
- understanding of global issues and power relationships;
- optimism and action for a better world (DEA, 2009).

The Wider Perspectives Module

This module for students in Year 3 of a four-year undergraduate course to qualify as a primary teacher in the UK explores citizenship in practice. Students reflect upon their own values and beliefs, assess the aims and purposes of education, and develop a philosophy of teaching statement. The module introduces students to various dimensions of education for global citizenship such as Service-Learning, development of partnerships both locally and internationally, comparative education and education for sustainable development. Underpinning pedagogical approaches such as experiential learning and participatory methodologies are analyzed. The introductory theoretical component leads into a period of project planning. In this second phase of the module, students identify an educational issue they would like to explore in a school or another learning context and then spend a minimum of ten days in community engagement in this local or global setting chosen from:

- international teaching placement (Hope College, Michigan, USA; St Xavier's College, Mumbai, India; Angier, France; Forest Schools, Norway);
- community engagement locally or globally (beyond the classroom);
- Service-Learning in schools (supporting schools to promote community cohesion, sustainable schools; curriculum enrichment and whole-school approaches to the global dimension).

In recognizing and supporting the diversity of learning needs, students are also encouraged to organize their own project and pursue issues with which they are concerned. Examples of local projects include researching a police programme to promote community cohesion and monitoring the support offered by housing association trusts to adults with learning difficulties. One group of students worked closely with SOS Children, the international charity and long-standing partner of Liverpool Hope University, to produce educational materials that challenge approaches to educating about the developing world that reinforce patronizing and charitable perspectives. These materials are now available on the SOS Children UK website and are being used by SOS volunteers in schools across the country.

Students have the opportunity to complete either a semester abroad or a short placement at one of Liverpool Hope's partner institutes listed above. Placements in diverse educational settings challenge student assumptions underpinning their own philosophy of education. Students also reconsider educational issues beyond the school campus such as child poverty, sustainability, diversity, disability, racism and terrorism. For this experience to be mutually transformative, it is important that students work in conjunction with the providers in the setting to develop a project which meets the educational needs of children in the setting or members of the local community. This also enables community engagement to be a critical learning experience as advocated by Rosenberger. He argued that students need the opportunity to choose needs or issues in the community that connect to the module content. This can facilitate dialogue (with stakeholders in framing and defining the problem) and action (to engage in problem posing education around the social, political and economic issues that arise in the community experience). (Rosenberger, 2000, p. 40).

Students are expected to be self-starting and independent but are supported through tutorial support by university staff during this time. This reflects the pedagogical approach to education for global citizenship advocated by Ian Barr (2005, p. 57) that enables students to experience the five learning modalities.

- Independent learning: promoting responsibility for learning.
- Learning as dialogue: encouraging cooperative learning.
- Learning as partnership: working across institutional and community divides.
- Learning as public good: developing commitment to social ends.
- Learning as lifelong: establishing dispositions and habits of mind.

At the end of the project, students share their eclectic experiences through a presentation in groups at a conference to celebrate their community engagement work. The module is structured to provide opportunities for students to act upon these new understandings as they embark on a five-week school placement at the end of the year. In this school-based learning, students are expected to demonstrate how education for global citizenship with a local and global perspective can be incorporated within their own teaching practice.

Data will now be presented that illustrates the ways in which structured experience of community engagement provokes both global and transformative learning. This draws on data collected after the module had run for one year: semi-structured interviews with a purposeful sample (Patton, 2002, p. 46) of students following their community engagement experience; and an end of module evaluation that included self-report items on global learning from a recent national survey of educators in the UK (DEA, 2009). Data is also presented from community partners to triangulate these findings. This final data set was unprompted and received via email communication with local, national and international placement mentors.

Transformative Learning

There are numerous examples of feedback from community partners both in the UK and overseas that comment on the impact of this module on student performance. An email from a professor of Elementary Education at Hope College, Michigan, confirms that a short placement in the USA had been a transformative experience for these students as described by Mezirow (1991):

> I viewed this group as being very reflective/thoughtful about their experiences in our discussions of what they were seeing and learning. This group of students struck me as more willing/able to engage with their thinking around their experiences. This continued as the visit went on. In particular, I was often asked questions that were beyond the superficial and went deeper into the why of things. (And they asked lots of questions ... which was great!). This seemed to result in a number of conversations that went well past 'we do it this way and you do it that way' ... and one of us is right and the other wrong. Rather, they were willing to suspend judgement and look at the issue we were discussing from a variety of viewpoints – setting aside preconceived notions based only on their familiarity with things. They had opinions, but they were willing and able to engage with me and their peers on the underlying principles, etc. – and to challenge their thinking. I wonder a bit if one of the reasons for some of this may be the projects that were due upon their return home ...

The concluding comments here validate the structure of the module, which requires students to put into practice their learning in their final school-based learning (SBL) and present a poster to peers. The students experience transformative learning as they critically reflect on presuppositions that have 'come to constrain the way they perceive, understand and feel about our world' (Mezirow, 1991, p. 14), leading them to reformulate these assumptions to 'permit a more inclusive, discriminating, permeable and integrative perspective' (Mezirow, 2009, p. 22). Alternative viewpoints provoke students to surface and examine their deeply held assumptions, values and beliefs about the role of education.

The students reflect upon how their philosophy of teaching statement has evolved as part of the module assessment. Their evaluations suggest that they felt that completing a teaching philosophy statement with peer support alongside a community engagement placement was particularly effective:

> I was a little daunted by writing a philosophy of teaching statement but it was really good to reflect on what sort of teacher you think you are and aim to be – it was good to read other students as well, to hear different views. The reflective work alongside the placement helped with this and has encouraged me to think deeper about not just what and how I teach but why we teach.

This demonstrates reflection upon underlying premises, a characteristic of transformative learning. This also provides evidence of mastery of a 'threshold concept' in education (Cousin, 2006). A number of students articulated how they had been challenged to look at the world in different ways:

> Through creating and taking part in this project, I have learnt a great deal. Perhaps most importantly, that we all look at the world primarily through our own eyes which means that our perspectives, values and thoughts will vary from those around us. Sometimes we need to look beyond what we know and see things through the eyes of others in order to fully understand and relate to them. I have realized we can learn about how other people perceive the world and how they live by empathizing with them.

Students found completing a reflective journal 'liberating'. One commented:

> I have since come to realize I must critically reflect on my school based experiences in order to adopt a teaching approach that diverges significantly from my existing teaching practice. I feel I am not being true to myself or my teaching philosophy if I continue to teach the way I have observed others teach, or indeed as I have found myself teaching.

Student feedback confirmed the module team had successfully promoted global learning with local and global dimensions (DEA, 2009) that moves beyond traditional understandings of global education: 'My philosophy of teaching statement has changed since beginning my project because now I see global education not as a subject on its own but a complete way of thinking, behaving and modelling.'

Global Learning

A survey at the end of the module completed by 149 students showed that the module was successful in meeting its aims of promoting global learning and the role of educators in challenging social injustice. At the start of the module, 82.8 per cent of students reported they had little or no understanding of global learning in the curriculum. By the end of the module, 81.8 per cent reported having above average understanding of global learning. At the start of the module, 78.8 per cent reported having little of no understanding of what they can do to make a difference in the world. By the end of the module, 84.9 per cent reported having a very good or excellent understanding of the role they can play.

The mid-module evaluation revealed that the taught module was successful in encouraging students to begin to think and act against social injustice:

> This module has exceeded my expectations. I find all the tutors highly enthusiastic about what they teach and very approachable. I feel inspired to go out and make a change in my own way. The community engagement project is a very exciting prospect.

Students clearly valued the opportunity to pursue their own individual project:

> I have enjoyed the focus on global aspects of learning and sustainable development in a placement we choose. This has allowed my own interests to grow and be incorporated in my current educational development.

The end of year evaluation revealed that students were themselves able to make connections between the WPE module and their professional practice:

> I like the context of the course. It is so relevant to our teaching methods and the current global issues occurring at the start of the 21st century. It feels like what we are learning has a purpose and will play an important role in my teaching.

It is also interesting as an individual as well as a teacher. I feel inspired by the course and excited to see what I have learnt.

The evidence presented above indicates that the Wider Perspective module has enhanced student learning and for some this has been a transformative experience. The students have also supported a number of partners across the UK. For example, the SOS Children UK schools coordinator commented that the resources produced by Hope students 'will be of great benefit to our development education programme. The lesson plans are innovative, creative and have clear messages. We are very appreciative of their work.'

Three case studies will now be presented to illuminate aspects of transformative global learning experienced by our future educators as part of this module. The first student developed understanding of diversity and community integration through attending international evenings in a local church. The second completed a project that raised awareness of Fairtrade in a local primary school and articulates the importance of 'connecting' with those locally and globally with whom we are interdependent. Finally, a student who taught in an SOS Children's Village, Lilongwe, Malawi, describes how his assumptions about the nature and role of education were overturned.

Case Study 1: Understanding Diversity through Attending Church International Evenings

My community engagement involved supporting my local church international evenings. The organizer had previously taught English at the church and has mainly taught wives of men who have brought their family over for a job or have sought asylum in the UK. She now has a network of women and lets them know when the monthly events are on. She also visits the families and I go along with her sometimes. The attendees' nationalities range from countries in Africa to the Middle East and China. Most of the attendees of the international evenings are women aged 20–40 with their children, with numbers ranging from 40 to 70 in the church hall.

For the dinners, often women from a certain country will come early and cook their own food (recently all of the women from Yemen cooked food in their local style), then it is served to everyone else who attends and we provide games and activities for their children. The women mostly chat to each other through the evening though a few church members also come to get to know the women.

The local context is that the women who attend usually struggle to get to know anyone in their community beside people from their own culture who speak their native tongue. Most of the women wear hijabs or burkhas and feel isolated from the Western culture they live in and also often don't wish to integrate through a perceived clash of values. There are few opportunities to meet local people, and barriers of language/confidence often prevent this. A lack of understanding cultures (from both sides, from the local population and also from the families who have emigrated or claimed asylum) leads to more fear or isolation.

I have been informed about how difficult it is to become part of a local community when coming from a different culture. I have been able to see living in Liverpool from a completely different perspective, one that I could possibly never experience or know myself but am now able to understand a bit more. I have fewer prejudices or uninformed judgements regarding people emigrating to the UK with little knowledge of my culture or willingness to adapt to my culture, which can be threatening or upsetting to me. I have been able to find a commonality and a way to relate through food, socializing and sharing in community. I now have access to women who, on the surface, seem very different to me. I had found this frustrating in the past because I enjoy learning about other cultures and I dislike seeing people who are isolated or rejected from society. This has given me an opportunity to relate and spend time with women like this and have seen a side of the global issue of fundamentalist Islam and the isolation and clash of values which often fuel the issues. I believe that this lack of community integration is one of the factors contributing to the issues seen in the London train and bus bombing and I have been able to see one of the small steps to finding a solution. The experience has helped me to re-evaluate the role that education must play in responding to our diverse and complex world.

Case Study 2: Connecting with Others through Fairtrade

My wider perspectives placement was at a local primary school in Liverpool and the aim was to introduce Fairtrade to the children in a child friendly manner and to make the issue relevant to seven to eight year olds in a school that is culturally homogenous. We wanted to show that there are things that both student teachers and pupils can do to make the world a fairer place. The project was run concurrently by one of my peers in a school for children with special educational needs. We wanted to help children to use their newly developed understanding to contrast localities both locally and globally.

Everything covered within the project led up to a meeting between the two schools to celebrate our understanding of the issues involved. This was an event which exceeded our expectations and brought everything we had explored together wonderfully. The children were fascinated with each other and enjoyed being together – one child even picked up a Fairtrade banana and asked another if they knew the journey that it had been on, obviously feeling proud of their new knowledge. The day was particularly successful in challenging the children in mainstream education to understand that those with learning difficulties are capable of learning and achieving although they may do so in a different way.

Through creating and taking part in this project I have learnt a great deal: perhaps, most importantly, that we all look at the world primarily through our own eyes which means that our perspectives, values and thoughts will often vary from those of the people around us. We are all individuals and this should be celebrated, but sometimes we need to look beyond what we know and see things through the eyes of others in order to fully understand and to relate to them. We can learn about how other people perceive the world and how they live by empathizing with them. As children develop their ability to empathize with others, they become more able to understand the emotions behind certain behaviours and attitudes and form stronger connections with others. As citizens of many communities, including both the local and the global community, we should develop our ability to empathize and utilize this in order to connect with people, places and situations – and then we can begin to make a positive contribution.

Case Study 3: Transforming Perspectives through Volunteering Overseas

John undertook three weeks' teaching in the primary and secondary schools attached to the SOS Children's Village in Lilongwe, Malawi's capital city. The SOS village is home to around 150 orphaned and abandoned children, and over 1,000 children come from across the city to learn in the school. The village is also home to Lilongwe Medical Centre, which includes a clinic, children's rehabilitation programme and counselling service. It was John's first time to travel outside of the UK.

His contribution within the school transformed aspects of his professional knowledge, skills, values and beliefs. For example, his assumptions about teaching, learning and the purpose of education were challenged:

> For the first time I actually questioned what education was for. How would completing their Grade 12 exams help these young people function in society? I can honestly say I'd never thought about that before. It has fundamentally shaped my approach in school and in the classroom.

During this brief immersion overseas he questioned his Western-centric outlook with its emphasis on consumerism, materialism and individualism: 'There's more of a community feel, well, in all the villages, that we've been to, than there is here ... people are more tolerant! They take time with each other.' Relationships with individual teachers or community members challenged his thinking. He comments in his diary: 'These were people I am spending time with, getting to know. It is invaluable to begin to understand things from this very different perspective.' John began to see the teachers he was working with as fellow learners as opposed to recipients of aid. He became aware of the reciprocal nature of interactions:

> We soon realised that the approach 'this is how you should do it' was totally inappropriate. When we were marking the books we sat in the staff room with the class teachers and had a look at the work and discussed it, we tried to involve them as much as we could and we all learnt a great deal.

John described his experience as 'liberating' and a 'journey of self discovery' but also recognized that this process of reflection had exposed him:

> In that environment I was no longer defined by all the things and people that define me at home. I initially felt like I was stripped of the things that make me who I am. It was extremely formative.

John was acutely aware of the difficulties in assimilating this transformed outlook when he returned to the UK:

> There are things when you come back you can't change ... it's such a rush-rush lifestyle over here, it's all about work, work, work ... better yourself ... how good can you get your life. My family commented themselves that I was far more tolerant on my return to the UK.

John, however, began to recognize his extended citizenship role at both local and global levels. This challenged him to reconsider the role of education in combating inequality:

> I think it's so important to educate people, smashing the silly stereotypes that they have built up, some of the stereotypes that I had. As a teacher in school I am in quite a privileged position to do exactly that. We need to educate ourselves, and we need to think, think for a change.

Conclusion

Liverpool Hope University (LHU) has a rich tradition of local and global community engagement initiatives (Bamber et al., 2008) that continue to provide a form of education for global citizenship. The recent introduction of the extra-curricular Service and Leadership Award (SALA) at this institution emphasizes local action and provides accreditation for extra-curricular activity. Recent research (Bamber et al. 2012) suggests that students who register on the SALA have characteristics, personal predispositions and attitudes that differ from those who choose not to register. Recognition of the need to embed service within the curriculum is made explicit in the LHU's most recent Learning, Teaching and Assessment Strategy, which includes the goal of enabling students to become confident learners by 'providing opportunities for a rounded education that shapes life and vision, such as intercultural learning, experience of other cultures and contexts, engagement in service and voluntary work' (Norton, 2009, p. 5).

The development of a teaching philosophy statement alongside a community engagement project followed by a period of school-based learning (also known as teaching practice), as exemplified here, is a potent combination that provokes deep learning. As a pedagogical approach it is not unproblematic. Despite completing a teaching philosophy statement, students do not always make links between their community engagement and their emergent professional identity. Students need further support to incorporate their learning within their ongoing teaching practice. Practically, facilitating community engagement demands institutional support. In this case, the development of both local and international partnerships has been justified through articulating the ways in which this approach lives out the mission of the university and vision of the Faculty of Education. Finally, educators should be cognisant that this approach may reinforce rather than overturn incomplete world-views and existing stereo-types, for example as regards poverty and diversity. Nevertheless, data has been presented here that challenges the perception that it is only through interna-tional community engagement that students can challenge their presuppositions and become ambassadors for global education. The 'Wider Perspectives in Education' module provides a successful model that embeds Service-Learning and global learning within the curriculum and has the potential to transform the personal and professional world-views of our future educators.

References

Bamber, P., Bourke, L. and Clarkson, J. (eds) (2008), *In safe hands; guiding principles for International Service-Learning.* Stoke on Trent: Trentham.

Bamber, P., Bourke, L. and Lyons, M. (2012), 'Global Citizens: Who are they?' *Education, Citizenship and Social Justice.* (forthcoming)

Bamber, P. and Hankin, L. (2011), 'Transformative learning through service-learning: no passport required'. *Education and Training*, Vol. 53, Issue 2/3: 190–206.

Barr, I. (2005), *In the Situation of Others. The Final Evaluation Report on the Department for International Development's Initiative on Embedding the Global Dimension in Initial Teacher Education 2001–2005.* Unpublished report.

Cousin, G. (2006) 'Threshold concepts, troublesome knowledge and emotional capital: an exploration into learning about others', in J. H. F. Meyer and R. Land (eds), *Overcoming Barriers to Student Understanding: Threshold Concepts and Troublesome Knowledge.* London and New York: Routledge.

DEA / IpsosMORI (2009), *Teachers Attitudes Towards Global Learning.* London: DEA.

Mezirow, J. (1991), *Transformative Dimensions of Adult Learning.* San Francisco: Jossey-Bass.

—(2000), *Learning as Transformation.* San Francisco: Jossey-Bass.

—(2009), 'Transformative learning theory', in J. Mezirow, E. Taylor and Associates, *Transformative Learning in Practice.* San Francisco: Jossey-Bass, pp. 18–32.

Norton, L. (2009), *The Learning, Teaching and Assessment Strategy for Taught Undergraduate Degree 2009–2012.* Unpublished document, Liverpool Hope University. Available at: http://www.hope.ac.uk/learningandteaching/lat.php?page=s trategy&current=strategy [accessed 24 June 2011].

OXFAM (2006), *Education for global citizenship: A guide for schools.* [online]. Available at: http://www.oxfam.org.uk/education/gc/files/education_for_global_ citizenship_a_guide_for_schools.pdf [accessed 6 May 2010].

Patton, M. Q. (2002), *Qualitative Research and Evaluation Methods.* London: Sage.

Rosenberger, C. (2000), 'Beyond empathy: Developing critical consciousness through service-learning', in C. O'Grady, *Integrating Service-Learning and Multicultural Education in Colleges and Universities.* Mahwah, NJ: Lawrence Erlbaum, pp. 23–44.

Tellez, K. (2000), 'Reconciling service-learning', in C. O'Grady, *Integrating Service-Learning and Multicultural Education in Colleges and Universities.* Mahwah, NJ: Lawrence Erlbaum, pp. 71–92.

8

The Transformative Potential of Service/ Community-Based Learning in Initial Teacher Education: A Case Study from Ireland

Josephine Boland and Elaine Keane

Introduction

The homogeneity of the teaching profession, particularly with respect to ethnicity and class, is an international phenomenon. Student teachers' limited personal experience of diversity compounds the issues arising from this trend. In the context of an increasingly multicultural society, responding to the diverse realities of contemporary post-primary schools is a challenge for which many newly qualified teachers are ill-prepared. Service/community-based learning (S/CBL) is a potentially transformative pedagogy which can create effective spaces for experiential learning, particularly working with minority and disadvantaged groups. Within teacher education, it also offers rich opportunities for interrogating core values of the teaching profession – democracy, social justice, equality and inclusion. 'Learning to Teach for Social Justice' (LTSJ) – a Service-Learning course within the Postgraduate Diploma in Education (PGDE) in the National University of Ireland, Galway – is designed with that aim in mind. It represents one element of evolving partnerships between the School of Education and local community organizations. Enabling factors include a strong emphasis on professional values by the newly established Teaching Council (the statutory body with responsibility for the profession), an institutional culture which supports and valorizes civic engagement and a developing alliance of community organizations and teacher educators committed to social justice and civic engagement.

In this chapter we critically explore opportunities and challenges involved in embedding this pedagogy within a programme of teacher education, with attention to context and with reference to relevant theoretical perspectives and research. It is informed by our experience implementing S/CBL within teacher education in Ireland, a research study on the process of embedding civic engagement within the higher education curriculum and an independent evaluation of LTSJ. We offer perspectives of students, community partners and academics which we believe will resonate in other contexts. Finally, we consider the potential and sustainability of S/CBL as a transformative pedagogy for diversity and social justice in teacher education.

Context

Teacher education and intercultural education in Ireland

In recent years there has been an explicit commitment in national policy documents to social justice and related values within teacher education, as manifest in the Teaching Council of Ireland's Codes of Professional Practice and Professional Conduct:

> Teachers in their professional role show commitment to democracy, social justice, equality and inclusion. They encourage active citizenship and support students in thinking critically about significant social issues, in valuing and accommodating diversity and in responding appropriately. (Teaching Council of Ireland, 2007, p. 19)

In its review of initial teacher education programmes in Ireland, the Teaching Council includes a focus on 'teaching in a multicultural environment' (OECD, 2009). The recently launched Intercultural Education Strategy 2010–2015 (Department of Education and Skills and Office of the Minister for Integration, 2010) stresses the role of teacher education in the development of an intercultural learning environment. The strategy emphasizes the necessity of building the capacity of all education providers to ensure 'that inclusion and integration within an intercultural learning environment become the norm' (ibid., p. 2). Actions identified include reviewing the intercultural education component of both initial teacher education and continuing professional development and filling any gaps in provision.

Diversity and homogeneity

Irish society has undergone massive transformation in the last decade largely as a result of the 'Celtic Tiger' economic boom and the significant immigration which accompanied it. In tandem with these developments, Irish schools have evolved from a relatively homogeneous to a heterogeneous student intake (Smyth et al., 2009). Concerns have been expressed, however, about a developing 'ghettoization' in the school system, evident in the concentration of large numbers of newcomer students in some schools with very few in others (ibid.; Byrne et al., 2010).

In terms of catering for diversity, the inclusion of Travellers within the Irish education system remains one of our long-standing challenges. Travellers are Ireland's indigenous ethnic minority group, with an estimated 40,129 members of the community living in the country in 2008 (All-Ireland Traveller Health Study Team, 2010). They now have almost full participation at primary school level and there is a high rate of transfer from primary to post-primary. However, retention at post-primary continues to be problematic (Byrne and Smyth, 2010). Barriers to participation and achievement include poor living conditions and poverty, a perception of prejudice on the part of the settled community, a perceived culture clash between Traveller and settled teenagers, lack of visibility of Traveller culture in formal curricula, low teacher expectations and little family history of literacy and education (Hourigan and Campbell, 2010; Lynch and Lodge, 2002).

Despite increasing diversity among our school-going population, the teacher population has remained homogeneous. Internationally, females predominate, particularly at primary level (OECD, 2009), and female applicants and entrants to post-primary teacher education in Ireland considerably outnumber males (Heinz, 2008). The teaching profession and student teacher bodies are predominantly white and of the majority ethnic group, both internationally (Zumwalt and Craig, 2005) and in Ireland (Heinz, 2008; Leavy, 2005; Devine, 2005). While, internationally, teachers have typically come from the working and lower middle classes (Zumwalt and Craig, 2005), in Ireland, there has been an over-representation of those from farming backgrounds, rural areas and middle-class backgrounds (Heinz, 2008; Drudy et al., 2005). Hence, there is a considerable 'diversity gap' between our teaching and pupil populations, especially given increasing immigration in recent years. In light of that, an Advisory Group noted it was 'highly desirable to ensure greater participation in teacher education by students from diverse backgrounds, including those who are disadvantaged, students with special needs and candidates from ethnic minorities' (Advisory Group on Post-primary Teacher Education, 2002, p. 101).

Key principles, Concepts and Relationships

Experiences with and beliefs about diversity

It is claimed that having prior 'cross-cultural experiences' is an important factor influencing the extent to which concepts relating to diversity are embraced (Castro, 2010). One implication of a lack of diversity within the teaching population, however, is that teachers have very little prior experience with minority and disadvantaged groups. In Ireland, Leavy (2005) found that 59 per cent of her participating pre-service primary teachers had no exposure to members of the Travelling community, 65 per cent had no contact with refugees or asylum seekers and 20 per cent never had a conversation with a non-Irish national.

Research has found that pre-service teachers hold deficit assumptions and express negative views about minority and marginalized groups and these are particularly manifest through low expectations (Sleeter, 2008). In Ireland, such negative views are expressed most in relation to Travellers (c.f. Clarke and Drudy, 2006; Leavy, 2005). What Causey et al, (2000) refer to as 'naïve egalitarian' beliefs – based on individualistic and meritocratic assumptions – are evident as pre-service teachers try to explain differential achievement within education (Mueller and O'Connor, 2007). They are reported as lacking a 'critical consciousness' (Castro, 2010, p. 200) about the pervasiveness, sources and implications of structurally-embedded inequalities in society, and, in particular, their impact on the educational experiences of different student groups. Pre-service teachers also tend to lack understanding about their own position in terms of ethnicity, culture and class and the implications of this for teaching diverse groups (Mueller and O'Connor, 2007; Allard and Santoro, 2006).

Teachers in Ireland report feeling unprepared for teaching in diverse contexts and claim they are ill-equipped to deal with the challenges presented by a diverse student body and that they lack understanding about how to make the teaching and learning environment more inclusive (Smyth et al., 2009; Devine, 2005). Serving teachers, particularly those of significant experience, have had little exposure to ideas regarding social justice and cultural diversity. Many teachers qualified at a time when intercultural education was not part of teacher education (Department of Education and Skills and Office of the Minister for Integration, 2010). Intercultural education guidelines for both primary and post-primary schools (NCCA, 2006) were not accompanied by in-service support. The need for continuous professional development opportunities for teachers in the area of diversity and social justice is widely acknowledged (Department of Education and Skills and Office of the Minister for Integration, 2010; Smyth et al., 2009; Keane, 2009).

Two broad approaches to education for diversity are acknowledged within initial teacher education: an integrated/infusion approach, where principles of inclusion and diversity are infused right throughout the programme, and a bolted-on approach, where the overall programme structure and content remain unchanged and an extra element is added in. While the latter approach is more common, Zeichner et al. (1998) advocate the former. While teacher education in Ireland includes a focus on intercultural education, research suggests that attitudinal change, and the building of the 'critical consciousness' mentioned earlier, are more effectively accomplished through direct 'in the field' experience and engagement, accompanied by critical discussion and reflection. The OECD (2009, p. 45) report on migrant education in Ireland emphasizes the importance of 'moving from an understanding of intercultural education in theory to its characteristics in practice'. This is where S/CBL – with the powerful combination of field-experience and reflection – has the potential to be a transformative pedagogy for diversity and social justice.

Transformative models and reciprocal partnerships

Proponents of S/CBL highlight the benefits to students in terms of their academic performance, enhanced self-esteem, career knowledge and sense of social/civic responsibility (Eyler and Giles, 1999; Kenny et al., 2001). Iles (2007) concludes that, while it poses many challenges, the pedagogy provides students with an opportunity to bring together academic knowledge and work experience with compassion and empathy. While sustained partnerships between higher education institutions and community organizations may lead to longer-term benefits for the particular organization or sector, there is a notable dearth of literature offering a convincing empirical basis for such claims.

The defining characteristics of S/CBL are well addressed elsewhere in this volume. For the purpose of this discussion, however, it is valuable to draw an important distinction regarding potential, with particular reference to *transformative* potential (Welch, 2006; Butin, 2010). 'Transactional' models are generally characterized by an exchange process, with the community in receipt of a service and students in receipt of academic credit for demonstrated learning. Transformative potential for students can be achieved where experiences lead to greater understanding, empathy and capacity for critique. 'Transformative' models which focus on community or societal outcomes, however, also aim to question and to change the circumstances, conditions, values or beliefs which are at the root of community's or society's need (Welch, 2006). Having such ambitious outcomes has implications for the design of the learning experience, the role of academics, the nature of the relationship with relevant community partners and the conditions which need to be in place to ensure sustainability. We will argue that transformative outcomes for students, community and society are not mutually exclusive and can be interrelated, even where attitudinal change for students may be a primary focus.

Establishing and maintaining partnerships represents one of the most challenging aspects of S/CBL, particularly in terms of the time and effort involved and where partners have diverse expectations. Arising from their study of partnerships in education, Billett et al. (2007) identify principles which assist the process, including establishing and maintaining shared goals and a capacity for partnership work based on trust. Ward and Wolf-Wendel (2006), however, highlight the preponderance of 'doing for' over 'doing with' and point to a lack of critical attention to how differences in motivation lead to different perspectives on partnerships. They critique representations of 'community' within the S/CBL literature, claiming that they perpetuate a construction of higher education as experts and of communities as beneficiaries of their remedies. While the voices of community partners have gained more attention in recent years (Stoecker and Tyyon, 2009), evidence of 'doing for' as the prevalent mode can be readily found in the literature and practice of S/CBL. Lounsbury and Pollack (2001) claim that this is an inevitable consequence where S/CBL is conceived of as a pedagogy with valuable, but primarily academic, outcomes for students. We suggest, however, that there is nothing inevitable about the outcomes of an S/CBL initiative. Opportunities may be found to strike a balance between valuable outcomes for students (academic and attitudinal) and for community partners – hence realizing transformative potential for both.

Significance of orientation for sustainability

Ultimately, the achievement of transformative potential is dependent on the willingness and capacity of academics to embed the pedagogy as an enduring feature of the curriculum. In a multi-site study of the process of embedding a civic engagement dimension in the higher education curriculum, 'orientation' to civic engagement was identified as central to sustainability (Boland, 2008). The concept of 'orientation' – attitudes, aims and action tendencies which influence the practice and the strategic conduct of individuals – has been used as a device for analyzing the motivations of academics involved in S/CBL (Boland, 2008). Embedding the pedagogy within the curriculum remains fundamentally dependent on the initiative and motivation of individual academics. No single factor accounts in a consistent way for variations in their capacity to sustain that commitment. While time and workload feature as significant factors, absence of recognition (and reward) seems more likely to act as a disincentive. The impact of these concerns is at its most acute where academics feel the pressure of multiple responsibilities. The combined impact of constraining factors tends to be greatest for collaborative projects with a strong ethos of partnership, where sustainability is more difficult to achieve. Exceptions to this generalization could be accounted for where academics held a strong civic 'orientation' or where civic values were central to the discipline, including teacher education. Moreover, commitment to sustainability was more likely where an academic conceived of civic engagement as an integral part of their academic role and identity. These findings – from a study involving a range of disciplines – have particular relevance when considering the sustainability of an initiative such as LTSJ.

Learning to Teach for Social Justice

Description

Learning to Teach for Social Justice (LTSJ) has been developed as part of the School of Education's commitment to learning and teaching though civic engagement. It provides student teachers on the Postgraduate Diploma in Education (PGDE) with the opportunity to engage in experiential learning opportunities in a real-world context while providing a service to the community, based on needs identified by the partner organization. The size of the one-year full-time PGDE cohort is typically 220 students. The experience is designed to connect with *Education, Diversity and Social Justice*, a core course within the PGDE. LTSJ aims to enhance the educational experiences of minority ethnic and other marginalized post-primary school pupils, while simultaneously supporting student teachers' development as educators committed to a social justice ethos. LTSJ is part of a wider commitment by the School of Education to civic engagement and initial teacher education.

LTSJ was initiated in 2006 as a non-credit-bearing elective element of the PGDE. Interested students (typically 15 to 20 each year) opted to work with one of our then two community partners in the provision of support to either Travellers or refugees and asylum seekers in various academic support-type settings. Since 2008, LTSJ has been further developed on a collaborative basis as a formal credit-bearing elective course with two additional community partners, both of whom also run homework clubs in areas of Galway city characterized by disadvantage. Experiential learning is the primary mode of learning, which takes place in the community-based partner organization, at times negotiated between the student teacher and the organization.

Learning outcomes emerged from a tripartite dialogical process involving the School of Education, the community partner organizations and students. It is expected that on completion of this experience and the associated assessment, the student teacher will be able to:

- adapt their developing pedagogic skills to a one-to-one teaching situation;
- critically reflect on issues of educational disadvantage and interculturalism from another's perspective;
- consider the impact of culture and tradition on expectations and experiences of education;
- use educational technology as a creative and motivational resource;
- engage professionally with a partner organization, students and parents;
- cope with the level of uncertainly that is a feature of an informal and relatively unstructured learning environment;
- review their own personal philosophy of teaching;
- communicate their learning from the experience to others.

Tutorial sessions are provided on campus to prepare students for, and support them during, the experience, to encourage reflection and to plan how best to communicate their learning. Preparation is also provided by each partner organization. Minimum requirements include demonstration of satisfactory engagement with the community organization (including the completion of at least 20 hours), participation in the campus-based tutorial sessions and contribution to a collective sharing of their learning. Once minimum criteria have been met, student achievement is graded on performance in a reflective paper.

Our longest-standing community partner is the Galway Traveller Movement (GTM), which is strongly committed to improving the lives of the Travelling community through education. Most PGDE students have opted to work with the GTM's 'Pavee Study' homework club. This club is run in the GTM offices four nights per week during the school year, is supervised by Traveller parents and targets post-primary pupils from the Travelling community from schools throughout the city. Student teachers supervise the completion of homework and provide general academic support, alongside others working in a volunteering capacity. Members of GTM contribute to the School of Education's programmes (as do other community partners) and they are actively involved in another project relating to education for social justice. One of the teacher educators works closely with the GTM's education committee on policy matters. Members of the School have provided ICT training to 'Pavee Study' Traveller pupils and supervisors on campus. Other opportunities to extend the relationship are being explored.

Perspectives of Students, Academics and Community Partners

Outcomes and opportunities

Evidence of some of the outcomes from LTSJ can be gleaned from a number of sources. In addition to completing individual assessments, students have shared their collective learning in posters and conference presentations (PGDE students, 2009, 2010). An independent external evaluation was undertaken of LTSJ, based on interviews with teacher educators and community partners and a survey of students (Keating, 2009). Some of the findings provide an insight into the outcomes, opportunities, limitations and challenges.

First, it is significant that the rationale for LTSJ derives from an identified community need, a commitment to social justice and a teacher educator's sense of academic identity.

> One of the things that I wanted to do was to try and see if there was some way we could tackle educational underachievement for minority groups in schools and at the same time try to support student teachers in their development in terms of a social justice ethos ... I would see it as part of my role in terms of diversity and teacher education. (teacher educator in Keating, 2009)

For the teacher educators concerned, it offered the opportunity to develop a very different relationship with a small group of students and gain valuable insights into how students perceive themselves as teachers. It also offered an opportunity to appreciate the different lenses through which we view the world, to draw on complementary skills and expertise as partners in the project and to promote professional development in the field.

> I've learned a lot from my colleague about sociological theories and ways of looking at disadvantage – such as the discourse of 'naive egalitarianism' – as she feels passionately about disadvantage and stereotyping and the exclusion of Travellers within the educational system. (teacher educator in Keating, 2009)

Evidence from the students' testimonies was broadly very positive, notwith-standing the challenges encountered in working in a relatively unstructured environment. They benefited from the opportunity to experience diversity in a positive and safe environment.

> What I liked best was getting the opportunity to experience diversity and in particular to meet the children and their parents. Prior to being involved in the Pavee Study, I had little or no chance to meet with Travellers. It was also great to work with a small number of students. (student teacher in Keating, 2009)

Students claim that they have 'learned to leave preconceptions behind' (PGDE students, 2009). They have seen, at first hand, that difficult relationships between some Traveller students and some teachers can lead to educational disadvantage and that cultural differences impact on pupils' attitudes to education. They learn that relationship-building is central to teaching and learning and they gain greater confidence in approaching issues relating to cultural diversity in the classroom. There is clear evidence of transformative outcomes for students, for example in terms of enhanced capacity for insight and empathy.

> ... because I have gained an insight into their culture, I have more patience and more understanding when they become distracted or unmotivated. But I know that they need as much encouragement and as much motivation as students that have high expectations of themselves. (PGDE student, 2008–9)

The partnership is valued by the community partner on a number of levels. In the homework club they get committed student teachers working on a *pro bono* basis. As a result of the 'Pavee Study', Traveller parents have noted that their children are more engaged in their school work, are happier going to school, and are getting more positive reports from schoolteachers. Traveller pupils have had an opportunity to experience a far more positive relationship with teachers than most of them have previously experienced at school. Perceiving the profession in a more positive light may encourage Traveller pupils to consider it as a viable future profession for themselves. The potential for promoting a sense of agency for all concerned is keenly felt: 'Education is power and once Travellers become more educated they will be better able to understand the power and decision making structures that exist and affect their lives and subsequently will be able to influence these decisions' (community partner in Keating, 2009).

It is also a positive experience for GTM members, most of whom are Travellers themselves, to meet student teachers committed to supporting diversity. Overall, the relationship with the university is highly valued.

> The benefits in particular have been huge, especially working with people within the University ... One of the main benefits of this project is that the University are taking [diversity training] on board and linking in with organizations such as the GTM where we have the expertise to give feedback. (community partner in Keating, 2009)

The opportunity for members of GTM to contribute to the PGDE programme and to present at events attended by senior university figures is very important.

> [We] gave a talk at the end of year presentation with the Registrar of the University and this type of validation and exposure is hugely important for us. This type of work and exposure is one of the more positive projects that we engage in, as many of the other issues such as accommodation can present us in a negative light. (community partner in Keating, 2009)

Community partners also have certain expectations arising from their university alliance which indicate potential for reciprocity and for longer-term systemic outcomes.

> The university has the potential to influence existing schools as they have a network of principals ... The Department of Education and Science would be more open to an invitation from the university to discuss the issues, than [to] an invitation from the Galway Traveller Movement. (community partner in Keating, 2009)

Challenges and limitations

The problems associated with 'fitting it all in' featured for academic staff, community partners and students. Collaboration proves very time-consuming when parties to the process work to different schedules and priorities. The community partners also experience their own challenges associated with resourcing and the priority that needs to be afforded to other pressing matters for the community they serve. Concerns about sustainability are evident, especially given the challenge associated with gaining recognition for S/CBL as a legitimate teaching and learning strategy, for students and for themselves as academics.

> ... it is difficult to see how one or two people could continue to sustain this year in year out due to the level of work and time commitments, especially if it is to expand ... More formal recognition for this work would be great. At the moment, nothing else is moved from your work to allow this, it is all extra. (teacher educator in Keating, 2009)

Some progress was made in enhancing the legitimacy of S/CBL as a valid and valued means of teaching, learning, research and scholarship by the strategic involvement of senior management figures in end-of-year student presentations, by participating in conferences and through publications (Keane and Boland, 2009, Boland et al., 2009; Boland, 2010).

One of the main limitations in terms of impact, however, is that LTSJ remains an elective rather than a core element of the PGDE, taken by a relatively small proportion of the cohort – to date, less than 20 students each year.

> I have always worried that with this work the way it is at the moment, we are preaching to the converted. Student teachers who [elect to enrol in LTSJ] are already positively disposed to diversity. How do we do this in such a way that we manage to get the people who have negative attitudes towards Travellers? (teacher educator in Keating, 2009)

The feasibility of mainstreaming the S/CBL experience as a mandatory element of the programme for all 220 PGDE students seems doubtful. The organizational challenges and the difficulty in sourcing suitable S/CBL opportunities with an explicit social justice dimension are considerable. There is also some doubt about the prospect of involving all staff in the initiative as 'not all have the same attitude towards this line of work' (teacher educator in Keating, 2009). Student teachers themselves have conflicting views about the desirability of making it mandatory.

The community partners recognize, however, that providing an S/CBL experience or whole-class lectures on interculturalism is insufficient as a response, signalling the need to target practising teachers in order to realise transformative outcomes throughout the education system.

The existing [school] environment also has to change [in tandem] with the work we are currently doing, otherwise the benefits of our work can get lost ... young/ new teachers will find it very hard to challenge existing attitudes as they are so ingrained and as a result may conform in order to fit in themselves. (community partner in Keating, 2009)

Conclusion

In the context of initial teacher education, S/CBL offers transformative potential both for student teachers and for the partners to the process. It can lead to significant change in student teachers' beliefs about diversity and enhance their confidence and competence in catering for diversity within their classrooms. It has the potential to develop the 'critical consciousness' that Castro (2010) speaks of as so often lacking among student teachers. It is our view that experiential learning of this nature also offers the potential to enhance student teachers' sense of agency, giving them a deeper appreciation of how they can serve as agents of change in the schools in which they work. For minority and marginalized pupils, their involvement in homework club settings with student teachers can enhance their engagement and achievement in education, ultimately contributing to equality in education. A further potentially transformative outcome is the possibility of encouraging hitherto marginalized young people to consider entering the teaching profession. Increasing diversity of the teaching profession could have a number of important benefits, including better preparation of young people for living in a multicultural society and the provision of role models for ethnic minority children.

Where S/CBL is underpinned by reciprocal partnerships between teacher educators and community partners, the potential for longer-term transformative change can be realized – some benefits to the community partners were evident in LTSJ. The opportunity for experiential professional development for teacher educators arising from this work is one outcome which receives very little attention, but in our case was notable.

One of the unresolved issues concerns whether or not to 'mainstream' S/ CBL within initial teacher education. On the one hand, one could argue that for it to be truly transformative, it must be available as an experience in which *all* student teachers participate. Logistical barriers to the mainstreaming of an S/CBL experience with a social justice ethos are, arguably, prohibitive. There is also a risk – in attempting to 'mainstream' S/CBL – of a drift towards a more 'transactional' model. Maintaining a meaningful reciprocal partnership between a School of Education and community providers could prove much more challenging.

Teacher education programmes are increasingly criticized for being overloaded. An alternative to a 'bolted-on' strategy is to promote an 'infusion' approach to intercultural education, such that social justice principles would underpin the philosophy and practice of the teacher education programme and the relevant academic discipline/school. Should this approach be adopted, then significant professional development would be required to ensure that all teacher educators were themselves educated in and committed to the implicit values and methods of S/CBL as a pedagogy for diversity and social justice. These issues raise important questions, first, as to what should be 'core' to initial teacher education in terms of knowledge, skills and values, and second, as to how to create the appropriate learning experiences which can facilitate their development.

The sustainability of LTSJ – in its current guise – will be subject to a range of factors, some of which are outside the influence of the university and the community partners. The civic orientation of the academics concerned, the focus on student attitudinal development and the extent to which diversity and social justice are central to the values of the profession all augur well for the sustainability of the initiative. The logistical challenges involved in collaborative work, while considerable, are surmountable. The context, however, within which the partners work – in terms of competing demands, increasing range of responsibilities, diminishing resources and the privileging of certain kinds of performance in academic life – poses a more significant threat.

We argue, nonetheless, that service/community-based learning constitutes a potentially transformative pedagogy for diversity and social justice in challenging contexts. For student teachers, it contributes to their preparation as agents of change in today's challenging school and classrooms contexts. The process of embedding the pedagogy in the curriculum makes visible issues of diversity and social justice for all teacher educators. The very existence within the university of 'Learning to Teach for Social Justice' as a community-engaged pedagogy encourages us all to question the conditions, practices, values and beliefs which are at the root of inequality in society.

References

Advisory Group on Post-primary Teacher Education (2002), *Report of the Advisory Group on Post-primary Teacher Education*. Dublin: The Stationery Office.

Allard, A. and Santoro, N. (2006), 'Troubling identities: teacher education students' constructions of class and ethnicity'. *Cambridge Journal of Education*, 36 (1): 115–29.

All-Ireland Traveller Health Study Team, School of Public Health, Physiotherapy and Population Science, University College Dublin (2010), *The All-Ireland Traveller Health Study: Our Geels. Summary of Findings*. Dublin: Department of Health and Children Available online at: http://www.drugsandalcohol.ie/13791/2/TravellerfindingsSUMMARY_LR_All%5B1%5D.pdf [accessed 12 November 2010].

Billett, S., Ovens, C., Clemans, A. and Seddon, T. (2007), 'Collaborative working and contested practices: forming, developing and sustaining social partnerships in education'. *Journal of Education Policy*, 22: 637–56.

Boland, J. (2008), *Embedding a Civic Dimension Within the Higher Education Curriculum: A Study of Policy, Process and Practice in Ireland*. Edinburgh: University of Edinburgh Press.

—(2010), 'Teaching and learning through civic engagement: prospects for sustainability in teacher education'. *Issues in Educational Research*, 20: 1–20.

Boland, J., Keane, E. and McGinley, H. (2009), 'Learning to teach for social justice: lessons from initial teacher education in Ireland'. *International Conference for Service-Learning in Teacher Education in Teacher Education*. Galway, June 2009.

Butin, D. W. (2010), *Service-learning in Theory and Practice: The Future of Community Engagement in Higher Education*. Basingstoke: Palgrave Macmillan.

Byrne, D., McGinnity, F., Smyth, E. and Darmody, M. (2010), 'Immigration and school composition in Ireland'. *Irish Educational Studies*, 29 (3): 271–88.

Byrne, M. and Smyth, E. (2010), *No Way Back? The Dynamics of Early School Leaving*. Dublin: The Economic and Social Research Institute and the National Council for Curriculum and Assessment.

Castro, A. (2010), 'Themes in the research on preservice teachers' views of cultural diversity: Implications for researching millennial preservice teachers'. *Educational Researcher*, 39: 198–210.

Causey, V., Thomas, C. and Armento, B. (2000), '"Cultural diversity is basically a foreign term to me": The challenges of diversity for pre-service teacher education'. *Teaching and Teacher Education*, 16 (1): 33–45.

Clarke, M. and Drudy, S. (2006), 'Teaching for diversity, social justice and global awareness'. *European Journal of Teacher Education*, 29 (3): 371–86.

Department of Education and Skills and Office of Minister for Integration (2010), *Intercultural Education Strategy 2010-2015*. www.into.ie/ROI/Publications/.../Intercultural_education_strategy.pdf. (Accessed 20 November 2011).

Devine, D. (2005), 'Welcome to the Celtic tiger? Teacher responses to immigration and increasing ethnic diversity in Irish schools'. *International Studies in Sociology of Education*, 15 (1): 49–70.

Drudy, S., Martin, M., Woods, M. and O'Flynn, J. (2005), *Men and the Classroom: Gender Imbalances in Today's Schools*. London and New York: Routledge Falmer.

Eyler, J. and Giles Jnr, D. E. (1999), *Where's the Learning in Service-learning?* San Francisco: Jossey Bass.

Heinz, M. (2008), 'The composition of applicants and entrants to teacher education programmes in Ireland: Trends and patterns'. *Irish Educational Studies*, 27 (3): 223–40.

Hourigan, N. and Campbell, M. (2010), *The Teach report – Traveller education and adults: crisis, challenge and change*. Athlone: National Association of Travellers' Centres.

Iles, J. (2007) 'Service-learning and reflective practice at Roehampton University, London' in L. Mc Ilrath and I. Mac Labhrainn (eds), *Higher Education and Civic Engagement – International Perspectives*. Aldershot: Ashgate.

Keane, E. (2009), 'Frictional' relationships ... tension in the camp: Focusing on the relational in under-represented students' experiences in higher education'. *Irish Educational Studies*, 28 (1): 85–102.

Keane, E. and Boland, J. (2009), *A Pedagogy for Diversity in Higher Education? The Transformative Potential of Service/community-based Learning in Initial Teacher Education. Valuing Complexity: Celebrating Diverse Approaches to Teaching and Learning*. Maynooth: All Ireland Society for Higher Education.

Keating, M. (2009), *External Evaluation of Service-learning within the PGDE: Learning to Teach for Social Justice*. Galway: Quality by Design.

Kenny, M. E., Simon, L. A. K., Kiley-Brabeck, K. and Lerner, R. M. (2001), *Learning to Serve: Promoting Civil Society Through Service-learning*. Dordrecht: Kluwer.

Leavy, A. (2005). '"When I meet them I talk to them": the challenges of diversity for preservice teacher education'. *Irish Educational Studies*, 24 (2–3): 159–77.

Lounsbury, M. and Pollack, S. (2001), 'Institutionalizing civic engagement: Shifting logics and the cultural repackaging of service-learning in US higher education'. *Organization*, 8: 319–39.

Lynch, K. and Lodge, A. (2002), *Equality and Power in Schools: Redistribution, Recognition and Representation*, London: Routledge/Falmer.

Mueller, J. and O'Connor, C. (2007), 'Telling and retelling about self and "others": how pre-service teachers (re)interpret privilege and disadvantage in one college classroom'. *Teaching and Teacher Education*, 23 (6): 840–56.

NCCA (2006), *Intercultural Education in the Primary School, Guidelines for Schools*. Dublin: NCCA.

OECD (2009), *Reviews of Migrant Education*. Ireland, Paris: OECD.

Postgraduate Diploma in Education Students (2009), *Learning to Teach for Social Justice '08–'09*. Presentation to the School of Education. Galway: NUI.

Postgraduate Diploma in Education Students (2010), *Learning to Teach for Social Justice: PGDE perspective '09 –'10*. Service-learning Student Conference. Galway: NUI.

Sleeter, C. (2008), 'Preparing White teachers for diverse students', in M. Cochran-Smith, S. Feiman-Nemser and D. J. McIntyre (eds), *Handbook of Research on Teacher Education: Enduring Questions in Changing Contexts* (3rd edn). New York: Routledge and Association of Teacher Educators, pp. 559–82.

Smyth, E., Darmody, M., McGinnity, F. and Byrne, D. (2009), *Adapting to Diversity: Irish Schools and Newcomer Students*. Dublin: ESRI.

Stoecker, R. and Tyyon, E. (eds) (2009), *The Unheard Voices: Community Organization and Service-learning*. Philadelphia, PA: Temple University Press.

Teaching Council of Ireland (2007), *Codes of Professional Conduct for Teachers*. Dublin: The Teaching Council.

Ward, K. and Wolf-Wendel, L. (2006), 'Community-centered service-learning: moving from doing for to doing with'. *American Behavioural Scientist*, 43: 767–80.

Welch, M. (2006), *Service-learning as Deeper Education*. Hodson Bay, Athlone: Service-learning Academy.

Zeichner, K., Grant, C., Gay, G., Gillette, M., Valli, L. and Villegas, A. (1998), 'A research informed vision of good practice in multicultural teacher education: design principles'. *Theory into Practice*, 37 (2): 163–71.

Zumwalt, K. and Craig, E. (2005), 'Teachers' characteristics: Research on the demographic profile', in M. Cochran-Smith and K. Zeichner (eds), *Studying Teacher Education: The Report of the AERA Panel on Research and Teacher Education*. Mahwah, NJ: Lawrence Erlbaum, pp. 111–56.

9

Service-Learning Experience for the Development of Inclusion: A Case Study from Spain[1]

Esther Luna

Introduction

This chapter has its origins in a broader research programme in Citizenship Education which is being undertaken by the Intercultural Education Research Group[2] (GREDI) at the University of Barcelona (Spain). Our starting point is that of a dynamic, active and committed conception of citizenship, which, as a consequence, implies a rather more practical than theoretical way of addressing education issues, and an approach which is more responsive and more committed to the process of social transformation as opposed to being engaged in the simple transmission of information. Our objective is the development of an active citizen, one who is aware of his or her responsibilities and commitments to the community starting with the most immediate expression of this in either the school or the local neighbourhood (Bartolomé et al., 2002; Cabrera, 2002).

The challenge which is presented by the idea of an active citizenship education process leads directly to the issue of the need to create new educational and participative spaces. Civil society in all its various forms and guises – the neighbourhood, neighbourhood groups and associations, work groups, and so on – can be transformed by an appropriate educational strategy into a revitalized and revalued space which offers an ideal context for the educational development of a collective identity at different levels and in a variety of contexts.

As Gentili (2000) and Luque (1995) indicate, local communities, neighbourhoods and cities are generally recognized as privileged spaces for the development of active citizenship and for the promotion of participation and involvement. However, for a community to be a development site for a sense of belonging and for the exercise of an active citizenship, it is also necessary that the community sees itself as such. It is necessary to *promote the participative capacity from within the educational spaces themselves*, thereby facilitating the process knowledge of and access to the community's resources. It is also beneficial to promote community involvement through promoting connections between the individuals and the groups of which the community is composed.

What is involved then is the creation of what Kisnerman (1986, p. 70) terms a 'community feeling', a feeling which is characterized by a convergence of interests, needs, values and shared responsibilities with the others who share the same social space (Luque, 1995). Without doubt what is involved is a new challenge for educational action in which different educational levels and institutions come together, as Inglehart (1996) points out, with the responsibility of educating citizens who will have a high level of autonomy and an interest in participating fully and critically in public life. Pateman (1970) also believes that citizen participation has an educational function in that it allows the individual to gain democratic experience and to develop a feeling of community.

What Citizen Participation are we Talking About?

The differing conceptions of participation deployed by Carr and Kemmis (1988), Folgueiras (2005), Lipman (1991), Paul and Elder (2005), Pérez Ledesma (2000), Rebellato (2000) and Schön (1997) lay special emphasis on the need to offer education for an active, committed and responsible participation. If we take the idea of Folgueiras (2005, p. 87) then what we understand by participation is:

> ... a citizenship right, a collective social action which generates a sense of commitment and at the same time a feeling of shared responsibility which facilitates involvement in decision making, creates opportunities for the development of capacities and favours or expresses a feeling of identity or of community, always insofar as this is put into practice within a framework of equality.

The writer also highlights in her definition the importance of starting from one's own experiences and those of the other participants. In this way they outline the topics to be dealt with and thus encourage the establishment of horizontal relations, thereby facilitating an equalitarian dialogue. In this way active participation becomes 'a social and educational process which seeks change transformation and social improvement, whether on an individual or a collective basis' (Folgueiras, 2005, p. 87).

Taking as our starting point the Folgueiras analysis of the citizen participation construct, we have identified four fundamental elements – each interrelated with the others – which transform the concept into a key tool for social and educational transformation:

- participation as a citizenship right insofar as the process develops a collective and social action;
- participation as a responsibility to the extent that it implies a commitment and a shared responsibility;
- participation as an improvement tool since it creates opportunities for capacity development;
- participation as a necessity since it favours the feeling of belonging to a community.

These four elements are both generated and achieved at various levels at one and the same time and have as their objective an overall understanding. That is to say, an effective citizenship participation is not born only from an individual, nor from civil society as a totality, nor from an institution, but rather from the combination of the three, thereby maximizing the synergies between each one (Cabrera, 2002; Flanagan, and Faison 2001; and Yates and Youniss, 1998).

Our interest in this approach brings us to consider citizenship participation in an educational context – which, despite the difficulties involved in establishing a participative educational framework in the school, is both necessary and possible – given that the school is the formative public space for citizens-in-the-making (Ianni, 2003). In this sense, we would like to explore what part the school can play in helping the child to learn and exercise citizenship participation.

Service-Learning as a Methodology to Develop Citizen Participation

The innovative methodological proposal known as Service-Learning connects with the key elements of Folgueiras' citizenship analysis construct referred to in the previous section. It is characterized by a learning process which transcends the traditional limits of classroom-based activity. It is a methodology and a way of learning which is derived from a new model of the relations between school and community, one which offers to all those involved (pupil, teacher, family, community representatives, etc.) the opportunity to develop participative citizenship competences committed to the collective project of creating a society which is more just, more egalitarian, more inclusive and more diverse.

Service-Learning may be defined as an educational process which emphasizes academic learning linked to some form of community service project. It involves 'academic learning-work in the community' where both parties benefit from a mutual learning process. In order to indicate the key characteristics of Service-Learning, we will cite the opinions of three recognized specialists in the field: Exley (2004), Furco (2003) and Tapia (2006). All three authors make important conceptual contributions about Service-Learning, of which five are outlined below.

- *It is student centred.* S/he takes responsibility for planning the necessary actions to be taken, as well as carrying out necessary project evaluation and follow-up.
- *It meets a felt need.* Service-Learning projects take as their point of departure a real need in a specified community. The student needs to become aware of the needs of the community via a number of sources (newspapers, interviews, surveys, archives, invited speakers, etc.) in order to identify a topic or need around which an activity could be organized.
- *It is planned within the curricular programme.* Service-Learning projects not only aim to meet a social need, but also aim to improve the quality of school-based learning, which means they have a systematic educational intent. According to Smink and Duckenfield (1998), there are two ways of facilitating the curricular integration of Service-Learning activities: through the elaboration of projects which incorporate learning objectives (from the school to the community); or through analysis of community needs to develop projects which, if carried out, involve the actualization of curricular objectives (from the community to the school).
- *Action learning is integral to Service-Learning.* Any analysis of a given reality would lose its force and a great deal of its educational potential for making the student a socially aware citizen if the student did not carry through some kind of practical action as a response to the analysis.
- *Critical reflection is a prerequisite for Service-Learning.* Such reflection fuses learning inside and outside the classroom, thereby deepening and enriching the overall learning experience.

From the School to the Community: A Service-Learning Programme to Develop Citizen Participation

Our programme *From the School to the Community* (Cabrera et al., 2007) is designed to promote engaged citizenship within the schooling context using the methodology of Service-Learning. It has as its objective the development of the sense of belonging to a community as well as the activation of citizenship roles for secondary school students. In this way, two essential dimensions of being an active citizen are promoted: instilling an active awareness of one's community, as well as acquiring a set of skills, competences and attitudes which are integral to community involvement.

The *From the School to the Community* programme is structured around five modules. Each one involves a series of activities, with specified content. They are conducted in small or large groups (or in a combination of the two) and take place inside and outside of the classroom context in a way that promotes student autonomy. Unlike the traditional teaching situation, the teacher has more of a support role – in the context of the small group – and a management role – in the larger group – stimulating debate and consultation.

Evaluation of the Programme *From the School to the Community*

A process of evaluation was initiated to assess the effectiveness of the programme *From the School to the Community*. A variety of data gathering processes were used as part of the evaluative process, including observations and interviews of the various participants involved in the research, including students, teachers in the school and families.

A group labelled as 'conflictive, with low performance and low interest in academic content'

Some research (Folgueiras, 2005; Novella, 2005; ISEI-IVEI,[3] 2007; and Piédrola,[4] 2007) is indicative of a lack of participation among Spanish citizens and particularly among inhabitants of the province of Barcelona. It is fitting then that the programme 'From the school to the community' was carried out in a secondary school of Santa Coloma de Gramenet, on the outskirts of Barcelona, more specifically in the Singuerlín area of Santa Coloma. The particular school was chosen on the basis of accessibility for the researchers and of the school's interest in implementing the programme.

The school is recognized for its innovative practices. It caters for all key stages at secondary school (compulsory and 16+). Our programme was aimed at the compulsory stage, specifically a Year 10 class. Notwithstanding its innovative practices, the Year 10 class experienced a high level of absenteeism. It was also considered a troublesome and low-performing class with a general low level of interest in academic studies

At the beginning of the academic year, however, there was a high level of enthusiasm in both teachers and students that led to a high level of involvement in the teaching/learning process. However, this situation changed as the year progressed. The group started to display a negative self-image, both individually and collectively, since they started to resent being labelled as 'conflictive and poor performers'.

Taking all this into consideration, it is fair to say that the school presented a good opportunity to trial and validate our programme, the litmus-test of which would be the extent to which we were able to engage with the young persons who had become alienated from the schooling process.

Data collection procedures and sources of information

An analytic approach was taken to assess the overall effectiveness of the programme intervention. Table 9.1 (below) presents a synthesis of the techniques used and their related objectives. The associated information sources are also presented.

Research stages.

The research involves three stages: initial evaluation, the process itself, and the analysis of the results. For each of the stages the objectives, instruments, strategies and information sources are outlined in detail.

Initial evaluation

The initial evaluation had the following objectives.

- Adapt the programme to the needs and interest of the school.
- Analyze the initial viability of the project, examine the possibilities of carrying it out in practice and confirm that the basic requirements needed to carry the programme through to its conclusion are fulfilled.

Table 9.1: Data collection

Technique	Objective	Information Source
Questionnaire 1 'Citizenship'	Identify the key elements which configure the conception of citizenship in all its dimensions: democracy, living together, participation and belonging to a community.	Children in the two groups
Questionnaire 2 'Social and citizenship competences'	Evaluate the key dimensions of 'living together and citizenship competence'. Analysis of the impact of the programme on these dimensions.	Children in the two groups
School Head Interview	Gather information about the impact of the programme on the two groups[5] in the school.	School head
Teacher Interview	Gather information about the impact of the programme on the two groups.	Teaching staff
Student Interview	Obtain an in-depth description of the fundamental elements in the questionnaire (facilities and difficulties in the exercise of citizenship) as well as additional elements which are obtained during the application of the programme.	Children in the two groups
Participant Observation	Search intentionally for any concrete fact or event which may facilitate the gathering of parallel information which may be subsequently interpreted. Obtain meaningful data concerning the development of the programme during its application.	Classroom
No-participant Observation	Evaluate the life of the centre and establish its initial state.	Classroom School
Document Analysis	Conduct a diagnosis of the educational context at the school level.	Relevant documents
Materials Analysis	Approach the feelings, attitudes and reflections of the children over the process, as well as the skills acquired. Data which may be valuable for evaluating the process and outcomes of the programme.	Children in the two groups

- Analyze the initial state of the student sample in terms of the key dimensions of the programme.

In order to carry out this evaluation we utilized the following instruments and information-gathering strategies: document analysis, field diary, interview, classroom dynamics and questionnaires coming from different sources of information; and documentation from the school, head of school, student tutor and students.

Evaluation of the process

The objectives set for the evaluation of the process were the following.

- Assess the feasibility of programme implementation, analyzing the level of adequacy between the practical aspects, the theoretical framework and the design plan.
- Assess the achievements that were being obtained.

In order to achieve this, a variety of instruments and strategies for collecting and storing information were used, including a field diary, interviews, student portfolios and questionnaires. The information collected came from a variety of different sources, including students, teachers and families.

Evaluation of the results

In evaluating the results we set the following objectives.

- Understand the changes the programme produces in the students, both in the school and in the community.
- Identify 'good practices' in order to facilitate the optimum development of the programme for future implementation.

In pursuit of these objectives the following instruments and strategies were used in the information gathering process: field diary, student portfolios, and a questionnaire which was administered to both students and teachers as information sources.

Conclusions

By way of final conclusion, we will now focus on three key aspects of the research project's contribution as they relate to the objectives of the programme, especially in terms of what can be referred to as identified achievements for the participating students. These can be outlined as follows:

- the strengthening of the natural support networks;
- capacity building for active and responsible citizenship;
- the development and strengthening of individual and group identities.

The strengthening of the natural support networks

We can decisively conclude that the programme produced a remarkable improvement in relationships amongst the students themselves and particularly in their ability to recognize the value of collective action. Group work enabled them to enter a learning process which promoted a far better knowledge of their own community. At the same time, as Ichilov (2003) suggests, such processes involved the development of capacities for expression, discussion, deliberation, the negotiation of differences and the resolution of conflicts. In this way they nurtured an inclusive space which improved group functioning and mutual understanding.

At the same time, we have been able to see how work in small and large groups is able to foster collaborative dynamics amongst group members, where the emphasis moves towards the importance of learning to live and work jointly with others rather than in competitiveness (Camps, 1998). This collaboration invited the students to appreciate the value of collaborative engagements. Thus, as Novella (2005) argues, working collaboratively implies joint planning and constructing.

The programme then has developed two key aspects which may be considered essential for the creation of an inclusive space: the capacity for collaboration and mutual help between students, promoting a better classroom environment.

Preparation for active and responsible citizenship

The programme encouraged the students to experience democratic processes in the micro context of the classroom. This inculcated an active and responsible citizenship that respects the norms of community life while also promoting the development of critical judgement as well as social skills.

In terms of social skills, the students expanded their capacity for public speaking in addition to developing their organizational skills. They also honed their research and presentation skills, especially regarding the sourcing and delivery of statistical data. In addition, they developed their capacities for analysis, particularly in terms of identifying those elements that constitute the culture of a given neighbourhood. It was also in evidence that they had increased their capacity to effectively use the internet for information searches. As mentioned above, the programme's capacity to nurture active citizenship skills was also very much in evidence. It was noticeable, for example, that they acquired skills to analyze their communities' needs better and how to approach the local authority with a view to addressing them. As a result, they began to recognize and appreciate the roles that they could enact as active and participatory citizens, increasingly aware of the value of diversity and intercultural understanding that are the result of mutually collaborative engagements.

Students' behaviour reflected these values. This included interest in work, the level of group involvement, personal effort, positive conflict management, the skills needed to achieve consensus and also in the capacity to follow the rules and routines of the class.

Accordingly, this second dimension (preparation for an active and responsible citizenship) is directly related to the previous one (strengthening of natural support networks). As Novella (2005) asserts, the promotion of the natural support networks between students encourages the establishment of values, the development of skills and the acquisition of knowledge. Thus, developing common rules and values facilitates an improved level of group cohesion and involvement in the community, and encourages group identification, making community life more cohesive at both a classroom and community level (Bartolomé and Marín, 2005).

Individual and group identity

The feeling of success that the students experienced as a result of their engagement with the programme developed their self-esteem. For some of the students this invited additional engagement with the academic side of their lives that would not have been possible previously.

Regarding individual identity, it is worth mentioning that the programme encourages a positive sense of self-esteem among students insofar as it develops the latent potential of the student, socially (expressing their ideas) and academically (written and artistic expression). It also promotes companionship as a value and as a cooperative attitude, which was highlighted in the previous dimension. The promotion of the students' inherent sense of self-esteem encourages confidence for the completion of tasks. They also benefit from the positive recognition that accrues to such completions.

It is evident then that the programme promotes the acquisition of social capital through enhanced self-awareness and confidence-building of the students. Johnston et al. (1994) draw attention to the importance of collective group identity as a critical referent for the emergence of individual identity. This was also in evidence in our programme. The students came to perceive the classroom as a context in which their own individual identities could find expression.

The individual and group identity dimension affirmed that the programme encouraged the development of both individual and group identity amongst students. In addition to the three dimensions outlined above, which evidence the development of a sense of active citizenship among the students, it is also worth highlighting the adequacy of the Service-Learning methodology insofar as:

- it allowed the student to experience democratizing processes which encouraged their participation and the recognition of their needs and interests;
- it accentuated those values and citizenship practices associated with the concept of citizenship: commitment, intercultural dialogue, mutual respect, responsibility, equity and social justice;
- it stressed the dimension of citizenship as a process which is constructed via the process of putting it into practice, through meeting others, working together and acting as a citizen;
- it promoted the involvement of the student in tasks and activities that require participation and responsibility in decision-making processes, hence transforming the school into a privileged space of citizenship learning.

Therefore, it would be possible to say that Service-Learning as a methodological strategy is conducive to responding to the learning objectives of the citizenship participation educational programme. There is evidence to suggest that it is more facilitative of social transformation processes than the usual mechanisms for transmitting information.

Limits of the Research

The complex nature of the modern educational reality – diverse, complex and ever changing – is subject to limits and obstacles which cannot be ignored or forgotten (Mateo, 2001). Notwithstanding such obstacles, the manner in which they were addressed for this research project will be discussed in the following sections.

Environmental limits

Considering the environmental realities in which the research was conducted, the fact that it took place in a formal classroom context necessarily implies that its findings relate to that context, rather than what might be referred to as the informal one. Another environmental reality was the absence of cultural diversity within the student population involved with the research.

However, even if there was no evident cultural diversity in the group, the defining characteristics of the class were representative of a broader diversity: the learning rhythms, levels of problematic behaviour, school absenteeism rates and interests and needs of the group were all extremely diverse when compared with other groups of students in the same centre. It is also important to take cognizance of the fact that the responsibility for active, intercultural participation is a task which confronts all citizens, immigrants, non-immigrants, women, men, young people, adults, and so on (Bartolomé and Cabrera (2003 and 2007).

Technical limits

We refer here to the limits (both in quantity and quality) of the information gathered. The research overcame some of the inherent limits by using a variety of different (previously validated) strategies and instruments for information gathering, both in terms of quantitative and qualitative information. The use of technical support devices (recordings) permitted us to overcome the difficulties that some of the strategies (interviews, for example) would have presented; the use of IT resources for analyzing quantitative data (such as ATLAS-TI V.4.1) was also invaluable.

Limitations associated with the study object

First, the coordination of the teaching timetable with the community one was also a limit. This problem was largely overcome since it became an advantage rather than an obstacle given that it became a measure of the commitment of the student to the task which was to be carried out.

Second, time limits of the programme application made it unrealistic to observe the complete citizenship development process in the individual student. So although it was possible to observe the beginnings of the process, a complete nine-month course would have been necessary to observe the longer-term process. We should point out that we would have preferred to have been able to follow the process over a longer time scale, but doing so would have taken us beyond (both academically and temporally) the framework of a doctoral research thesis.[6]

Despite these limits, we should mention that the feeling of success and momentum generated by this initial application led to the programme being repeated in the following academic year (2006–7). However, the tutor then involved changed the centre, with the outcome that the programme was applied in the new destination school. The Town Hall of Santa Coloma de Gramanet is now actively considering continuing with this initiative.

This interest in continuing with the programme on the part of the local authority is also related to the theoretical evolution of the idea of participation. We consider that future efforts in this area should be directed towards network strategies from a community perspective, and a systematic process of collaboration and complementary activity between the various local organizations involved (Folgueiras, 2005). Coordination is a communitarian structure which seeks the collaboration in a stable and systematic form, avoiding duplication and competition for resources in order to make the common process more effective.

In addition to the limits already mentioned, we should point out that the small student sample –which might at first sight be considered to be a limit– was in fact converted into a virtue, allowing us to carry out an in-depth study, examining the individual impact on each and every one of the students.

Ethical and moral limits

We can assert, as far as the results obtained go, that in no way were the usual moral or ethical norms of research exceeded. We believe we in no way infringed the necessary level of respect which is owing to each and every student as a human being, and we respected in every case the individual interest of the student insofar as he or she expressed the will to participate in the activities proposed. This ethical commitment went as far as ensuring, in advance, the consent of the families concerned to have their children interviewed and photographed.

Finally, we would like to conclude by saying:

PARTICIPATION IS AN OPPORTUNITY FOR THE SOCIAL AND PERSONAL TRANSFORMATION OF BOTH THE INIDIVDUAL AND SOCIETY.

References

Bartolomé, M. and Cabrera, F. (2003), 'Sociedad multicultural y ciudadanía: hacia una sociedad y ciudadanía multiculturales'. *Revista de Educación, número extraordinario ciudadanía y educación,* 33–57.

—(eds) (2007), *Construcción de Una Ciudadanía Intercultural y Responsable. Guía Para el Profesorado de Secundaria.* Madrid: Narcea.

Bartolomé, M. (co-ed.), Cabrera, F., Del Campo, J., Espín, J. V., Marín, M. A. and Rodríguez, M. (2002), *Identidad y Ciudadanía: Un Reto a la Educación Intercultural.* Madrid: Narcea.

Bartolomé, M. and Marín, M. A. (2005), 'Las identidades cívicas y culturales: ejes clave para la construccion de una ciudadanía intercultural, en Sacavino, S. (Coord.) *Identidad(es) y Ciudadanía Intercultural. Desafíos para la Educación.* Consejo de Cultura en Brasil. Río de Janeiro: Novamerica.

Bhaerman, R., Cordell, K. and Gomez, B. (1998), *The Role of Service-Learning in Educational Reform.* Needham Heights, MA: Simon and Schuster.

Cabrera, F. (2002), 'Qué educación para qué ciudadanía', in E. Soriano (co-ed.), *Interculturalidad. Fundamentos, Programas y Evaluación.* Madrid: La Muralla, pp. 83–126.

Cabrera, F., Campillo, J., Del Campo, J. and Luna, E. (2007), 'Del centro educativo a la comunidad: materiales para el desarrollo de una ciudadanía activa', in M. Bartolomé and F. Cabrera (eds), *Construcción de Una Ciudadanía Intercultural y Responsable. Guía Para el Profesorado de Secundaria.* Madrid: Narcea, pp. 77–140.

Camps, V. (1998), *Educar en Valores: un Reto Educativo Actua.* Bilbao: Universidad de Deusto.

Carr, W. and Kemmis, S. (1988), *Teoría Crítica de la Enseñanza. La Investigación Acción en la Formación del Profesorado.* Barcelona: Martínez Roca.

Exley, R. J. (2004), 'A critique of the civic engagement model', in B. Speck and S. Hoppe (eds), *Service-Learning: History, Theory, and Issues.* Westport, CT: Praeger Publishers, pp. 85–97.

Flanagan, C. and Faison, N. (2001), 'Youth civic development: Implications of research for social policy and programs'. *Social Policy Report*, 15 (1): 3–14.

Folgueiras, P. (2005), *De la Tolerancia al Reconocimiento: UnPprograma de Formación Para Una Ciudadanía Intercultural*. [online]. Available at: http://www.tesisenxarxa.net/TDX-0613107-120403/ [accessed 23 June 2006].

Furco, A. (2003), 'Issues of definition and program diversity in the study of service-learning', in S. H. Billig and A. S. Waterman (eds), *Studying Service-Learning: Innovations in Education Research Methodology*. Mahwah, NJ: Lawrence Erlbaum Associates. pp. 13–33.

Gentili, P. (co-ed.) (2000), *Códigos para la Ciudadanía. La Formación Ética Como Práctica de la Libertad*. Buenos Aires: Santillana.

Ianni, O. (2003), *Teorias da Globalização*. Rio de Janeiro: Civilização Brasileira.

Ichilov, O. (2003), 'Education and citizenship in a changing World', in D. Sears, L. Huddy and R. Jervis (eds), *Oxford Handbook of Political Psychology*. Oxford: Oxford University Press, pp. 637–69.

Inglehart, R. (1996), 'Changements des comportements civiques entre generations: le rôle de l'education et de la secureté economique dans le déclin du respect de l'autorité au sein de la societé industrielle'. *Perpectives*, 4: 697–707.

ISEI-IVEI (2007), *La convivencia en los centros de secundaria. Un estudio de casos*. Bilbao: ISEI-IVEI.

Johnston, H., Laraña, E. and Gusfield, J. (1994), 'Identidades, ideologías y vida cotidiana en los nuevos movimientos sociales', in E. Laraña and J. Gusfield (coord.), *Los nuevos movimientos sociales. De la ideología a la identidad*. Madrid: Centro de Investigaciones Sociológicas, pp. 3–42.

Kisnerman, N. (1986), *Comunidad*. Buenos Aires: Humanitas.

Lipman, M. (ed.) (1991), *Filosofia a l'escola*. Philadelphia: Temple University Press.

Luna, E. (2010), *From the School to the Community: a Service-learning Program to Develop Active Citizenship*. Dissertation. University of Barcelona.

Luque, P. A. (1995), *Espacios Educativos. Sobre la Participación y Transformación Social*. Barcelona: EUB.

Mateo, J. (2001), *Investigació Educativa*. Barcelona: Departamento MIDE, Universidad de Barcelona (paper).

Novella, A. (2005), *La Participació Social de la Infància a la Ciutat: Estudi Sobre l'experiència de l'Ajuntament de Sant Feliu de Llobregat*. [online]. Available at: http://www.tesisenxarxa.net/TDX-0125107-102247/ [accessed 16 March 2006].

Pateman, C. (1970), *Participation and Democracy Theory*. Cambridge: Cambridge University Press.

Paul, R. and Elder, L. (2005), *Critical Thinking: Learn the Tools the Best Thinkers Use*. Upper Saddle River, NJ: Prentice Hall.

Pérez Ledesma, M. (ed.) (2000), *Ciudadanía y Democracia*. Madrid: Editorial Pablo Iglesias.

Piédrola, A. (2007), *La Participación del Alumnado Como Instrumento de Mejora de la Convivencia*. [online]. Available at: http://www.educaweb.com/noticia/2007/12/17/

participacion-alumnado-como-instrumento-mejora-convivencia-210687.html [accessed 15 January 2008].

Rebellato, J. L. (2000), *Antología Mínima*. La Habana: Caminos CMLK.

Schön, D. (1997), *El Profesional Reflexivo: Cómo Piensan los Profesionales Cuando Actúan*. Barcelona: Paidós.

Smink, J. and Duckenfield, M. (1998), *Action Research: an Evaluation. Guide Book for Teachers: Making the Case for Service-Learning*. St Paul, MN: NYLC.

Tapia, M. N. (2006), *Aprendizaje y Servicio Solidario en el Sistema Educativo y las Organizaciones Juveniles*. Buenos Aires: Editorial Ciudad Nueva.

Yates, M. and Youniss, J. (1998), 'Community service and political identity development in adolescence'. *Journal of Social Issues*, 54 (3): 495–512.

Notes

1   The translation of this chapter has been funded by the grant awarded to the Research Group on Intercultural Education, University of Barcelona, received by the Association for Research in Science Education under 'Calls for research groups 2010'.

2   For more information visit www.gredi.net.

3   ISEI-IVEI. Basque Institute for Educational Investigation and Evaluation.

4   The research, entitled *Participation as a tool to improve coexistence*, was carried out by Proyectos Sociales – Fundación Pere Tarrés, Ramon LLull University (Barcelona) during the 2006–7 academic year.

5   Group is defined as the class group.

6   The research presented in this chapter is the result of the author's doctoral research.

10

Learning in a Non-Formal Setting: The Development of Service-Learning in the Spanish Context

Gonzalo Silió Sáiz and Roser Batlle

Introduction

Can you learn by providing service to the community? Most of the answers to this question are likely to be affirmative. But, if we ask, 'What is learned?', the answers are likely much more disparate and diverse. We can agree that through such service experiences, we learn diverse competencies and lessons. However, we are not as conscious of *what* we learn or *how* we learn it. This is likely because community-based (or non-formal) organizations that promote and facilitate community service typically do not have individual learning and development as explicit objectives of their organizations. We believe that if such organizations adopted the methodology of Service-Learning (SL), they could take advantage of and benefit from the profound and lasting learning experiences that SL can foster for service providers (García Rodicio and Silió Sáiz, 2011).

Given that the practice of SL is as much about the learning to be acquired as the service to be performed, non-formal organizations should assess both the quality and impact of the service they offer as well as the learning that is promoted through the service. Consequently, they can claim their value as social organizations in a double vein: as both service-providing entities and as educational organizations. To be able to provide a quality service to the community requires certain understandings and competencies. Therefore, those who provide a community service should prepare themselves adequately to provide a quality service. It is this preparation that can help realize the maximum benefits of the service they provide (Trilla in Puig et al., 2009, p. 40).

Through SL, this preparation moves from being a functional, circumstantial requirement to becoming an explicit and valued objective. In SL, service is recognized as having broad value and benefit to society, not only because it addresses a need in the community but also because it builds within the service provider the capacity to become leaders and social entrepreneurs (Perold and Tapia, 2007). To this end, non-formal organizations can use SL to strengthen the civic and social purposes of education. In other words, they can help advance the belief that education is not only about advancing the learning of individuals, but that it also serves as a means to improve society.

In Spain, personal gains that might be realized from performing community service or voluntarism are often viewed with mistrust, given that inherent in the concept of service are altruistic intentions. However, the reality is that regardless of how altruistic their intentions might be, the majority of individuals who participate in community service often realize that their service experiences have left indelible marks on them. For many of them, they experience something intense and profound that transforms their lives and shapes their personal growth. And when the learning components are made more intentional, as is the case with SL, the potential for the service providers to benefit from the service experience can be more fully realized. Thus, we ask ourselves, what happens when there is more intentional pedagogical planning and evaluation of the learning in service activities? And what happens when service providers are more fully prepared to engage in SL activities? In the following pages, we discuss some possible answers to these questions. Overall, we believe that the service would advance in quality, the preparation would be more solid, and a growing sentiment of reciprocity would emerge. This growing sentiment of reciprocity, in particular, is important in that it would help reduce some of the paternalism in service activities and diffuse some of the prevailing power differentials between those who receive the service and those who provide it. Because of the balance that SL offers regarding its benefits to both the provider and the recipient of the service, all participants are more likely to recognize the benefits they have gained in providing service to others.

Within the Spanish mindset, service and learning are not typically thought of as being linked. The prevailing belief is that in order to learn or know more, one attends formal schooling. To be a good citizen or to engage in social action, one goes to non-governmental organizations (NGOs) or other non-formal community organizations. The practice of SL challenges this divided view by promoting the notion that knowledge and values not only can go together, but they can work synergistically to reinforce each other.

In this paper, we discuss the existing relationship between SL and the realm of non-formal education. We identify particular points of connection as well as the strengths and weaknesses of the relationship. In addition, we present three examples of SL projects in non-formal education, and we discuss the opportunity that SL offers to build relationships between formal education organizations (schools) and non-formal educational agencies. In particular, we analyze the applicability and potential of SL as an effective practice in non-formal educational settings.

Before we begin, we believe that it is important to explain what we mean by non-formal education. In the traditional definition of Coombs and Ahmed (1974), we define non-formal education as 'any organized, systematized, and educational activity, that takes place outside of the official system, to facilitate certain forms of learning with particular segments of the population, in adults as well as in children' (in Trilla, 1992, p. 11). We should note that while there are many entities outside of the official school system that are education-focused institutions, there also exist many other entities whose mission is not primarily educational, such as businesses, NGOs, cultural or environmental agencies, but which oftentimes include and offer organized educational functions. There are also organizations that have discovered that by adding some educational components to their work, their goals can be enhanced. An example of this is the Bank of Blood and Tissues of Barcelona, which in the past years has used SL as an educational tool to build a campaign to gain donors (Puig et al., 2009).

Because of the different ways that organizations operate and use educational initiatives, it is possible that the term 'non-formal education' may be incomplete or inadequate when referring to certain entities that develop a project of SL or that would benefit from using it. A term that could well encompass all of these organizations is the English term *community-based organizations* or *community-based projects*, which lacks an analogous term in Spain.

Because of this, when we speak of non-formal education, we refer to an entity or organization apart from the school that undertakes an activity that has educational components or at least attempts to do so. In this paper, we consider non-formal educational organizations that arrive at SL primarily through the goal of providing a service, as is described by Trilla (Puig et al, 2009, p. 40)

In their aim to better their action and impact, these non-formal educational organizations are beginning to see the value of incorporating intentional learning into the service experience. They have come to believe that doing so increases the quality of their projects and helps them reach the organizations' overall mission.

SL and Non-Formal Education: Old Ingredients, New Recipes

As early as 1974, the education system in Spain was divided into three realms: formal education, informal education and non-formal education (see Figure 10.1 below). In this paper, we focus on the last of these: non-formal education. Another classic definition that extends what has already been discussed in the introduction considers non-formal education as those educational activities that reinforce the formally organized education system, in order to educate with certain goals in mind regarding the support of a person, group or organization (Brembeck, 1973, in La Belle, 1980).

In this paper, we refer to the educational possibilities that different entities can develop outside of the school; this does not mean to say that they cannot cooperate, collaborate or complete formal educational activities from the non-formal realm. More so, we defend partnerships and working in networks where the school is a basic node and in many instances an essential node, since it has resources and legitimacy as an educational agent that does not compare with other institutions.

Figure 10.1: The three realms of education

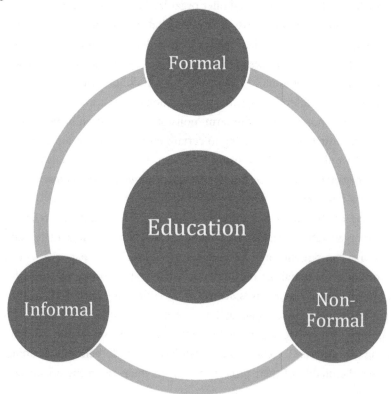

Stated in a simple way, SL is to learn by doing a service to society, to learn taking small actions to improve one's surroundings. According to the Centre for the Promotion of Service-Learning in Cataluña, SL is an educational activity that combines processes of learning and service to the community in a single, well-defined project where the participants learn through working with the real needs of the surrounding area with the intent of improving it (Puig et al. 2007).

We can establish that the two principal ingredients of SL are the *application of knowledge gained* to address the needs of the world that surrounds us (and, in this way, SL favours the development of lifetime knowledge) (Martín et al., 2010); and the *development of a service* that addresses the *felt needs* of the community where the activity takes place (Martín et al., 2010). Both of these ingredients are familiar practices and similar to the regular actions of organizations and other non-formal educational entities. This facilitates the use of SL and suggests that SL has the potential to be a well-accepted methodology that can be easily applied by these organizations.

Going a bit further, if we analyze the rest of the identified characteristics of SL, we can see that most are already present in the recipes developed in non-formal education. For example, these include the active role of the student in the development of the activity; the planning of the learning experiences and its connection with the educational curriculum; the organization; the reflection on what took place during the activity; the respect and recognition of diversity as a strength, and the capacity to generate alliances between people and institutions (Furco and Billig, 2002; NYLC, 2008; Puig, et al., 2007; Tapia, 2006).

Also, according to the results of the empirical works that examine its efficiency (Ammon et al., 2001; Melchior and Bailis, 2002; Furco, 2002; Billig and Klute, 2003; Billig and Eyler, 2003; National Service-Learning Clearinghouse, 2006; Moely et al., 2008), the two elements of the cocktail reinforce each other. Learning makes sense when it is applied to an act of solidarity, and the service is of higher quality and is more effective if the people who do it have been taught to carry it out to completion.

We can conclude that using SL in the realm of non-formal education is doubly attractive. On one hand, it is a methodology that shares elements and strategies already applied in the non-formal context, and, on the other hand, it enhances the essential objective of these organizations: service. In other words, SL reinforces the existing and offers new arenas for social action, with ingredients that are already familiar, offering the possibility of experimenting with new recipes. In addition, SL offers social organizations the opportunity to promote civic values and norms grounded in solidarity and responsibility in a very direct and efficient manner (Folgueiras, Luna and Puig, in press). As has already been proven by various investigations (Billig, Jesse and Root, 2006; Delp, Brown and Domenzain, 2005; Fielding, 2001; Morgan and Streb, 2003; Oldfather, 1995; Tapia, 2002), SL promotes the acquisition of values of solidarity and of civic responsibility in its participants.

SL has a marked social emphasis, derived just as much from the influence of the individual learners as from the context and surroundings where the service takes place. As a result, it might be considered a community development strategy (Birdsall, 2005; Muzak and Woollard, 2008; Worrall 2007) as well as an educational methodology. This approach gives it the added value to be a very useful and versatile tool that social organizations that plan to work in the community should have at hand. Another of the identifying aspects of SL that also has an influence in the community is the ownership that the participants assume in all the stages of the project: diagnosis, planning, execution and evaluation, getting a real sense of authentic participation and commitment to the project. This is to say, having a say in all that takes place in the group and in the project, reinforces the social ties and the human capital of our societies (Puig et al., 2007).

However, it is not our intention to present SL as a panacea that works for everyone. We simply understand that it is a good tool to learn through compromise – a process that requires some give and take. And since the non-formal educational organizations base their action in this compromise, we believe that the application of SL can be beneficial and ideal for them. This does not suggest that this is a substitute for necessary and important practices such as free play, sports, workshops, hikes, camping and excursions, and a long list of other activities that can complement SL.

Work in the non-formal arena is like a kaleidoscope, in that different topics, actions and interventions exist and are developed through a multitude of types and forms of arrangements. But all of these educational or supportive actions share some characteristics that limit and shape the social expectations of the said interventions. We have already debated in the previous pages the idea that only formal institutions can develop and provide learning experiences. In fact, we discussed previously that the intensity of the activity and the direct involvement of the individuals in the service facilitate the acquisition of learning through SL experiences (García Rodicio and Silió Sáiz, 2011). But we also need to mention that deliberately integrated reflection can serve as a valuable learning opportunity in a SL experience.

Reflection, an essential and implicit part of every SL project (Holland, 2001), is another way that SL can take advantage of the pedagogical value of service. This also points to the pedagogical value of the practices of service in non-formal education. Because of the great potential SL offers, it is imperative that approaches such as SL be developed in order to take advantage of the educational potential that such pedagogies and practices offer.

From Old Beliefs to New Opportunities

Even though it might be expected that a priori, the non-formal educational organizations could be the most predisposed to provide Service-Learning experiences to children and youth, this is not always the case. Sometimes one ends up questioning whether non-formal learning should assume this function. But often these questions are based on two reasons, or, perhaps, false assumptions, about non-formal education:

- The identity of the field as non-formal comes with assumptions about rigour, suggesting that non-formal learning is less related to that which is understood as 'real' learning.
- Non-formal learning is associated with free time, a concept that could even seem antagonistic to the idea of service.

When one considers that the principal mission of free time is to alleviate stress, it is expected that, above all, it be a time of maximum freedom and individuality for a person, since these dimensions are not always possible in other contexts and activities. From this point of view, an educational initiative of free time for youth and adolescents, that offers opportunities of Service-Learning, could be seen as instructionally inadequate. In fact, some sectors are reluctant to recognize and celebrate the proactive role of non-formal educational entities.

Even if this aspiration for non-formal education could be legitimate and reasonable, the educational realm of children and youth nonetheless is usually a web of misunderstandings or misperceptions.

- *The misperception that the main priority is to satisfy the spontaneous wishes of individuals*: this is to say, that in the time outside of the formal arena, boys and girls should choose what they want to do and what satisfies them. Without a doubt, one of the most significant values of free time is that children and teenagers can do what they please and simply develop their dreams. However, to choose, one has to have to have choices, such as different stimuli, and one has to be receptive and sensitive to one's surroundings. Otherwise, the options are no more than a routine, a validation of what is already established. Without complementary stimuli to their immediate desires, the boys and girls would never choose transformative activities, those that require additional effort, or activities in which they have to share with diverse classmates (for example, of other cultures or with other abilities). Such activities are enriching and can result in personal growth, but it is difficult to achieve them with practices that are only attempting to relieve stress. What's more, when individuals who have never participated in these types of activities do so, they often obtain great personal satisfaction, which encourages them to enroll in more group projects for the personal benefits as well as for the development of their social conscience (Yeh, 2010).

- *The illusion of not having commitments.* During their free time, boys and girls should not have to take on more commitments, but should feel free of obligations. It is obvious that living signifies a commitment to involve oneself, since it is the mere relationship with others that comes with putting forth effort and making commitments. Such commitments are freely chosen, but commitments nevertheless. Free time without a single obligation can only be understood as something empty, disconnected and inert given that even individual, autonomous projects come with challenges, obligations and ideas to develop. As a result, the idea of living without obligations, even during free time, is an illusion.

- *The misperception that free time has to be a time of play and diversion.* This misperception suggests that there is no room for learning experiences, much less for service. However, there is an extensive bibliography with an empirical base that has demonstrated the positive effect of play during the time of learning. For this reason, if we learn from service (Furco, 2011), we understand that we can develop a service in an enjoyable, gratifying and enriching way. This approach offers positive value for participants since their involvement ends up being enjoyable, which also increases the efficiency of their learning.

To counter these misperceptions, we are going to discuss the factors that facilitate the understanding of SL as a possible and desirable educational opportunity for children, youth and adults to do in their free time.

Our first argument is that the organizations can be in and of themselves SL projects, because the volunteers (supervisors and educators) of these entities are undertaking a service project in the community (educating people during their free time), which demands that they gain various understandings in order to carry out their work effectively.

The volunteers (supervisors and educators) are expected to be competent in the values and philosophy of the entity for which they work and everything else related to the knowledge and abilities needed to act as educators. No entity could complete their social function or their service to the community without significant training efforts of the youth educators. Furthermore, it is evident that the better trained they are, the greater the quality that they will be able to achieve with their service. As a consequence, any non-formal educational entity undertakes some form of SL practices whether they realize it or not (Puig et al., 2007).

But now we are going to focus on the projects' primary players (or leaders). Perhaps only the adults – educators and supervisors – can provide a service for others? Service actions to the community, or doing something to improve one's surroundings, should form an essential part of the educational 'menu' that is offered to our boys and girls. In fact, the pedagogy based on the design and development of projects led by the groups of boys and girls is an educational method very frequently used by non-formal education entities, and, at the same time, it is the closest thing they have to SL.

However, not all interesting projects that are organized and conducted by boys and girls constitute a service to the community. When the project does not have a service dimension for third parties, we cannot consider it SL, even if the learning experiences that the project provides are, in and of themselves, very valuable.

An example would be a group of boys and girls launching a financial project that involves the production and sale of artisan crafts with the goal of collecting funds to reduce the costs of their own summer camping trip. Obviously, the project is very valuable. It will promote responsibility and independence; it will require abilities that are academically interesting, such as calculus and hand dexterity; and it will probably benefit the youth in the group with the greatest economic difficulties. However, it will not exactly be a SL project because there are no 'third party' beneficiaries and the emphasis is placed, very legitimately, in a different place – to achieve for this same group a valuable and economically accessible educational experience.

Many boys and girls need to participate in projects of group utility such as the one mentioned above, making a commitment to a service for others. The effort that every project comes with, as well as the abilities associated with planning for the short and long term, requires of them certain effort or preparation, and for many it is easy to begin to commit if the beneficiary is oneself or a group of similar individuals.

But it is not always this way. Sometimes the complete opposite happens. Sometimes boys and girls feel more attracted to a project aimed toward serving others than to a project that would benefit their own group because they consider the altruistic project as more important and they get more satisfaction out of this type of commitment, especially when one's own group of equals is not very cohesive and has problems in its internal dynamics.

As such, the belief that it is always necessary to first establish group solidarity in order for the group to later be able to provide a service to the community does not always hold up. Precisely because having a project that transcends the group dynamics is often a way to strengthen it and build group cohesion.

What would we think, for example, of a non-formal educational organization where adolescents learn a wealth of games, learn about group dynamics, develop various skills, and deeply explore the marvels of our landscape, but never, never do anything for the community, never apply themselves to a social project, or never venture beyond the comfortable surroundings of their group of friends? We would think that they have done a part of their work very well, but that they haven't finished it. The discovery of the other and the experience of doing a service for the community should be present (which it is already) in the practice of non-formal educators and in the activities of boys and girls. The non-formal educational organizations carry SL in their mission and their 'DNA'.

Certainly, these organizations enjoy a privileged position to carry out SL projects. They seek to improve and deepen the projects because they are already carrying them out, albeit in a somewhat unsystematic way. We conclude with a discussion of the strengths and weaknesses that the inclusion of SL brings to non-formal education organizations (see Figure 10.2). We believe that entities will be encouraged to develop these practices when they feel they can, through SL, begin to recover the social dimension of education – the dimension that seeks to improve society, not only the individual agenda of each participant.

Three Examples of SL Practices from Non-Formal Education

Next, we present three SL examples, each coherent and well structured, which seek to foster diverse competencies for students by placing them in a service experience that seeks to address a cause (see Figure 10.3).

Strengths

The flexibility and diversification of the intervention modalities, aspects that multiply the possibilities to act.

The scarcity of bureaucratic processes, which facilitates decision-making and taking action in the environment, something that is much more complicated for the school.

The identification of the entities in the local area, which converts the act of giving something to the community into an act that furthers an institutional goal.

The growing public attention that these entities gain can increase confidence in them and build the social acceptance of their actions.

Weaknesses

The instability of the partnership, which compromises the quality of the projects and their continuity.

The insufficient training and preparation of the staff and professionals responsible for the pedagogical aspects of SL projects.

Precarious economic conditions, which threaten the continuity of the projects as well as their quality.

The outdated or inefficient practices of many organizations, which prevents opportunities to optimize technological innovations or ensure sustained, positive relationship with the public.

The dominant client mentality that many families and institutions hold, which can be in conflict with the idea of service.

Figure 10.2: Strengths and weaknesses of including SL in non-formal organizations

Project	Participants	Context
Youth in the neighbourhood	Youth in the organization convened by an association	Practices in the curricular field of Citizenship Education
Pasalacabra (*Passing the Goat*) (Martín and Serrano, 2010, pp. 184–96)	Youth in a secondary school who are convened by an association	Solidarity concert
Mina Gallarta	Youth from a youth centre	Field work as a summer activity

Figure 10.3: Service-Learning examples

In the three experiences, the teenagers:

- connected with a social need;
- raised their moral awareness when confronted with a challenge or a problem that they discovered in their surroundings;
- committed themselves to carrying out a social action to contribute to addressing the challenge or social need;
- learned many things as they acquired knowledge, exercised abilities, developed skills and deepened attitudes and values.

Project Youth for the Neighbourhood

Synopsis

The secondary school students convened during their free time in their neighbourhood club. Their neighbourhood is the Florida, in L'Hospitalet de Llobregat, close to Barcelona. The students participate in a training course for volunteers as part of their academic training so that they can then help the educators from the club to work with boys and girls outside of the school schedule, when their families are still at work or otherwise cannot be with them.

What is the social need being addressed?

The Florida is a neighbourhood with a high percentage of young immigrants with young sons and daughters. Fathers and mothers have to work until very late and they cannot tend to their children after school hours. For this reason, the neighbourhood club is overflowing, and the educators need help to meet the high demand.

How do they connect and how do they get involved in their surroundings?

The neighbourhood club and the secondary school have for some time collaborated in various educational projects. The teachers hope that the secondary school students, mainly immigrant youth, will apply themselves to community service duties as part of their development as citizens.

For this purpose, teachers and educators agreed to propose to the youth a concrete and real way of helping that the youth themselves could offer, if they were first prepared or trained. The students received the proposal directly from educators, who are mostly young adults. They could collaborate or refuse to help, but no student refused the proposal. They all committed themselves to complete a 12-hour classroom-based preparation and then continue with 40 hours of activities with the children at least one afternoon per week.

What does community service consist of?

To implement this project, they establish partnerships between the two educational agents in the neighbourhood: the secondary school and the neighbourhood club. The service consists of helping the educators tend to the smallest children for the two hours just after school ends. Together with educators, the youth go to the neighbourhood schools to wait for the children to get out at the end of the school day. The youth take them to the neighbourhood club, help them get a snack, clean up, do their homework, play, read, converse, and make crafts, and are responsible for picking things up.

What do they learn through this experience?

- Awareness and understanding of what childhood is like in the neighbourhood, which is part of the curriculum of citizenship education.
- Knowledge and abilities in games, readings, crafts, and of day-to-day routines.
- Communication and relationship-building skills that they practise in their work with young children, their families and the educators in the neighbourhood club.
- Organization and planning abilities, essentially, responsibility in following through with their personal commitments.
- Self-esteem and security in oneself.

In the words of Sheila, a 16-year-old student that participated in this project:

> Last year we had the opportunity to gain an understanding about how you need to treat young boys and girls in the neighbourhood club. The educators were always aware that I was also delighted in the orientation for volunteers.
>
> This experience was very gratifying, since while I help educators and I teach the children, I also learn a lot from them. This is a very beautiful activity to get a sense of the young children's world. I am learning how they behave and how to treat them.

> I had a great time and, at the same time, I realized that up to a certain extent, young ones can be grateful. I also can say that it's fulfilling to do things without the extrinsic motivation of profit or gain.

Project Pasalacabra (Passing the Goat)

Synopsis

Youth from diverse secondary schools, gathered by the Asociacion De Servicios Iniciativa Social (Association of Social Services Initiative – ADSIS) of the Carmelo neighbourhood in Barcelona, organize a concert to their liking, with the primary goal of building awareness in the neighbourhood and earning money to buy between three and four goats for an Ecuadorean region with nutritional problems.[1]

What is the social need addressed?

Hunger and malnutrition is one of the most prevalent social problems for the teenagers. Catzuqui de Velasco is a region in Ecuador with some of the greatest malnutrition problems for boys and girls.

How do they connect to and get involved in their surroundings?

The ADSIS foundation gets in touch with the different schools to propose to students that they get involved in this cause as volunteers and outside of school hours, to apply their capabilities and their enthusiasm for music and celebrations to plan the concert.

The youth are presented with a proposal from a cooperating doctor in Catzuqui de Velasco. Even though there is a fixed goal (the project has to do with creating a concert and the funds are for a specific population), everything else is yet to be defined. There will certainly be the challenge of participation and collective planning. They are asked to consider going beyond a musical event that fits their interests, including promoting particular musical groups or, simply, launching a huge celebration. The proposal suggests an option of donating the economic revenues that they gain. They will not invest it or distribute the money among themselves, nor will they use the money for an end-of-the-year trip; they will not pursue other perfectly legitimate ends though they may be very formative in and of themselves. Instead, they will labour to obtain revenues for a solidarity cause.

What constitutes community service?

To implement this project, they establish partnerships among three agents: the secondary schools, the ADSIS foundation and the population of Catzuqui de Velasco. The youth involved plan, execute and assess a popular concert for the neighbourhood, collecting not only revenue from the tickets, but also from the sale of arts and crafts and fair trade products, as well as a bar service during the concert. As an example of the impact of this project, 390 people attended one of the concerts and collected enough money to purchase four goats for milk production in Catzuqui de Velasco.

What do they learn from this experience?

- Improve their organizing and planning abilities as well as their capacity to work in groups.
- Make decisions.
- Accept ideas and different points of view.
- Take responsibility in the personal commitments they make.
- Learn technical skills related to organizing a concert: lights, sound, decorations.
- Plan the use of space.
- Create and maintain a budget.
- Knowledge and awareness of a social problem.
- Reflection upon the causes of the unjust situation.
- Concrete geographical knowledge related to the target population.

In the words of Raul, one of the students involved:

> We were presented with an opportunity to be leaders, to make decisions, to do something great. I suppose that was the key. With time, I have discovered that the final goal mattered the least of all. The experience, the first-hand experience of having carried the project forward, a project of this scope is one of those things you remember, that leaves a subtle and transparent mark on you, that causes a reaction, that at the very least, does not let you be indifferent. Then comes the day in which apart from obtaining the objective, that group of youth knew that we had carried the project out by ourselves, that we were capable,

that what took place was a precedent, that we had made another world possible. Why not think in much larger terms? Another world is possible, we demonstrated it.

Project Gallarta Mine

Synopsis

Teenagers in the neighbourhood club of the Bellvitge area, in the L'Hospitalet de Llobregat (close to Barcelona) carried out a small summer work camp in the Museum of Mining in the Basque country, at the beginning of a route throughout this territory. The work camp consisted of collaborating in the maintenance and restoration of different elements and exhibits in the museum.

What is the social need addressed?

Mining has been one of the key aspects of the Basque country's economic and cultural identity, but the industry is now in decline and runs the risk of its heritage being lost.

Fortunately, an association of ex-miners founded the Museum of Mining and has recovered a large number of pieces, tools, machinery and documents from the old iron exploration sites. The objective is to restore the industrial heritage and to help disseminate its historical memory. There is still much work to be done and they are grateful for volunteers.

How do they connect and get involved with their surrounding?

There is a route through the Basque country that is very popular in the summer and enjoyed by Catalan teenagers associated with youth organizations. It seems more like a group trip than an excursion or a classic camping trip. Nevertheless, they can easily fall into taking a touristic and consumption-driven approach to the route, an approach that offers little educational quality.

The teenagers of 14 to 16 years of age from the youth neighbourhood centre wanted to take part in this activity, something that was almost a ritual and emblematic to them. But at the same time, they expressed a desire to 'do something useful that is concrete'. They were a motivated and active group.

The educators working with the group of teenagers explored their options and found the possibility of combining the route with what we could call a 'work mini-camp' of four or five days through the Mining Museum.

When the teens found out from the educators about the possibility of collaborating with the Mining Museum and enjoying a few days on the route, they felt twice as thrilled. Their commitment was, therefore, to do a phase of solidarity work in the middle of a route discovering the Basque country. Both activities went well together, reinforcing one another.

What does community service consist of?

The service consisted of the restoration of the area around the Mining Museum: painting and restoring a few wagons and preparing the garden that would be used to display items in the outdoors. These tasks were completed under the supervision of volunteer ex-miners from the museum.

To implement this project, they established partnerships between two agents: those of the youth centre and those from the Mining Museum.

What can be learned from this experience?

- Increased awareness about the language, the culture, and the folklore of the Basque country.
- Discovery of a profession and an economic reality unknown to the majority of the youth.
- Organizational and planning abilities; the capacity to work in groups; responsibility in following through with their personal commitments; technical abilities in the restoration and conservation of the museum: cleaning, sanding and painting.
- Social skills in relating to and collaborating with older individuals.

In the words of the supervisors that accompanied the group on this experience:

> The teenagers' response to the trip was very positive. They greatly enjoyed participating in this restoration project at the mining museum and learning things about the culture of the Basque Country.

But they also commented that perhaps the experience was a bit short and the teenagers would have preferred participating in more restoration projects!

From the Formal to the Informal and Vice versa.

The heterogeneity of social organizations makes it practically impossible to create a classification of modalities in SL projects (Puig et al., 2007). There are many types of projects, some organized by themes while others are based on the ages of the participants. They also have varying spans and durations. Despite this fact, we could classify them according to the following two areas:

- projects that aim to reinforce scholarly processes;
- projects that seek educational objectives themselves without a reference to the school.

A social organization or non-formal educational entity can take part in an infinite number of service-learning projects with or without the school and in both cases, alone or in cooperation with other organizations. In any of these situations, the value and quality of their project can have the same legitimacy and desirability. But the advantage that SL provides is that it makes it possible to work in a network of four or more entities (Perold and Tapia, 2007), which confers a more global dimension to each entity's practice.

Projects Independent of Schools

Many educational projects taken up by social organizations are developed with little or no connection to schools. The dominant tendency up to this point has been to consider the school a self-sufficient institution that does not need any additional support at all from others, with the exception of the families and the students.

But, on the other hand, it is also the tendency of the community-based organizations and of the world of non-formal education to work in parallel to or with their backs to the school, and even at times in conflict with it. In any case, there are not many precedents of cooperation. And community service projects are not exempt from this lack of cooperation.

There are some reasons and situations that explain why it is sometimes so difficult to have cooperation between schools and social organizations. In the first place, these entities have different priorities. While for many social organizations, the primary reason for existing is to provide service to the community, for the school, such work is only one of many interesting possibilities for advancing educational practice. Schools view the community service practice as one that takes place in an open space and should be compatible with academic obligations that are often quite inflexible. Community service and SL are practices to which professors must dedicate large amounts of time and effort. Community-based social organizations operate with different norms and on different timetables from schools. This makes it difficult to form mutually beneficial partnerships. We have to admit that if all SL projects had to happen in collaboration with the school, probably very few would get started.

Second, the time of day when youth socialize and have free time (in the afternoons after classes, during the weekends and vacations) coincides with times in which the school is closed or the teachers are not present. Without a doubt, this makes it more difficult to share projects between both institutions; in particular, it complicates the distribution of tasks and responsibilities.

Finally, many teachers argue that non-formal educational entities should offer, precisely, activities and resources that are very different from what the school offers. They believe that if non-formal educational activities have nothing to do with what happens at school, students will end up feeling like they are in a different environment that is stimulating because it is not a school. For these reasons, many teachers think that cooperating does not make sense or is not necessary.

Nonetheless, at a minimum level of interaction, it would be desirable to have some coordination between the school and an enterprising, independent organization that can facilitate the coordination of the SL project. This coordination could consist of the following:

- *Information*: the entity informs the school or institute about the project in a way that is a little more in-depth than what could be communicated through a pamphlet or a poster.
- *Recognition*: the entity seeks from the school some recognition of the positive work being done or the educational legitimacy of the project, even if the school does not participate actively in it.
- *Promotion*: the teachers, seeing the project as interesting, promote it among the alumni and their families, so that the maximum number of students participate in it.
- *Connection*: the teachers are interested and apply themselves to promote the project, even if they do not participate directly in it. They establish some small connection with it, such as asking students for a written essay reflecting on the service afterward. This could be done in collaboration for the school magazine, for instance.

Projects Linked to the School

However complex the work may at times seem, social organizations should not abandon the vision of cooperating with the school without first having attempted it. The necessity of working in networks in a community, of combining efforts for social cohesion and educational quality, more than justifies investing efforts to change the norm of acting in isolation.

To start joint SL projects, the social organization needs a little better understanding of the teachers' educational priorities with regard to their students as well as to the academic content that most calls for practical application. For their part, the teachers might be interested in starting a collaborative project with an organization for different reasons or with various interests in mind.

As for the more concrete subject matter of the service itself, the social organization can provide a service that fits very well with determined curricular contents that are hard to apply in the classroom. For example, the environmental association of the neighbourhood offers youth the chance to plant trees in the riverbed. Such projects can foster learning about the environment that is part of the academic objectives of the course.

With regard to the general building of attitudes and values, the social organization can provide a service that interests the teachers because it fosters students' development of attitudes and abilities that are currently lacking. This illustrates another way that the subject matter of the service can contribute to other goals. For example, the community centre starts up a theatre group to act with populations who are most likely to be lonely (those living in nursing homes or hospitals). This project promotes self-expression and communication and also promotes discipline among boys and girls with special difficulties related to communication.

In summary, for a social entity to work through SL with a school, they should emphasize:

- utilizing the educational potential of the community;
- promoting the participation of the centres in the social and geographical environment;
- utilizing and creating social and educational networks;
- reinforcing the sense of belonging and cohesion in the area;
- making possible the interaction and communication between entities and their members (Puig et al., 2009).

All of these points centre on the benefits to the community and to the various stakeholders in the community. This is how social resources accumulate and how the social tissue is reinforced, which builds capacity for impact and supports the continuation of the mission.

Projects with other Organizations

Whether the social organization collaborates with the school or not, most of the time there will be a need to work at least with other organizations or public institutions. In the case of the work fields related to the environment, it is normal to come to an agreement with those who manage the public land regarding the type of work to be done. Usually, this is a public department. If a project deals with a type of social service or assistance, one should have an agreement with the hospital, nursing home or other institutions.

Essentially, spaces where a non-formal education entity can work in isolation, inventing services without being in contact with anyone else, do not exist (nor would this situation be a desirable one). But there can be diverse levels of work in networks, from the 'lightest' level in which technical agreements or simple coordination of efforts predominate, to the more profound levels in which the entities recognize each other as associates working together to develop the project and share objectives and resources in an authentic and cooperative relationship. As a consequence, SL is a good tool to encourage and facilitate collaboration and cooperation between various entities to reach a common objective (Abravanel, 2003).

Conclusion

Even though it arose from formal education, SL is attractive to many organizations that work in the non-formal arena (Perold and Tapia, 2007) for two principal reasons: because it improves the quality of the service offered and because it offers a formative experience to those who get involved in a project. It has an additional value in that it shapes future leaders and social entrepreneurs. Finally in this chapter, we believe it appropriate to conclude with four points that revisit the essence of what has been discussed so far and, at the same time, summarize the opportunities that applying Service-Learning projects through non-formal education offers.

1 The social organizations are of themselves authentic schools of active citizenship that promote actions of service and also educational actions.
2 SL should be a habitually used tool in the repertoire of interventions of a social organization because it fits with its reason for being and its way of doing.
3 SL provides an ideal space for cooperation between the different educational and social agents in an area, reinforcing the social cohesion and the goals of each party.
4 SL is a very useful tool to link the pedagogical action of the school with the assistance-focused actions of the organizations in the community.

Undoubtedly, when a social project recognizes and adds value as much to the cause that it pursues as to the learning that it provokes, this is 'Service-Learning'. The entities that work in the realm of non-formal education not only assume a social responsibility that is assistance-based in nature, but by adopting tools like SL they could rebuild their worth as educational agents. They are agents that provide added value since they emphasize not only self-improvement but also improvement in social development and the community.

References

Abravanel, S. A. (2003), *Building Community Through Service-learning: The Role of the Community Partner*. Denver, CO: Education Commission of the States.
Ammon, M. S., Furco, A., Chi, B. and Middaugh, E. (2001). *Service-learning in California: A Profile of the CalServe Service-learning Partnerships, 1997–2000*. Berkeley, CA: University of California, Service-Learning Research and Development Center.
Billig, S., and Eyler, J. (eds) (2003), *Deconstructing Service-learning: Research Exploring Context, Participation, and Impacts*. Greenwich, CT: Information Age Publishing.
Billig, S., Jesse, D. and Root, S. (2006), *The impact of service-learning on high school students' civic engagement*. Evaluation report prepared for the Carnegie Corporation of New York. Denver, CO: RMC Research Corporation.
Billig, S. H. and Furco, A. (2002), *Service-Learning through a Multidisciplinary Lens*. Greenwich, CT, Information Age Publishing.
Billig, S. H., and Klute, M. M. (2003), *The Impact of Service-learning on MEAP: A Large-scale Study of Michigan Learn and Serve Grantees*. Presentation at National Service.
Birdsall, J. T. (2005), *Community Voice: Community Partners Reflect on Service learning*. Available at: http://www.mc.maricopa.edu/other/engagement/Journal/Issue5/Birdsall.pdf [accessed 26 November 2006].

Coombs, P. H. and Ahmed, M. (1974), *Building new educational strategies to serve rural children and youth.* Second report on a research study for UNICEF prepared by the International Council for Educational Development.

Delp, L., Brown, M. and Domenzain, A. (2005), 'Fostering of youth leadership to address workplace and community environment health issues: A university-school-community partnership'. *Health Promotion Practice,* 6 (3), 270–85.

Fielding, J. (2001) 'Students as radical agents of change'. *Journal of Educational Change,* 2, 123–41.

Folgueiras, P., Luna, E. and Puig, G. (in press), 'Aprendizaje y servicio: estudio del grado de satisfacción de estudiantes universitarios', in *Revista de Educación,* 362.

Furco, A. (2002), 'Is service-learning really better than community service? A study of secondary school service', in A. Furco and S. H. Billig (eds), *Advances in Service-learning Research: Vol.1. Service-learning: The Essence of the Pedagogy.* Greenwich, CT: Information Age Publishers, pp. 23–50.

—(2011), *Securing Student Success through Service-Learning.* 20th National Conference: Hand in Hand: Service Learning and College Completion. Mesa, AZ.

García Rodicio, H. and Silió Sáiz, G. (2011), *Tomando la temperatura al Aprendizaje-Servicio. ¿Qué procesos de aprendizaje fríos y cálidos promueve?* Manuscript submitted for publication.

Holland, B. (2001), 'A comprehensive model for assessing service-learning and community-university partnerships'. *New Directions for Higher Education,* 114: 51–60.

Jones, S. (2003), 'Principles and profiles of exemplary partnerships with community agencies', in B. Jacoby and Associates (eds), *Building Partnerships for Service Learning.* San Francisco, CA: Jossey-Bass, pp. 151–73.

Kraft, N., and Wheeler, J. (2003), 'Service-learning and resilience in disaffected youth: a research study', in S. H. Billig and J. Eyler (eds), *Advances in Service-learning Research: Vol. 3. Deconstructing Service-learning: Research Exploring Context, Participation, and Impacts.* Greenwich, CT: Information Age Publishing.

La Belle T. J. (1980), *Educación no formal y cambio social en América.* Latina. Ed. Nueva Imagen. Méjico.

Leming, J. (1998), 'Adding value to service-learning projects'. *Insights on Global Ethics,* Autumn, 7.

Martin, X. and Rubio, L. (eds), *Prácticas de ciudadanía. Diez experiencias de aprendizaje servicio.* Barcelona: Octaedro, pp.184–96.

Martín, X., Rubio, L., Batlle, C. and Puig, J. M. (2010), 'Qué es aprendizaje servicio?', in X. Martín and L. Rubio (eds), *Prácticas de ciudadanía. Diez experiencias de aprendizaje servicio.* Barcelona: Octaedro, pp. 15–24.

Martin, X. and Serrano, L. R., (eds), (2010), *Prácticas de Ciudadanía. Diez experiencias de aprendizaje servicio.* Barcelona: Ministerio de Educacion Ciencia y Octaedro.

Melchior, A. and Bailis, L. N. (2002), 'Impact of service-learning on civic attitudes and behaviors of middle and secondary school youth: Findings from three national evaluations', in A. Furco and S. H. Billig (eds), *Advances in service-learning research: Vol. 1. Service-learning: The essence of the pedagogy.* Greenwich, CT: Information Age Publishers, pp. 201–22.

Moely, B. E., Furco, A. and Reed, J. (2008), 'Charity and social change: The impact of individual preferences on service-learning'. *Michigan Journal of Community Service-Learning*, 15 (1): 37–48.

Morgan, W. and Streb, M. (2003), First do no harm: The importance of student ownership in service-learning. St. Pauls, MN: *Metropolitan State Universities, 14* (3), 36–52.

Muzak, J. and Woollard, L. (2008), 'Finding the fit: Community partners as co-educators in community service-learning', in D. E. Clover and C. McGregor (eds), *Community-University Partnerships: Connecting for Change.* Proceedings of the Third International Community-University Exposition (CUexpo 2008).

National Service-Learning Clearinghouse (2006), *Impacts and Outcomes of Service-Learning in K-12 Settings: Selected Resources.* Washington, DC: Corporation for National and Community Service.

National Youth Leadership Council (NYLC) (2008), *K-12 Service-Learning Standards for Quality Practice.* Saint Paul, Minnesota, National Youth Leadership Council.

Oldfather, P. (1995), 'Songs "come back most to them": Students' experiences as researchers'. *Theory into Practice, 34* (2), 131.

Perold, H. and Tapia, M. N. (eds) (2007), 'Servicio Cívico y Voluntariado in Latinoamérica y el Caribe'. *Service Enquiry/Servicio Cívico y Voluntariado.* Buenos Aires: Centro Latinoamericano de Aprendizaje y Servicio Solidario.

Puig, J. M., De la Cerda, M., Graell, M., Martín, X., Muñoz, A., Trilla, J., Gijón, M., Rubio, L., Palos, J., Batlle, R., Bosch, C. and Climent, M. T. (2009), *Educación y compromiso cívico.* Barcelona: Graó.

Puig, J. M., Battle, R., Bosch, C. and Palos, J. (2007), *Aprendizaje servicio. Educar para la ciudadanía.* Madrid: Octaedro.

Puig, J. M. and Palos, J. (2006). 'Rasgos pedagógicos del aprendizaje-servicio'. *Cuadernos de Pedagogía, 357:* 60–3.

Rubio, L. (2009), 'El aprendizaje in el aprendizaje servicio', in J. M. Puig (ed.), *Aprendizaje servicio. Educación y compromiso cívico.* Barcelona: Graó, pp. 91–106.

Tapia, A. (2002), 'Una propuesta contra el fracaso escolar', *B/ Ilustre Colegio Oficial de Doctores y Licenciados en Filosofía y Letras y en Ciencias, 133,* 10–12.

Tapia, M. N. (2006), *Aprendizaje y servicio solidario en el sistema educativo y las organizaciones juveniles.* Buenos Aires: Ciudad Nueva.

Trilla, J. (1992), 'La educación no formal: definición, conceptos básicos y ámbitos de aplicación', in J. Sarramona (ed.), *La educación no formal.* Barcelona: CEAC,.

—(1993), *La educación fuera de la escuela. Ámbitos no formales y educación social.* Barcelona: Ariel.

Worrall, L. (2007), 'Asking the community: A case study of community partner perspectives'. *Michigan Journal of Community Service Learning*, 14: 5–17.

Yeh, T. L. (2010), 'Service-learning and persistence of low-income, first-generation college students: An exploratory study'. *Michigan Journal of Community Service Learning*, 16, 2: 50–65.

Note

1 For more information about this project, visit www.adsis.org and the page of the experiences www.aprenentatgeservei.cat.

11

Service-Learning in the Australian Values Education Program

Terence Lovat

Abstract

Service-Learning has been a constant feature of the various projects that have functioned under the umbrella of the *National Framework for Values Education in Australian Schools* (DEST, 2005). In the two-stage project titled *Values Education Good Practice Schools Project* (DEST, 2006 and DEEWR 2008), involving 312 schools in 51 clusters, several clusters focused specifically on Service-Learning as their prime values pedagogy. In the major evaluation project, *Project to Test and Measure the Impact of Values Education on Student Effects and School Ambience* (Lovat et al., 2009b), involving both quantitative and qualitative methodology, Service-Learning was shown to be a particularly effective means of maximizing the impact of values pedagogy on all aspects of student achievement. This chapter will briefly explore the thinking that lay behind the Australian programme, the generalized results of its projects and the place of Service-Learning as an essential element within it.

Introduction

This chapter will provide an overview of the major stages of development of the Australian Values Education Program and the various research and practice projects that emanated from it. It will illustrate, through reference to these, how Service-Learning came to be seen as a particularly vital force in the achievement of the goals of the programme. It will then focus on the findings, anecdotal and empirical, that highlight the Service-Learning component, including through the formal evaluation (Lovat et al., 2009b). The chapter will show the development of thought and evidential trail that led to Service-Learning being defined by one of the project reports in the following way:

> Service-learning is a pedagogy that aids the development of young people as they learn to engage in the worlds of others and then participate in civic service. It is a form of experiential learning which is integrally related to values education, and helps young people to empathise, engage and take their place as civic-minded, responsible, caring and empowered citizens in our community. (DEEWR, 2008, p. 34)

Values Education Study

Since the early 1990s, each state and territory education system in Australia has been actively promoting its system and teachers as inculcators of the essential values that define being Australian and being a global citizen. The Australian government placed its seal on the development through its 'Civics Expert Group' report (DEETYA, 1994). It is now commonly accepted that an essential component of public education's responsibilities is to be found in the work of inculcating values in its students. In short, public education is now defined as a comprehensive educator, including being an inculcator of personal morality and cohesive citizenry. Furthermore, curricula related to civics, citizenship and values education have been designed and trialled in a variety of forms, both free-standing and integrated into mainstream syllabuses.

The Australian government report, *Values Education Study* (DEST, 2003), represented an important step in this process. The report's Executive Summary asserted that values education 'refers to any explicit and/or implicit school-based activity to promote student understanding and knowledge of values [and] to inculcate the skills and dispositions of students so they can enact particular values as individuals and as members of the wider community' (p. 2). The study consisted of 50 funded projects designed in part to serve as the case study data for the report. While these projects differed markedly from each other and functioned across all systems of education, most of them had in common a focus on practical behaviour change and social outreach as tangible outcomes.

The government report was initially endorsed by the Ministerial Council on Education, Employment, Training and Youth Affairs (MCEETYA), a group that represents all state and territory education ministers in association with the federal minister. At the meeting that endorsed its terms of reference, MCEETYA noted the following:

- that education is as much about building character as it is about equipping students with specific skills;
- that values-based education can strengthen students' self-esteem, optimism and commitment to personal fulfilment; and help students exercise ethical judgement and social responsibility;
- that parents expect schools to help students understand and develop personal and social responsibilities (DEST, 2003, p. 10).

The preamble to the draft principles, which was developed as a result of the study, stated explicitly that 'schools are not value-free or value-neutral zones of social and educational engagement' (DEST, 2003, p. 12). Among the draft principles was one that spoke of values education as part of the explicit charter of schooling, rather than in any way incidental to its goals. It also made it clear that values education is not designed merely as an intellectual exercise but is aimed at changing behaviour by promoting care, respect and cooperation. Through the report, the fullness of the potential positive effects of values education became evident for the first time, including its capacity to enhance students' sense of their place in the world and their responsibilities to their wider communities. Teacher testimony cited in the report spoke of values education impacting on student welfare; social justice; community service; human rights; intercultural awareness; environmental sustainability; mutual respect; cohesion and peace; social, emotional and behavioural well-being; building communities; student resilience; student engagement; student self-management and building a learning community (Lovat, 2009; Lovat et al., 2010a). The modern agenda of values education as a means of instilling comprehensive forms of student engagement was opened up by the nature and direction of the report, a feature that was then built on in the *National Framework for Values Education in Australian Schools* (DEST, 2005).

The National Framework

In the 2004 federal budget, $A29.7 million dollars was allocated to build and develop a national values education programme, guided by the *National Framework for Values Education in Australian Schools* (DEST, 2005). The

Framework's guiding principles were explicitly connected with the charter for schooling explicated by federal, state and territory ministers in the *National Goals for Schooling in the Twenty First Century* (MCEETYA, 1999), the so-called 'Adelaide Declaration'. The Adelaide Declaration represented a marked shift in educational philosophy as it had progressed in the later part of the twentieth century. The declaration effectively challenged the instrumentalist and reductionist tendencies of much educational research of the second half of the twentieth century and a range of late twentieth century reports that had tended to narrow the goals of schooling around job and career preparation, with similarly narrow perspectives on the kinds of competencies and outcomes required of effective learning. In contrast, the declaration was explicit about the comprehensive role that schools should play in matters of personal integrity and the development of citizenship: 'schooling provides a foundation for young Australians' intellectual, physical, social, moral, spiritual and aesthetic development' (MCEETYA, 1999).

The Framework built on the broad perspectives offered by the Adelaide Declaration in making the specific link with values education as a means of facilitating its lofty and comprehensive goals for schooling. It spoke of values-based education as a way of addressing some of the social, emotional, moral, spiritual and aesthetic developmental issues that schooling tends to neglect. Specifically, it stated that such education has potential to strengthen students' optimism, self-esteem, sense of personal fulfilment, ethical judgement and social responsibility. The Framework rationale made explicit reference to the language of quality teaching as both supporting and being enhanced by values education. This led to the proposition that values education and quality teaching comprised a nexus, referred to thereafter as a 'double helix effect' (Lovat and Toomey, 2009), that sees the learning that characterizes quality teaching (intellectual depth, communicative competence, empathic character, self-reflection) more readily and easily achieved in the learning ambience created by values education. Furthermore, the comprehensive reach of the Framework offered the conceptual grounding for the later insight that the impact of values education on quality teaching was most palpable in those sites that incorporated into their pedagogy an intentional and well-crafted Service-Learning programme. Hence, we would come to describe the interface of values education, quality teaching and Service-Learning as a 'troika' working together in the interests of student well-being (Lovat et al., 2009a).

The 'Troika' of Values Education, Quality Teaching and Service-Learning

Since the early 1990s, there has been a concentration of effort aimed at maximizing student achievement in school education and rectifying the debilitating effects of failure. In 1994, a Carnegie Corporation Taskforce on Student Achievement (Carnegie Corporation, 1996) drew on new research in a variety of fields, including the emerging 'new neurosciences' (Bruer, 1999), to refute the narrow assumptions and findings of conventional educational research and to assert that effective learning requires a response that is as much about affect and sociality as about cognition. Indeed, increasingly, elements of neuroscience are suggesting that affect and sociality (sociability, social development) are inherently part and parcel of the entity we describe as 'cognition'. In so doing, the Carnegie report redefined learning to incorporate into the notion of 'intellectual depth' matters of communicative competence, empathic character and self-reflection as being at least as significant to learning as the indisputably important technical skills of recall, description, analysis and synthesis. The report represented a watershed moment that, in many respects, marked the beginnings of a new era of thought about schooling's potential to impact on matters of personal integrity and the social engagement of its students.

The Carnegie report illustrated well in its rhetoric that effective learning is inherently values-filled, that it entails a pedagogical imperative that social, emotional, spiritual and moral aspects of human development must be incorporated in any meaningful notion of intellectual depth. Herein, a values approach to learning is seen to be an indispensable adjunct to any learning environment if student well-being, including their meaningful social engagement, is to be maximized. As Carnegie postulated, the nurturing of empathic character is a foundational characteristic of effective learning. Without it, learning is impaired. For Carnegie, this was the real reason that failure was such a common feature of American schooling. It was not so much to do with native intelligence or with matters of social disadvantage. It was that the assumptions of educational systems were based on a deprived understanding of intelligence and the consequent pedagogical practices of their teachers were therefore founded on inadequate theories of learning. Hence, Carnegie proposed that it was not students, but schools, that fail.

The evidence emanating from the neurosciences on which Carnegie drew has been sharpened in the work of Antonio Damasio (Damasio,

2003; Immordino-Yang and Damasio, 2007). Damasio's main interest is in the *neurobiology* of the *mind*, especially concerning those neural systems that underpin reason, memory, emotion and social interaction. His work is associated with the notion of the cognition/affect/sociality nexus, a way of conceiving of emotional and social development as not being separate from, but inherently part of, all rational processes:

> Modern biology reveals humans to be fundamentally emotional and social creatures. And yet those of us in the field of education often fail to consider that the high-level cognitive skills taught in schools, including reasoning, decision making, and processes related to language, reading, and mathematics, do not function as rational, disembodied systems, somehow influenced by but detached from emotion and the body. (Immordino-Yang and Damasio, 2007, p. 3)

The scientific rigour of experimental work of this kind is causing educationalists to rethink many of their assumptions about a range of developmental issues, including that of learning itself. Damasio's work points to the need for new pedagogy that engages the whole person rather than just the cognitive person in its narrowest sense. Damasio has demonstrated that sociality enjoys an interactive nexus relationship with the brain functions known as cognition and affect. That is, there can be no cognitive and emotional development without corresponding social development.

Similarly, the work of Daniel Goleman (1996, 2001 and 2006) is associated with concepts of social and emotional intelligence, and hence social and emotional learning (SEL). Goleman has demonstrated in his work that social intelligence (SQ) and emotional intelligence (EQ) are at least as vital to sound cognition as the more familiar notion of IQ (intelligence quotient). The implication is that IQ, a notion that has been prominent in teaching, is not fixed, free-standing and determinative of student achievement as an isolated factor. It is rather highly contextualized and dependent on other factors about one's current state of well-being of body, mind and social being. As such, the effects normally associated with IQ can be impacted on by well-informed, well-constructed pedagogy that is designed to engage the whole person. Goleman has shown that social intelligence is not a separate entity from other forms of intelligence. It functions conjointly with other forms to constitute the very entity we describe as 'intelligence'. Without it, intelligence is impaired.

In like manner, Robert Sternberg (2007) was not only critical of the traditional IQ test but actually devised a more sophisticated intelligence test based on his broader theory of intelligences. Sternberg sees cognition as part of a broader mix of human factors, involving the analytic, synthetic and practical, implying a fuller range of human capabilities than is understood by the more limited and rationalistic notions of intelligence. These research findings illustrate why it is that attending to matters such as trust, care and encouraging relationships in schools can have such a positive impact on learning in general (Bryk and Schneider, 2002; Rowe, 2004). Furthermore, there is now a vast store of evidence from values education research that the establishment of a positive, caring and encouraging ambience of learning, together with explicit discourse about values in ways that draw on students' deeper learning and reflectivity, has power to transform the patterns of feelings, behaviour, resilience and academic diligence that might once have been the norm among students (cf. Benninga et al., 2006; Hawkes, 2009; Lovat and Toomey, 2009; Lovat and Clement, 2008a, 2008b). Furthermore, there is increasing evidence that it is in those sites where an intentional and carefully managed Service-Learning component is included that this transformation is most pronounced.

It is pertinent therefore to examine those elements of values education research that have focused specifically on Service-Learning and the consequent nurturing of empathic character, sociality and social intelligence. Service-Learning is characterized by a pedagogy that combines community service with reflection on action (Furco and Billig, 2002). Studies at school level have shown that such pedagogy has a positive impact on student behaviour and moral awareness, resulting in improved attitudes towards their social responsibilities and civic engagement (Halfacre et al., 2006; Berkowitz et al., 2008; Hart et al., 2008). Furthermore, research has demonstrated that the intense reflection on service to the community that characterizes the well structured Service-Learning programme produces responses consistent with advanced cognitive development and improved academic awareness (Eyler, 2002; Novak et al., 2007; Waldstein and Reiher, 2001). In turn, other studies have shown that this strengthened cognitive capacity and intellectual commitment can result in improved academic achievement (Kraft and Wheeler, 2003; Michael, 2005; Scales et al., 2006; Strage, 2004; Tannenbaum and Brown-Welty, 2006). Much of the evidence captured in the research and practice of the projects emanating from the Australian National Framework, cited above, is consistent with these wider international findings. Central among the Australian projects from which such findings emanate is the *Values Education Good Practice Schools Project* (VEGPSP).

Service-Learning in the Australian Values Education Project

The National Framework referred to above impelled a number of important projects related to best practice in schools, teacher education, parents and other stakeholders and resources. The largest project, the *Values Education Good Practice Schools Project* (VEGPSP), impacted on 316 Australian schools in 51 clusters. The schools were drawn from all sectors across all states and territories, with many of the clusters consisting of schools from across the sectors of public, private and religious. Throughout its two stages, VEGPSP involved over 100,000 school students and over 10,000 teachers. At its core were the 51 Cluster Leaders (senior teachers) and their University Associates (academic mentors). Between these two functions, the research and practice nexus of the project was assured.

Service-Learning was a constant feature of VEGPSP. In the report on the first phase of the project (DEST, 2006), comprising 166 schools in 26 clusters, several of the cluster projects focused explicitly on social outreach and engagement mes that were identified increasingly with the ambience and intention of Service-Learning. The many definitions of Service-Learning to be found in the literature were narrowed down to the following working definition:

- service to others integrated into cross-curricular programmes;
- a learning context where the concept of service is both explicit and implicit;
- a two-way learning process – that is, there is explicit reciprocity between the school and the outside community (DEST, 2006, p. 156).

Teaching and teacher education

Outreach ventures included working in aged care centres, reading programmes for people in hospitals, developing safe travel programmes for students going to and from schools, environmental projects and the development of 'Student Action Teams' linked to the work of the Red Cross. Typical of the remarks of students involved were the following quotations:

- 'I have learnt different values.'
- 'I learnt about care and compassion' (DEST, 2006, p. 157).

Meanwhile, one teacher made the following observation:

> The overall confidence of the students grew as they gained an understanding of the needs of the residents and they came away feeling a sense of achievement and greater understanding. This then flowed into the conversation and written

responses gained after the trip. The students showed compassion to the circumstances the residents lived in and wanted to discuss other ways they could help. (DEST, 2006, p. 157)

In one of the school sites where, according to best practice guidelines, reflective discussion and dialogue preceded and followed the outreach experiences, pre-service reflection with students revealed apprehensiveness about the potential for the experience to have any meaning for them. In contrast, reflection after the event illustrated the comprehensiveness of the project's impact on them. By the time the students had undertaken their projects, however, the comments exhibited marked change, as seen in the following quotations:

- 'Understanding because you need to know how people feel and what they think.'
- 'I value my life and understanding.'
- 'Don't take life for granted because it is too short.'
- 'I now value my youth and have more respect for the elderly and the way they live.'
- 'There are values in everything. I just didn't realize it before' (DEST, 2006, p. 161).

And, in one particularly direct and personal response which illustrates how important personal experience can be:

From all of the people in the respite centre, I saw how they respected me and they tolerated how hopeless I was. They were so patient it was unbelievable. I really respect them and I tried to do my best because it was so important to them – all of those values things really. (DEST, 2006, pp. 160–1)

In the report of the second phase of the project (DEEWR, 2008), comprising 25 cluster projects around 151 participant schools, the potential of Service-Learning as a means of achieving the full effects of values education was the subject of greater recognition. The Executive Summary of this project proffered the following in relation to enhancing student agency:

The Stage 2 cluster experiences speak convincingly of the critical importance of enabling and providing opportunities for student agency. Although present in many of the Stage 1 projects, the role of student empowerment and agency in values education practice has been significantly highlighted in Stage 2. Starting from the premise that schooling educates for the whole child and must necessarily engage a student's heart, mind and actions, effective values education empowers student decision making, fosters student action and assigns real student responsibility. Effective values education is not an academic exercise; it needs to be deeply personal, deeply real and deeply engaging. In many of the Stage 2 projects students can be seen to move in stages from growing in knowledge and understanding of the values, to an increasing clarity and commitment to certain values, and then concerted action in living those values in their personal and community lives. (DEEWR, 2008, p. 11)

The reference to student agency in the report denoted a new awareness of the importance of building into values education programmes overt and well organized social outreach opportunities. Furthermore, the growing realization of the value-added nature of such opportunities was seen when the report referred to the specific values education goal of fostering intercultural under-standing and literacy around matters of social inclusion and exclusion:

Stage 2 speaks more specifically and extensively than Stage 1 on the use of values education to foster social inclusion within school communities. A number of cluster projects demonstrate how some of their values education practices can provide both the tools and the common ground for positively engaging with the diversity and difference that arises from a multitude of cultures, faiths, ethnicities, abilities, and geographic and socioeconomic circumstances, and which can marginalise groups from mainstream learning. These Stage 2 cluster projects show that values education is uniquely placed as a vehicle to work across these different forms of 'divide', and to provide opportunities for social inclusion, fostering social cohesion, developing intercultural and interfaith understanding, and engaging the disengaged. (DEEWR, 2008, p. 11)

The report identified, for a range of cluster projects, the centrality of Service-Learning pedagogy to the project's intentions. For example, one cluster of schools took a global education focus on children's working conditions in Third World countries. The resultant action took the form of student campaigns to alert consumers to manufactured goods that were the product of child labour. In another cluster, engagement with disadvantaged groups in their own community led to organized activities to address loneliness and deprivation. Both examples were seen to portray growth in empathic character on the part of students, an essential learning outcome related directly to the goals of enhanced citizenship capacity. On the basis of such evidence, the report proffered:

Service-learning is a pedagogy that aids the development of young people as they learn to engage in the worlds of others and then participate in civic service. It is a form of experiential learning which is integrally related to values education, and helps young people to empathise, engage and take their place as civic-minded, responsible, caring and empowered citizens in our community. (DEEWR, 2008, p. 34)

The link between growth in student engagement, on the one hand, and greater academic attention and enhancement, on the other hand, was noted quite early on in the development of the Australian programme. Without these links being especially explicit, as early as the first phase of VEGPSP, teacher testimony was including comments like the following:

> Everyone in the classroom exchange, teachers and students alike, became more conscious of trying to be respectful, trying to do their best and trying to give others a fair go. We also found that by creating an environment where these values were constantly shaping classroom activity, student learning was improving, teachers and students were happier and school was calmer. (DEST, 2006, p. 120)

By the time VEGPSP had matured into the second phase, these links were being made more often and were more prominent in the participants' minds. In the latter report, we read:

> In an important development from the Stage 1 Final Report inferences, which talked about having something worthwhile to teach in the values domain, the Stage 2 cluster experiences drill deeper and report on the effects on students of what was taught, and link it to increased student agency. Teachers assert that increased student agency makes schooling more meaningful, enjoyable and relevant to students' lives. Student agency refers to empowering students through curriculum approaches that:

- engage them;
- are respectful of and seek their opinions;
- give them opportunities to feel connected to school life;
- promote positive and caring relationships between all members of the school community;
- promote wellbeing and focus on the whole student;
- relate to real-life experiences;
- are safe and supportive. (DEEWR, 2008, p. 40)

In this statement, we begin to sense an awareness of and confidence in the vital links between holistic and effective student agency and the wider goals of learning inherent to the school, including its foundational charter around academic learning. Herein, we see demonstrated evidentially the postulation made at the outset, namely that values education can no longer be seen merely as a moral imperative but also as a pedagogical one. In light of the Damasio thesis around the nexus of cognition, affect and sociality, this can hardly be surprising. In the second phase of VEGPSP, we read:

> The Stage 2 cluster experiences accord with research findings in the field of social-emotional learning and its relation to building academic success. Zins et al. (2004) conclude that safe, caring and orderly environments are conducive to learning; that caring relations between teachers and students foster a desire to learn and a connection to school; and that socially engaging teaching strategies focus students on their learning tasks. (DEEWR, 2008, p. 41)

Testing the Troika Thesis

Across the three years in which the VEGPSP projects rolled out, the nature of the resulting evidence was shifting from being purely qualitative to having a quantitative edge, albeit lacking formal instrumentation and measurement. These latter were brought to bear in the *Project to Test and Measure the Impact of Values Education on Student Effects and School Ambience* (Lovat et al., 2009b). In this study, there was interest in all of the claims being made around student effects, with a dedicated focus on arguably the most contentious claims, namely those around student academic improvement. Granted the high stakes around this claim, the study was characterized by intensive quantitative as well as qualitative methods of analysis. The main items of measurement included school ambience, student–teacher relationships, student and teacher well-being, and student academic diligence, with much attention being paid to the pedagogies and general strategies that contributed positively around these items.

The mixed methods approach took the form of a sequential explanatory design (Creswell et al., 2003). In this study, quantitative data were collected over two time-periods and analyzed. Qualitative data were collected during the second phase and were analyzed separately to help explain and elaborate on the quantitative results. The qualitative data helped to refine and explain the statistical results by incorporating more detailed information from the perspectives of the research participants. Student, staff and parent pre- and post-surveys were administered in order to obtain quantitative and qualitative data about the effects of the values education programme on student behaviour and engagement as well as classroom and school ambience. The results of the analysis of the teacher surveys revealed that teachers perceived statistically significant improvements on the three aspects of student behaviour that were assessed. These included academic engagement (t = −3.89, p <.05), inclusive behaviour (t = −2.31, p <.05) and responsible behaviour (t = −2.15, p <.05) (Lovat et al., 2010b). These results, together with the related qualitative data, then informed the claims made around the four items of measurement, namely, school ambience, student–teacher relationships, student and teacher well-being, and student academic diligence.

Concerning the matter of school ambience, qualitative evidence was elicited that confirmed earlier claims that values education impels a '"calmer" environment with less conflict and with a reduction in the number of referrals (of behaviour problems)' (Lovat et al., 2009, p. 8). With regard to student-teacher relationships, there was evidence of a 'rise in levels of politeness and courtesy, open friendliness, better manners, offers of help, and students being more kind and considerate [and] greater respect' (ibid., p. 9). About student well-being, the report provided evidence of 'the creation of a safer and more caring school community … self-regulation and enhanced self-esteem' (ibid., p. 10). Arguably, the most unexpected evidence was that concerned with the factor of student academic diligence. Here, the report spoke at length about students 'putting greater effort into their work and "striving for quality", "striving to achieve their best" and even "striving for perfection" … taking greater pride in their work and producing quality outcomes' (ibid., p. 6). The report concluded:

> Thus, there was substantial quantitative and qualitative evidence suggesting that there were observable and measurable improvements in students' academic diligence, including increased attentiveness, a greater capacity to work independently as well as more cooperatively, greater care and effort being invested in schoolwork and students assuming more responsibility for their own learning. (Lovat et al., 2009b, p. 6)

Included in the report was considerable evidence of the role that Service-Learning played as an element of the values education pedagogy under investigation:

> The notion of service-learning was implicit in many of the activities which schools introduced to develop students' responsibility and respect for others and the environment … Thus, students were able to put the values into practice

in functional and purposeful ways while making a meaningful contribution to the school environment. (Lovat et al., 2009b, p. 34)

The report noted that the general effects of enhanced social consciousness and empathic character, which have been identified in values education generally, were particularly strong features of the results where Service-Learning was an explicit and intentional component of the programme:

> Service-learning ... engages students in action-based activities where they can apply their curriculum learning in direct service to others or their community. It combines principles of constructivist learning with a very practical manifestation of empathy and social justice in the form of giving to others or contributing to worthwhile social change. (ibid., 2009b, p. 183)

> ... 'service-learning' allowed head, hands and hearts to be involved in a values based partnership. (ibid., 2009b, p. 208)

> ... service-learning [means] putting what has been learned about values into active practice. (ibid., 2009b, p. 227)

Furthermore, it was noted that Service-Learning was a particularly powerful pedagogy in strengthening the often noted link between values education and academic achievement:

> Uniformly, teachers report that doing something with and for the community increases the students' engagement in their learning. This resonates with an interesting but relatively novel proposition in education: when students have opportunities to give to their community, to something beyond themselves, it changes their attitude to the learning tasks. (ibid., 2009b, p. 183)

Conclusion

Research around effective learning has shown how much more holistic an enterprise it is than can be conveyed merely by concern for technical knowledge. In the research that underpins such a claim is the increasing evidence being provided in the field of values education, among which research the Australian evidence is substantial, comprehensive and empirically tested. Within this research evidence, there are clear indicators that the role of Service-Learning as a values-related pedagogy has potential to be especially effective in impelling the wider effects of learning at which values education is directed. These wider effects include those related to improved student behaviour, strengthened teacher–student relationships, the better learning ambience of the school and enhanced citizenship capacity. In this respect, Service-Learning can be seen to be more than a marginal or dispensable extra among the range of potential pedagogies but, indeed, to be central to effective pedagogy in general.

References

Benninga, J., Berkowitz, M., Kuehn, P. and Smith, K. (2006), 'Character and academics: What good schools do'. *Phi Delta Kappan*, 87: 448–52.

Berkowitz, M., Battistich, V. and Bier, M. (2008), 'What works in character education: What is known and needs to be known', in L. Nucci and D. Narvaez (eds), *Handbook of moral and character education*. New York: Routledge, pp. 414–30.

Bruer, J. (1999), 'In search of ... brain-based education'. *Phi Delta Kappan*, 80: 648–57.

Bryk, A. and Schneider, B. (2002), *Trust in Schools: A Core Resource for Improvement.* New York: Russell Sage Foundation.

Carnegie Corporation (1996), *Years of Promise: A Comprehensive Learning Strategy for America's Children* (executive summary). New York: Carnegie Corporation of New York.

Creswell, J. W., Plano Clark, V. L., Gutmann, M. and Hanson, W. (2003), 'Advanced mixed methods research designs', in A. Tashakkori and C. Teddlie (eds), *Handbook of mixed methods in social and behavioural research*. Thousand Oaks, CA: Sage, pp. 209–40.

Damasio, A. (2003), *Finding Spinoza: Joy, Sorrow and the Feeling Brain*. New York: Harcourt.

DEETYA (Australian Government Department of Education, Employment, Training and Youth Affairs) (1994), *Whereas the People: Civics and Citizenship Education*. Canberra: Civics Expert Group.

DEEWR (Australian Government Department of Education, Employment and Workplace Relations) (2008), *At the Heart of What We Do: Values Education at the Centre of Schooling – The Final Report of the Values Education Good Practice Schools Project – Stage 2*. Melbourne: Curriculum Corporation. Retrieved on 3 November 2011 from http://www.curriculum.edu.au/verve/_resources/VEGPSP-2_final_3.pdf.

DEST (Australian Government Department of Education, Science and Training) (2003), *Values Education Study* (Executive summary final report). Melbourne: Curriculum Corporation. Retrieved on 3 November 2011 from http://www.curriculum.edu.au/verve/_resources/VES_Final_Report14Nov.pdf.

—(Australian Government Department of Education, Science and Training) (2005), *National Framework for Values Education in Australian schools*. Canberra: Australian Government Department of Education, Science and Training. Retrieved

on 3 November 2011 from http://www.curriculum.edu.au/verve/_resources/
Framework_PDF_version_for_the_web.pdf.

—(Australian Government Department of Education, Science and Training) (2006), *Implementing the National Framework for Values Education in Australian Schools. Report of the Values Education Good Practice Schools Project – Stage 1: Final Report, September 2006.* Melbourne: Curriculum Corporation. Retrieved on 3 November 2011 from http://www.curriculum.edu.au/verve/_resources/VEGPS1_FINAL_REPORT_081106.pdf.

Eyler, J. (2002), 'Reflection: Linking service and learning – Linking students and communities'. *Journal of Social Issues*, 58: 517–34.

Furco, A. and Billig, S. (eds) (2002), *Service-Learning: The Essence of the Pedagogy*. Greenwich, CT: Information Age Publishing.

Goleman, D. (1996), *Emotional Intelligence: Why it can Matter more than IQ*. New York: Bantam Books.

—(2001), *The Emotionally Intelligent Workplace*. San Francisco: Jossey Bass.

—(2006), *Social Intelligence: The New Science of Social Relationships*. New York: Bantam Books.

Halfacre, J., Chessin, D. and Chambless, M. (2006), 'Service-Learning and student attitudes'. *Academic Exchange Quarterly*, 10: 226–31.

Hart, D., Atkins, R. and Donnelly, T. (2006), 'Community service and moral development', in M. Killen and J. Semetana (eds), *Handbook of Moral Development*. Muhwah, NJ: Lawrence Erlbaum Associates, pp. 633–56.

Hart, D., Matsuba, M. and Atkins, R. (2008), 'The moral and civic effects of learning to serve', in L. Nucci and D. Narvaez (eds), *Handbook of Moral and Character Education*. New York: Routledge, pp. 484–99.

Hawkes, N. (2009), 'Values and quality teaching at West Kidlington Primary School', in T. Lovat and R. Toomey (eds), *Values Education and Quality Teaching: The Double Helix Effect*. Dordrecht, The Netherlands: Springer, pp. 105–20.

Immordino-Yang, M. and Damasio, A. (2007), 'We feel, therefore we learn: The relevance of affect and social neuroscience to education'. *Mind, Brain, and Education*, 1: 3–10.

Kraft, N., and Wheeler, J. (2003), 'Service-learning and resilience in disaffected youth: A research study', in S. Billig and J. Eyler (eds), *Deconstructing Service-Learning: Research Exploring Context, Participation, and Impacts*. Greenwich, CT: Information Age, pp. 213–38.

Lovat, T. (2009), *What Works: Values and Wellbeing Pedagogy as Best Practice?* Keynote Address at Australian Government National Values Education Conference, Canberra, ACT, Australia. Retrieved on 3 November 2011 from http://www.valueseducation.edu.au/verve/_resources/2009_National_Values_Education_Conference_Report_FINAL.pdf. pp. 18-24.

Lovat, T., and Clement, N. (2008a), 'The pedagogical imperative of values education'. *Journal of Beliefs and Values: Studies in Religion and Education*, 29: 273–85.

—(2008b), 'Quality teaching and values education: Coalescing for effective learning'. *Journal of Moral Education*, 37: 1–16.

Lovat, T., Clement, N., Dally, K. and Toomey, R. (2010b), 'Addressing issues of religious difference through values education: An Islam instance'. *Cambridge Journal of Education*, 40: 213–27.

Lovat, T., and Toomey, R. (eds) (2009), *Values Education and Quality Teaching: The Double Helix Effect*. Dordrecht, The Netherlands: Springer.

Lovat, T., Toomey, R. and Clement, N. (eds.), (2010a), *International research handbook on values education and student wellbeing*. Dordrecht, Netherlands: Springer.

Lovat, T., Toomey, R., Clement, N., Crotty, R. and Nielsen, T. (2009a), *Values Education, Quality Teaching and Service Learning: A Troika for Effective Teaching and Teacher Education*. Sydney: David Barlow Publishing.

Lovat, T., Toomey, R., Dally, K. and Clement, N. (2009b), *Project to Test and Measure the Impact of Values Education on Student Effects and School Ambience. Report for the Australian Government Department of Education, Employment and Workplace Relations (DEEWR) by The University of Newcastle*. Canberra: DEEWR. Retrieved on 3 November 2011 from http://www.valueseducation.edu.au/values/val_articles,8884.html.

MCEETYA (1999), *Adelaide Declaration on National Goals for Schooling in the Twenty-first Century*. Canberra: Ministerial Council on Education, Employment, Training and Youth affairs. Retrieved on 3 November 2011 from http://www.curriculum.edu.au/mceetya/nationalgoals/.

Michael, R. (2005), 'Service-learning improves college performance'. *Academic Exchange Quarterly*, 9: 110–14.

Novak, J., Markey, V. and Allen, M. (2007), 'Evaluating cognitive outcomes of service learning in higher education: A meta-analysis'. *Communication Research Reports*, 24: 149–57.

Rowe, K. J. (2004), 'In good hands? The importance of teacher quality'. *Educare News*, 149: 4–14.

Scales, P., Roehlkepartain, E., Neal, M., Kielsmeier, J. and Benson, P. (2006), 'Reducing academic achievement gaps: The role of community service and service-learning'. *The Journal of Experiential Education*, 29: 38–60.

Sternberg, R. (2007), *Wisdom, Intelligence, and Creativity Synthesized*. New York: Cambridge University Press.

Strage, A. (2004), 'Long-term academic benefits of service-learning: When and where do they manifest themselves?' *College Student Journal*, 38: 257–61.

Tannenbaum, S. and Brown-Welty, S. (2006), 'Tandem pedagogy: Embedding service-learning into an after-school'. *The Journal of Experiential Education*, 29: 111–25.

Waldstein, F. and Reiher, T. (2001), 'Service-learning and students' personal and civic development'. *The Journal of Experiential Education*, 24: 7–13.

Zins, J., Weissberg, R., Wang, M. and Walberg, H. (eds) (2004), *Building Academic Success on Social and Emotional Learning: What does the Research Say?* New York: Teachers College Press.

12

Shaping Professional Teacher Identities through Service-Learning in Australia

Anne Power

University students engaged in Service-Learning have been found to demonstrate greater complexities of understanding than a non-Service-Learning comparison group; and when this was combined with reflection they were able to effectively analyze more complex problems related to teaching (Eyler and Giles, 1999). The programme Professional Experience 3 (known as PE3 in the Master of Teaching Secondary Course) at the University of Western Sydney requires pre-service teachers to complete 60 hours of work in a Service-Learning context that directly addresses social disadvantage. Partners include state government departments, non-governmental organizations and an array of educational and community sites. Each year, up to 500 students complete a PE3 placement before beginning work as teachers, many of them in disadvantaged schools or settings. Geographically, the scope of PE3 incorporates rural and remote placements and urban placements in Greater Western Sydney. Pre-service teachers work with indigenous students, with refugees and with newly arrived migrants in areas where educational disadvantage is identified. Consequently their pre-service experiences contribute to the shaping of professional teacher identities that are responsive to local needs of communities and individuals.

The Professional Experience 3 programme is distinctive in that it is embedded in a graduate entry programme and is mandatory for all Master of Teaching Secondary (MTeach) students. In this unit of study, students are required to reflect on their experiences and these reflections make reference to learning in a real context. Additionally, the programme is distinctive through the complexity of its multiple strands and its emphasis on 'turning around' success for learners in disadvantaged circumstances. This chapter critically explores the reflections of pre-service teachers engaged with PE3 as they create their own professional teacher identities and discover how Service-Learning can be life changing for adolescents in challenging educational contexts.

Introduction

The University of Western Sydney (UWS) is situated on six campuses serving the community of Western Sydney. The Master of Teaching Secondary Programme is located at Penrith, below the Blue Mountains. As Sydney has sprawled westward, Greater Western Sydney (GWS) has become one of its most diverse regions, with a patchwork of poor and prosperous places (Morgan, 2007). It has government-funded social housing, where the most disadvantaged including new immigrants and indigenous families may take up residence. In close proximity to the affluence associated with 150 of the nation's top 500 companies, there are large community sectors that are low in socio-economic status. Over a period of years, reports (Murphy and Watson, 1997; Mee, 2002; Fagan and Dowling, 2005) consistently show that low household income and employment levels characterize the lives of a significant number of people living in Western Sydney. Access to employment opportunities is constrained by transport (Hurni, 2007). Crime, and pertinently youth crime, rates tend to be above state average (Reid, Sproats and Singh, 2006). It is in this diverse context that the UWS pre-service teachers commence their shaping of their professional identities.

Professional Teacher Identities

People develop their identity in interaction with others but express their professional identity in their perceptions of who they are, who they want to become and what they do as a result of this interaction (Beijaard et al., 2005). Professional identities determine with whom a person will interact in a knowledge-sharing activity, and their willingness and capacity to engage in 'boundary crossing interactions' (Wenger, 2000, p. 239). A person's professional identity encompasses the set of attributes, beliefs, values, motives and experiences by which they define themselves in their professional lives (Ibarra, 1999). This is what Professional Experience 3 (PE3) is positioned to influence in pre-service teachers towards attributes of empathy and action grounded in social justice.

The PE3 Service-Learning Model

The Master of Teaching Secondary Programme at the University of Western Sydney prepares future teachers with learning experiences beyond the classroom. In PE3, pre-service teachers complete 60 hours of volunteer work in a Service-Learning context, working with individuals and small groups of adolescents. Their students may have physical or intellectual disabilities, literacy deficiencies or learning constraints, problems of self-esteem or disengagement. There are many challenges that arise: tutoring the educationally disadvantaged; nurturing leadership; dealing with violence and bullying; engaging students with autism and cerebral palsy; re-energizing adolescent learning in alternative locations; exploring global issues; experiencing rural schools; teaching in different countries; supporting international and overseas trained peers; and teaching refugee and indigenous students. PE3 enriches the learning that pre-service teachers undertake in their conventional block practicum placements in schools by enabling them to develop skills and deep understandings of personalized learning. In other Australian universities, there are programmes that engage in some of the contexts that PE3 encompasses but the site of the University of Western Sydney is chosen for this study because of the complexity of its strand offerings (Gannon, 2009, 2010; Naidoo, 2008, 2009, 2010; Power, 2008, 2010a, 2010b).

The strand offerings are varied. *Refugee Action Support* involves UWS students in providing tutoring to high school students who have come to a Western country without much prior experience of formal schooling. There are also a range of tutoring opportunities offered in schools and public libraries. *Crossing Borders* provides support for tertiary students whose previous university experience was in a different language and culture. *Global Ripples* is a tiered mentoring programme in which UWS students mentor high school students, who in turn mentor primary school students. The mixed age groups work together on a global education project, discovering the differences between, for example, medical facilities in First and Third World countries.

There are a range of mentoring strands that cater for high school students at risk of disengaging as well as for smooth transitions from primary to high school. *Beyond the Line* gives urban UWS students the chance to experience teaching in rural settings. *Maximising Potential* is a leadership coaching programme in which UWS students coach a group of senior high school students in their achievement of a community project. *Community Action Support* offers UWS students the opportunity to spend time with the Aboriginal community of Tennant Creek in the Northern Territory and teach in the school. *Social Clubs* gives UWS students the opportunity to work with students with Autism Spectrum and learn appropriate strategies to communicate and run activities with them. Academics support students as strand leaders, leading training for the specific strand, monitoring progress and writing a report on their development.

Service-Learning and Authentic Pedagogy

Service-Learning (or community engagement) has the dual aim of enriching learning and strengthening communities. The core concept is the combination of service objectives and learning objectives, with the intention that the activity positively affects both recipient and provider of the service (Furco and Billig, 2002; National Commission on Service-learning, 2002). However, Professional Experience 3 needs to not only provide a positive experience for the pre-service teacher but also relate this experience to quality pedagogy. Until recently, little consensus existed about how to define and measure quality pedagogy because of the difficulty in isolating the effects of a specific teaching technique. More recently, researchers have identified general characteristics of pedagogy that have meaning in real classrooms. These characteristics can be sustained organizationally by schools and have demonstrated effects on learning outcomes for all students. The quality of authenticity is located in an environment of constructivist learning with high standards of intellectual quality (Newmann et al., 1996). Moreover, authentic pedagogy has been found to produce achievement effects in students across a range of different social backgrounds (Newmann et al, 1996). Newmann's research had a considerable impact on two strands of Australian educational research: Productive Pedagogies (Hayes et al., 2000) in Queensland, and the Quality Teaching model (NSW Department of Education and Training, 2003) in New South Wales (NSW).

Researchers Wiggins (1993) and Mueller (2006) believe that there should be a 'real world' element involved in learning and that there should be tasks that allow students to apply essential knowledge and skills. This chapter considers Service-Learning as an exemplar of authentic pedagogies (Newmann et al, 1996). In its aim of enriching learning and strengthening communities, it extends beyond classroom and school confines, embracing a 'real world' element.

The Power of Reflection

Through written self-reflection, pre-service teachers engage in critical self-monitoring as they attend to their learning experiences. They write their experiences and shape their own professional identities as they develop what their teaching philosophy will be. Research shows that teachers and pre-service teachers who engage in guided reflection have the potential to improve the sustainability of productive change within schools (Bulajeva, 2003). Service-Learning has positive effects on university students' sense of social responsibility, enabling them to work with adolescents who have disengaged from formal schooling (Kahne et al., 2000). Disengaged adolescents have been found to be motivated by project-based learning (Munns et al., 2006). When adolescents were encouraged to recognize their achievements through self-monitoring reflective processes they were more likely to continue such reflective practices (Silverman and Cassaza, 2000), making the benefits of reflection spread to providers and recipients of Service-Learning.

Research suggests that reflection is more effective when reflection prompts are given, towards developing critical or higher levels of reflective thinking (Bean and Stevens, 2002). The documented evidence throughout this chapter is drawn from pre-service teacher reflections that observe their own completed service through the lens of the Professional Teaching Standards (NSW Institute of Teachers, 2005). Critical exploration of the reflections of the pre-service teachers reveals them to be of benefit to both provider and recipient. Comprehensive reflections, completed as part of assessment processes for the unit, indicate that UWS pre-service teachers have engaged deeply with issues of access and engagement in education. Their reflections encompass their actions to counter disadvantage relating to poverty, linguistic and cultural diversity, special needs and learning difficulties.

The Influence of Professional Teacher Standards

A framework for pre-service teacher reflection adopted the Professional Teacher Standards to establish an ongoing language of professional learning that has the potential to become part of a teacher's regular practice. Since its establishment in 2005, the New South Wales Institute of Teachers has joined the international movement for a renewed focus on professional learning for teachers (NSWIT, 2006). At UWS, the PE3 self-reflection has been mapped against Standards 1, 4 and 6, enabling students to articulate their learning in PE3 in terms of the Graduate Professional Standards that are now mandatory in NSW. The chosen standards are shown in Table 12.1 below:

- Demonstrating knowledge of learning (Standard 1).
- Communicating effectively (Standard 4).
- Continually improving professional knowledge and practice (Standard 6).

Pre-service teachers used a series of questions as prompts for self-reflection on Standards 1, 4 and 6 in relation to community Service-Learning.

Subsidiary questions:
What surprised you about your learning in your community setting?
What goals did you set for yourself in your Service-Learning activities?
What do you believe the participants in your Service-Learning project learned?
What did you learn?
How will the experience shape you as a teacher in a classroom?

The questions prompted the pre-service teachers to analyze their goal-setting for their learning and their own reactions to their Service-Learning (community

Table 12.1: UWS Professional Teacher Standards

1.1.2 Demonstrate research-based knowledge of the pedagogies of the content Taught.
1.1.3 Design and implement learning sequences using knowledge of NSW Syllabus Documents.
4.1.1 Communicate clear directions to students about learning goals.
4.1.3 Listen to students and engage them in classroom discussion.
6.1.1 Demonstrate a capacity to reflect critically on and improve teaching practice.

engagement) experiences. For research analysis, academics also used the three standards to categorize the written reflections.

Challenges faced by PE3 Students

Tutoring the educationally disadvantaged

Students in many state schools in Western Sydney tend to have minimal access to additional tutoring and other curriculum value-adding that characterizes more privileged schools. UWS pre-service teachers have been the mainstay of tutoring centres that have opened in particular school sites. In such work, the focus is on learning (Standard 1), evidenced by reflections about designing ways to assist students improve their learning abilities. In one-to-one and small group situations involving students with gaps in their education and challenging home lives, the pre-service teachers apply their practical and theoretical knowledge to meet students' specific needs.

Research confirms that project-based learning that engages students in authentic experiences can 'turn around' students who are disaffected and disengaged in the school environment (Munns et al, 2006). In response to a local high school's requests asking if pre-service teachers could provide targeted tutoring for Higher School Certificate (HSC) students, pre-service teachers staffed a Senior Study Centre. This required pre-service teachers to work individually and in small groups with students, using their working knowledge of the intricacies of the syllabus and assessment demands, before they had experience teaching at the HSC level in mainstream classes. The project at this school has been extended to a parallel Junior Study Centre where pre-service teachers work under the supervision of learning support specialists on literacy and numeracy intervention programmes for students in years 7–10. UWS pre-service teachers became part of a proactive response that endeavoured to individualize learning for students. 'Deanne's' reflection encompassed both Standard 1 on learning and Standard 4 on communication when she said:

> I got to know the girls I was tutoring, found out what they liked about Chemistry, what they liked to do outside school and what they aimed to do after school. I also learned they were being bullied in the Chemistry class and hated going to Chemistry, even though they enjoyed the subject itself. I drew the attention of the Head Science teacher to the situation and collaboratively found a solution to the difficulty. I also was able to catch the girls up on work

they hadn't completed. The girls went from failing Chemistry to passing their Year 11 exams with flying colours. I felt this was the most rewarding moment in my life. I felt that taking time to understand the students I was working with made them more comfortable and open to learning. (student reflection, 2009)

Nurturing leadership

Leadership capacity building for young people has been an explicit focus of one of the PE3 strands. In Maximising Potential, a partnership strand with an organization called *Future Achievement Australia*, pre-service teachers are trained as leadership coaches and work with young people on projects that focus on their local communities. Reflecting about Standard 4 on communication, 'Terri' said:

> I became confident about communicating with and motivating kids in their acquisition of leadership skills. I did the placement in between my two school practicum sessions and felt the benefit when I faced my Year 11 class in my final practice teaching block. I valued learning some proactive coaching tools and the opportunity of 'walking alongside' high school students in areas of personal leadership challenges. (student reflection, 2008)

The coaching strand focuses on adolescents being able to articulate learning goals and put them into action. Hence, the coaching is towards high school students identifying goals and the processes which will help them achieve them. The UWS coaches meet after sessions with high school students to consider collectively how goals are being met. Coaches work one-on-one or one-to-small group in this endeavour. This strand has enabled pre-service teachers to enhance their understanding of their own capacities and skills, while they have been engaged in identifying and nurturing leadership capacities in school students.

Violence and bullying

At one school in Western Sydney, gender-specific mentoring was introduced and initially young male future teachers were matched with boys at risk. The pre-service teachers were trained in anti-violence programmes and worked with their mentees on reducing aggressive and bullying behaviours. Standard 4 on communication was prominent in 'Ashley's' reflection:

The group of students I mentored from Year 8 and Year 9 were challenging behaviourally but I worked to develop their trust in me, helping them research in the library, playing sport with them and learning to cook together. In one class, one of my mentees was not having a good day and started to act up with the woodwork teacher. I got the teacher's consent to take the student outside for a 'cooling down' talk. He was disappointed in not being able to go on a field trip and, while I sympathised, I told him that needed to be handled outside of the class. Getting him to talk and listening to him made him feel better and he went back to class and behaved. What I have learned from this experience is going to stay with me throughout my teaching career. I have a new-found perspective on how to approach students and understand their needs for a more meaningful learning environment. (student reflection 2009)

In learning, communication and explanation are very important, as is the formulation and ownership of goals. The role of the teacher is one of facilitator, understanding, reinterpreting, synthesizing and incorporating suggestions. 'Matthew' said:

Most students I mentored were returning from suspension and it was my role to help integrate them back into the classroom, assisting them with their work. I felt this benefited me as I gained first-hand experience of what these students were thinking and feeling upon their return to the classroom. I found that the majority of time these students were off task because they did not fully understand the activity they were supposed to be doing. Consequently I worked to ensure student understanding of content. By creating a strong relationship with the students based on trust, I could tell that the mentoring experience was making a difference. Most of the students realized that they had behaviour problems at school and that they needed to change them. More importantly they wanted to change them. I was there to support and give them a little structure and guidance in achieving their goals of correcting their behaviour. The entire experience will greatly contribute to my development as a teacher. (student reflection 2009)

The boys' programme has since been extended to female pre-service teachers mentoring girls. Pre-service teachers have become trusted confidantes and motivators for their mentees.

Engaging students with autism and cerebral palsy

A focus on equity and diversity is provided via several strands that focus on special education. The Autism Spectrum Disorder Social Club invites pre-service teachers to engage more profoundly with young people with special needs in the development of social functioning that is a prerequisite for their academic success. The partner organization is Autism Spectrum Australia, and PE3 students interact with the Social Club participants, organizing talent showcases, guest speakers, exhibitions and project-based learning for these adolescents.

Another strand located within the university campus is a direct partnership with parents whose children have cerebral palsy. On the university campus, the Mittiga Centre was built as a partnership between UWS and the Spastic Centre of NSW. Students with cerebral palsy and associated disabilities attend the centre for physiotherapy, speech, occupational therapy and some learning assistance. PE3 students who have studied principles and practices of inclusive education can choose to work one-on-one in homes under the supervision of parents to assist these young people to succeed at school. Home-based provision is essential as many students have access to assistive technologies that are not available in other contexts. Over time, pre-service teachers develop more sophisticated understandings of students' needs and capabilities (Standard 4, communication) and, following this experience, several PE3 students have expressed the desire to change their career plans to become special education teachers. Reflecting on communication, 'Violet' said:

> With exposure to students who are affected by physical and intellectual disabilities, I have experienced firsthand the challenges associated in basic communication between teachers and students. I also had the opportunity to experience students who suffer from attention deficit disorders and, more importantly, how to implement behavioural strategies to manage any disruptions during class time. Overall I had an extremely challenging and rewarding time. (student reflection, 2009)

Alternative sites for adolescent learning

Pre-service teachers have linked with 39 alternative sites, initially through a partnership with Learning Choices Next Generation, established by the Dusseldorp Skills Forum in 2006. In these sites, they have worked with students who have been excluded or partially excluded from mainstream schools. This is a programme that requires the pre-service teacher to plan with a budget. Consequently, they learn not only the identification of learning goals but also the design of achievable projects and the selection of resources to support students' learning (Standard 6, teaching practice). For the pre-service teachers, the assessment tends to be visible in a completed project that in turn informs their further planning. Reflecting on her professional practice, 'Michelle' said:

> Seeing a vision, a community project, go from plan to product was very enlightening. The students and I realized that you can make a difference. The experience shaped the way the students and I thought about the routines of life, the definition of leadership and what it means to be successful. Success is not just the end result but the steps you take to get there. I benefited greatly from this unit for my teaching practice and as a person as well. I gained a better understanding of students at risk, the circumstances some of the students are facing and the reason why they are disengaged. I also developed strategies to re-engage them in my lessons. This was a very positive experience for me and I am thankful to have had the opportunity to learn and grow into a teacher who is better equipped to cater to students at risk in my mainstream classroom. (student reflection, 2008)

Negotiated interest-based projects are at the centre of this strand and students have produced short films, music recordings, physical theatre performances, booklets and magazines of their own writing, created résumés and job applications, repaired bicycles and built and raced model cars. Each project has embedded literacy, numeracy and personal development outcomes and is intended to orient school students towards re-entry to schools or other educational institutions.

The Learning Choices model has since informed a number of emerging partnerships which are responding to engagement issues relating to recent changes to the school leaving age. PE3's newest partnership is with JobQuest, coordinated by a recent UWS graduate, to run a series of programmes that aim to keep young people in education and direct them towards work-related training. This partnership allows UWS pre-service teachers to assist in skilling young people for the emerging sustainability industry via the *National Green Jobs Corps*. They also help young people to prepare for apprenticeships via the *Australian Apprenticeships Access Programme*.

Exploring global issues

Global Ripples is a tiered mentoring programme, in partnership with an AusAid-supported NSW Global Education project at UWS. Pre-service teachers mentor high school students who in turn mentor primary school students as they collaborate on group-devised projects addressing the five learning emphases of global education: interdependence and globalization; identity and cultural diversity; social justice and human rights; peace building and conflict resolution; and sustainable futures. Each of the projects is presented to wider audiences through showcases at the university and in the Penrith community. 'Evan' said:

> Through the Global Ripples project I experienced expanding my capacities as a teacher. I discovered that students participate differently under different contexts, and in the context of project making, students take on self-directed learning. I realize that teachers are mentors that can impact and develop a student's leadership, not only in the area of his studies, but also in all other areas of his life, and potentially for the rest of his life. This Professional Experience 3, Global Ripples, has given me experience that I will definitely develop in my future career as a teacher. (student reflection. 2009)

Experiencing rural schools

Rural regions are consistently identified as educationally disadvantaged and are designated 'hard to staff' by the Department of Education and Training (DET). The *Beyond the Line* strand in partnership with the DET enables urban teacher education students to have an experience in a rural or remote school. The UWS pre-service teachers investigate equity issues related to rural education in the sites they visit. They create resources that stay in the school and are tailored to meet needs identified by that particular site. For many pre-service teachers, spending time in a rural community can provoke change in their direction and career aspirations. Reflecting on his teaching practice, 'Tim' said:

> On my last night in Coonabarabran reflecting back on these days I find myself smiling. I've met teachers, locals and students who look at this town as a blessing. These are people embracing this lifestyle and accepting country life for everything it offers. I see students doing work that far exceeded my expectations and I see a vibrancy that I never expected. That dread in the pit of my stomach that I have had ever since I signed those scholarship papers and said I'd go west has eased; the optimism in this underprivileged region of our state has opened my contemptuous eyes. (student reflection, 2009)

Teaching in Malaysia and China

Particular PE3 strands have an understanding of educational diversity that has a more international orientation. In the Overseas Professional Experience

Programme, pre-service teachers have been placed in schools in Penang, Malaysia and in Ningbo, China. In these strands, UWS pre-service teachers travel as a supervised cohort to teach English in the host Chinese university and in response to a policy mandating English instruction in secondary Malaysian schools. Reflecting on his professional practice, 'Andrei' said:

> This experience has taught me that, when teaching students whose second language is English, you have to be prepared to break activities down and use a lot of scaffolding. The most success was when literacy learning was based in other activities. I have learned that students need to be comfortable before quality learning can take place. At the start, the students that I taught were shy and lacking self-confidence. However with each session the students opened up more, understanding at a quicker pace and the learning improved exponentially. (student reflection, 2009)

In each of these sites, pre-service teachers learn about different educational contexts and how to identify and meet student needs in different circumstances. Constructivist pedagogies are redesigned to take account of cultural contexts and expectations. Pre-service teachers become flexible and adept at reading contexts, identifying and building on prior learning.

Supporting international and overseas trained students

The *Crossing Borders* strand also addresses international issues of equity and diversity. It is directly linked to the university's plan to improve the learning experiences of international and overseas trained students (from Asia, the Middle East and Africa) within the MTeach degree itself. In this strand, students are matched with international student peers in the same course, in order to assist with identified adjustment issues relating to their course of study in an unfamiliar university context and to NSW schools where the international pre-service teachers will complete practicum placements. The peer mentors are trained in learning support and cultural sensitivies. The mentees may self select for the programme but students at course commencement are particularly encouraged to take advantage of the programme. Reflecting on communication, 'Neil' said:

> 'Akbar' had many difficulties settling into university. We explored the university library together and I gave him lessons in sending emails and using a USB for storage of files. I think my best work was in Crossing Borders. The idea that someone needs my help prompts me to think more. I want to apply this to my

everyday teaching. To make an impact on a person's learning, I need to accept different learning abilities. (student reflection, 2010)

This strand is linked to the Australian Universities Quality Assurance theme of internationalization which emphasizes quality management of experiences for international students studying onshore. *Crossing Borders* presents one way in which curriculum can become internationalized to meet the needs of diverse groups of learners.

Teaching refugee students

Particular strands of PE3 focus on specialized areas of current need in education. Refugee Action Support (RAS), for example, began with the realization that UWS students were increasingly being asked in various community sites to work with refugee students in areas in Western Sydney where the Sudanese community had rapidly expanded. In state schools, second language support in Intensive English Centres is time-limited and terminates at the end of Year 10. Transitions into mainstream secondary schooling and into senior schooling were proving difficult for Sudanese students. In partnership with the Australian Literacy and Numeracy Foundation (ALNF), a training programme focusing on cultural knowledge and sensitivity, English as a Second Language (ESL) and literacy strategies were devised and in 2007 UWS students began working in homework centres in four local high schools. Since that time, RAS has more than doubled the number of schools in which it is located and the model has expanded to other Australian universities. The impact of RAS has been recognized by the Refugee Council of Australia as exemplifying good practice in educational intervention for young refugees. In its report, ALNF claimed that 90 per cent of student participants improved academic results (ALNF, 2010). Significantly, impacts on pre-service teachers have been notable. The UWS pre-service teachers reflect on the opportunity to know and respect the backgrounds of the students with whom they work in this unit – their social, ethnic and cultural backgrounds. 'Lucy' said:

This programme expanded my understanding of diversity and social issues that are critical to the collective development of society. The training prepared us to handle the demands of multi-dimensional classrooms. Most refugees arrive here from developing countries and difficult pasts. RAS puts a human face to the contentious issue of asylum seekers. The experience taught me that we teachers often make assumptions about the prior learning of students but we should make no assumptions without assessment. It drew attention to the sustainable support needed to make learning occur through the creation of a safe and reliable learning environment for all. (student reflection, 2010)

Reciprocal learning with indigenous students

Community Action Support (CAS), developed in 2009 in partnership with Australian Literacy and Numeracy Foundation (ALNF) and the local Indigenous Language Centre, focuses attention on indigenous educational outcomes in remote Australia. It matches pre-service teachers with Year 11 students of Aboriginal descent at Tennant Creek High School and supports these young people with their own educational aspirations and as they take up leadership roles as cross-generational bilingual literacy tutors with local Aboriginal primary school children. Pre-service teachers spend five weeks in Tennant Creek. After their stay, the UWS group continue to provide support via distance education technologies. Reciprocal learning and respect are key features of this strand, reinforced with high expectations of educational outcomes and aspirations. For pre-service teachers from urban Australia and from non-indigenous backgrounds, CAS has provided a profound and powerful learning opportunity about the practical meaning of reconciliation. The core of the reflections that are completed in Professional Experience 3 are to do with improving teaching practice (aspects of Standard 6) through to the creation of a safe environment in which adolescents can experience respect and rapport. Disaffected students have often missed this. For the UWS students, the first priority is this element – the creation of an environment in which students can collaborate and enjoy feelings of successful learning. 'David' said:

> Working with a small group of students allowed me to see that students who appear to be struggling with set tasks might simply not demonstrate their understanding for cultural reasons (whether youth culture or Indigenous). This programme brings Indigenous and non-Indigenous closer by teaching in dual languages. The experience has helped me learn that teaching and learning must always be flexible and self-critical. (student reflection, 2009)

Conclusion

This chapter has critically explored the reflections of pre-service teachers as they discovered how Service-Learning could shape their own professional teacher identities and also provide adolescents in challenging educational contexts with life-changing experiences. Whatever strand the UWS student undertakes, the common thread in their reflections is their growth as a teacher and facilitator of learning. Professional Experience 3 is underpinned by an overt commitment to ensuring equity in educational access and outcomes for young people from diverse backgrounds. The UWS School of Education explicitly sets out to develop futures-oriented dispositions in its graduates, including a sense of social justice and empathy and a commitment to equitable outcomes for all of the learners for whom they have responsibility (*School of Education Strategic Plan, 2010–2015*). Community partnerships and the engaged learning that takes place in PE3 are key strategies for ensuring that pre-service teachers develop such dispositions. Pre-service teachers have changed their career paths as a result of PE3. On graduation, many have obtained subsequent ongoing employment at their PE3 site, they have headed new non-governmental programmes, and they have started partnerships with PE3 in new schools when they began working as full-time teachers. The opportunities afforded by PE3 placements are producing a generation of new teachers who have more sophisticated understandings of how educational opportunities are often inequitably distributed among communities. Through deep engagement with young people from very diverse backgrounds and situations, beginning teachers acquire skills to work more effectively and recognize that, as teachers, they can make a difference in young people's lives.

References

Bean, T. and Stevens, L. (2002), 'Scaffolding reflection for preservice and in-service teachers'. *Reflective Practice*, 3 (2): 213–27.

Beijaard, D., Meijer, P., Morine-Dershimer, G. and Tillema, H. (eds) (2005), *Teacher professional development in changing conditions*. Dordrecht, the Netherlands: Springer.

Bulajeva, T. (2003), 'Teacher professional development in the context of school reform'. *Journal of Teacher Education and Training*, 2: 39–45.

Darling-Hammond, L. (2006), 'Securing the right to learn: Policy and practice for powerful teaching and learning'. *Educational Researcher*. (35), 7: 13–25.

Eyler, J. and Giles, D. (1999), *Where's the Learning in Service-learning?* San Francisco, CA: Jossey-Bass Publishers.

Fagan, B. and Dowling, R. (2005), 'Neoliberalism and suburban employment: Western Sydney in the 1990s'. *Geographical Research*, 43: 71–81.

Ferfolja, T. and Naidoo, L. (2010), with Australian Literacy and Numeracy Foundation (ALNF) *R N. (2010) Supporting Refugee Students through the Refugee Action Support Program*. Penrith, NSW: University of Western Sydney Press.

Furco, A. and Billig, S. (eds) (2002), *Service-learning: The Essence of the Pedagogy*. Greenwich, CT: Information Age Publication.

Gannon, S. (2009), 'Into the (textual) west'. *English in Australia*, 44 (3): 29–38.

—(2010), 'Service-learning as a third space in pre-service teacher education'. *Issues in Educational Research*, 20 (1).

Hayes, D., Lingard, B. and Mills, M. (2000) Productive Pedagogies. *Education Links*, 60, 11–13.

Henke, R., Chen, X., Geis, S. and Knepper, P. (2000), *Progress Through the Teacher Pipeline: College Graduates and Elementary/Secondary School Teaching*. Washington, DC: National Center for Education Statistics.

Hurni, A. (2007), 'Marginalised groups in Western Sydney: the experience of sole parents and unemployed young people'. *Social Research in Transport (SORT) Clearinghouse*. Accessed 14 August 2009 from: http://www.sortclearinghouse.info/research/117.

Ibarra, H. (1999), 'Provisional selves: Experimenting with image and identity in professional adaptation'. *Administrative Science Quarterly*, December 1999.

Kahne, J., Westheimer, J. and Rogers, B. (2000), 'Service-learning and citizenship: Directions for research'. *Michigan Journal of Community Service-learning*, 7: 15–24.

Mee, K. (2002), 'Prosperity and the suburban dream: Quality of life and affordability in Western Sydney'. *Australian Geographer*, 33: 337–51.

Morgan, G. (2007), 'A City of Two Tales: Distinction, dispersion and dissociation in Western Sydney'. *American Sociological Review*, 35 (3). Accessed 18 June 2010 from: http://www.uws.edu.au/__data/assets/pdf_file/0019/7174/Morgan_Final.pdf.

Mueller, J. (2006), *The Authentic Assessment Toolbox*. Accessed 14 August 2009 from: http://jonathon.meuller.faculty.noctry.edu/toolbox/standradtypes.htm.

Munns, G., Arthur, L., Downes, T., Gregson, R., Power, A., Sawyer, W., Singh, M., Thistleton-Martin, J. and Steele, F. (2006), *Motivation and Engagement of Boys: Evidence-based Teaching Practices: A Report Submitted to the Australian Government Department of Education Science and Training*. Canberra, ACT: DEST. Available from: http://www.deewr.gov.au/schooling/boyseducation/pages/publications-conferences-websites.aspx

Murphy, P. and Watson, S. (1997), *Surface City: Sydney at the Millenium*. Sydney: Pluto Press.

Naidoo, L. (2008), 'Supporting African refugees in Greater Western Sydney: a critical ethnography of after-school homework tutoring centres'. *Education Research for Policy and Practice*, 7 (3): 139–50.

—(2009), 'Developing social inclusion through after-school homework tutoring: a study of African refugee students in Greater Western Sydney'. *British Journal of Sociology of Education*, 30 (3), 261–73.

—(2010), 'Engaging the refugee community of Greater Western Sydney'. *Issues in Educational Research*, 20 (1).

NCSL (National Commission on Service-learning) (2002), *Learning in Deed: The Power of Service-Learning for American Schools*. New York: NCSL.

Newmann, F., Marks, H. and Gamoran A. (1996), 'Authentic pedagogy and student performance'. *American Journal of Education*, 104: 280–312.

NSW (New South Wales) Department of Education and Training (2003), *Quality teaching in NSW public schools: Discussion paper*. Sydney.

NSW Institute of Teachers. *Professional Teaching Standards*. Accessed 3 March 2007 from: http://www.nswteachers.nsw.edu.au/Main-Professional-Teaching-Standards. html.

Power, A. (2008), 'In action: Future educators in a NSW project'. *Pacific-Asian Education*, 20 (1): 47–54.

—(2010a), 'Editorial: Special edition: Service-learning in teacher education'. *Issues in Educational Research*, 20 (1). Retrieved on 28 January 2011 from http://www.iier. org.aul.

—(2010b), 'Community engagement as authentic learning: Sustainable change through reflection using professional teacher standards'. *Issues in Educational Research*, 20 (1).

Reid, C., Sproats, E. and Singh, M. (2006), *Schools Noticing, Intervening and Preventing Youth Crime Through Building Emotional Capital*. Sydney: University of Western Sydney.

Silverman, S. and Cassaza, M. (2000), *Learning and Development: Making Connections to Enhance Teaching*. San Francisco, CA: Jossey-Bass Publishers.

Stewart, D., Sun, J., Patterson, C., Lemerle, K. and Hardie, M. (2004), 'Promoting and building resilience in primary school communities: evidence from a comprehensive "health promoting school" approach'. *International Journal of Mental Health Promotion*, 6 (3): 23–33.

Vickers, M., Harris, C. and McCarthy, F. (2004), 'University-Community engagement: Exploring service-learning options within the practicum'. *Asia-Pacific Journal of Teacher Education*, 32 (2): 129–41.

Wenger, E. (2000), 'Communities of practice and social learning systems'. *Organization*, 7 (2): 225–46.

Wiggins, G. (1993), *Assessing Student Performance: Exploring the Purpose and Limits of Testing*. San Francisco, CA: Jossey-Bass.

Conclusion

Timothy Murphy and Jon E. C. Tan

When we began this collection our idea was to find a way to showcase the significant international work that has been taking place that utilizes Service-Learning approaches. With the concept of Service-Learning being somewhat new to the UK, we felt that, given the nature of our own work, it was opportune to draw together international research and scholarship that helped illuminate the ways in which the intersections of learning, pedagogy and community were being negotiated. To all of our contributors we would, thus, like to say thank you for sharing your knowledge and experience and enabling us to draw upon your expertise. We hope that in reading this volume, it will provide us all with food for further thought that will invigorate our future endeavours in the development of Service-Learning both as a powerful learning experience and as a pedagogical approach. As one of the cornerstones of Service-Learning is its emphasis on building critical reflection into these learning experiences, it is perhaps appropriate that we now reflect on what this collection of case studies represents to us as editors.

Significantly, each of the works represented here speaks of the need for authenticity – the ways in which we interconnect learning with real issues, ones that are meaningful to all those involved. Reflecting on the role of the educator, one could envision it as being an interpreter and facilitator of learning, working to provide a crossing-point between curriculum and the world beyond the 'classroom'. At the same time, building a closer and ultimately inextricable bond between what happens inside and outside of the 'classroom' suggests that both the 'outside' and the 'inside' are powerful components in the generation of knowledge that can contribute equally. That said, recognizing the ways in which such contributions can operate equally brings into sharp relief many difficult questions that sit at the heart of a consideration of education in socially-just terms. Perhaps more challenging here is the recognition of how curricula at all levels, and in all national contexts, foregrounds and rewards the acquisition of certain knowledge. But whose knowledge and whose voice? What comes across strongly, in the cases presented here, is the sense that the use of directed experiential learning pedagogies, such as that represented by what we know as Service-Learning, acts as a catalyst for learners to question their presupposed ideas about the world and others. Perhaps most importantly, such approaches act to turn the reflective lens on ourselves and enable us to interrupt those internalized discourses that attempt to explain social and educational inequalities as being about individual circumstances and beyond our influence.

What is clear from our reading of the contributions of all the authors is that we can occupy those democratic spaces in which we can challenge our thinking and envision a set of different social relations. Through dialogue, critical reflection and active civic engagement we can develop new collaborations between learners, pedagogues and communities that enrich us all and enable us to take our next democratic steps together.

Index